GUNSLINGERGIRL

DA PRESENTS

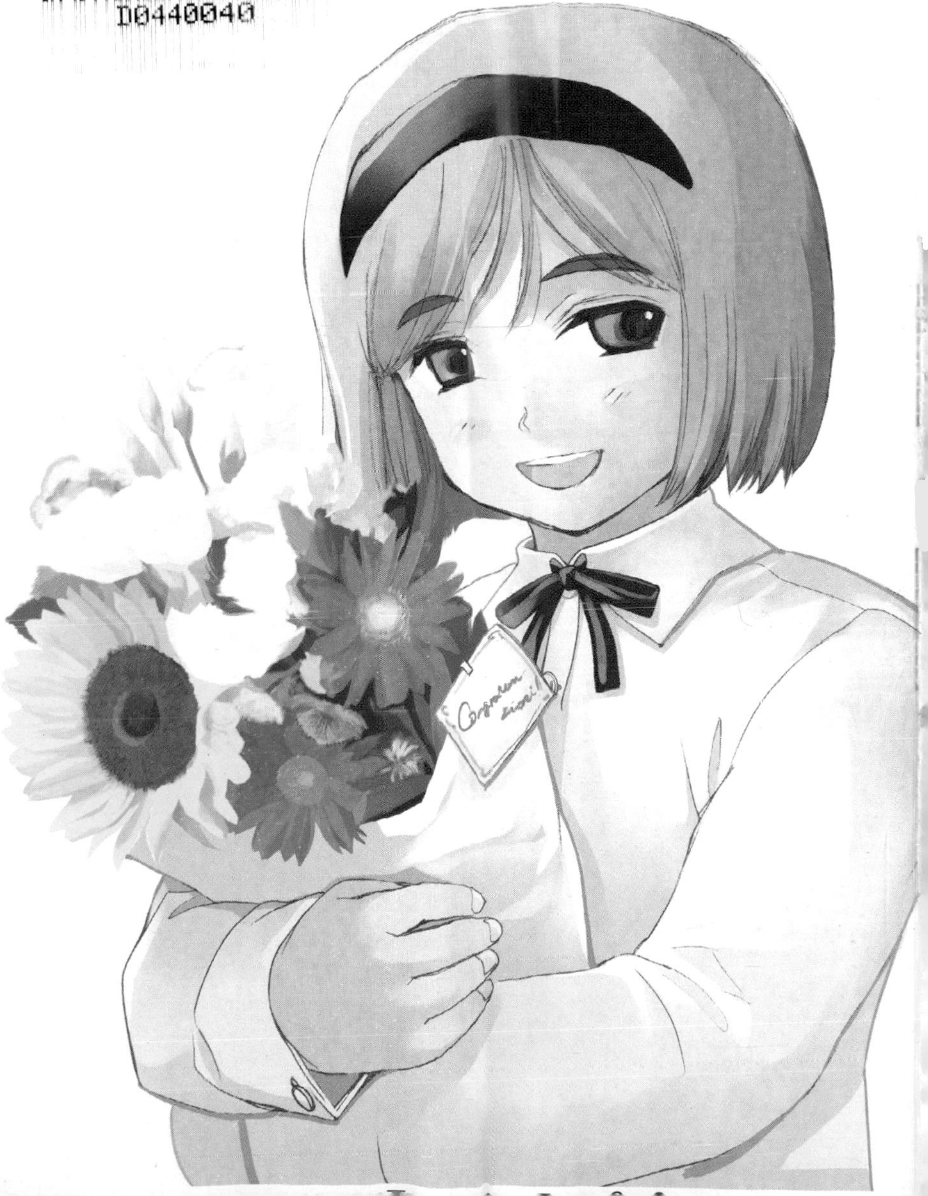

C O N T E N T S

Vol.3

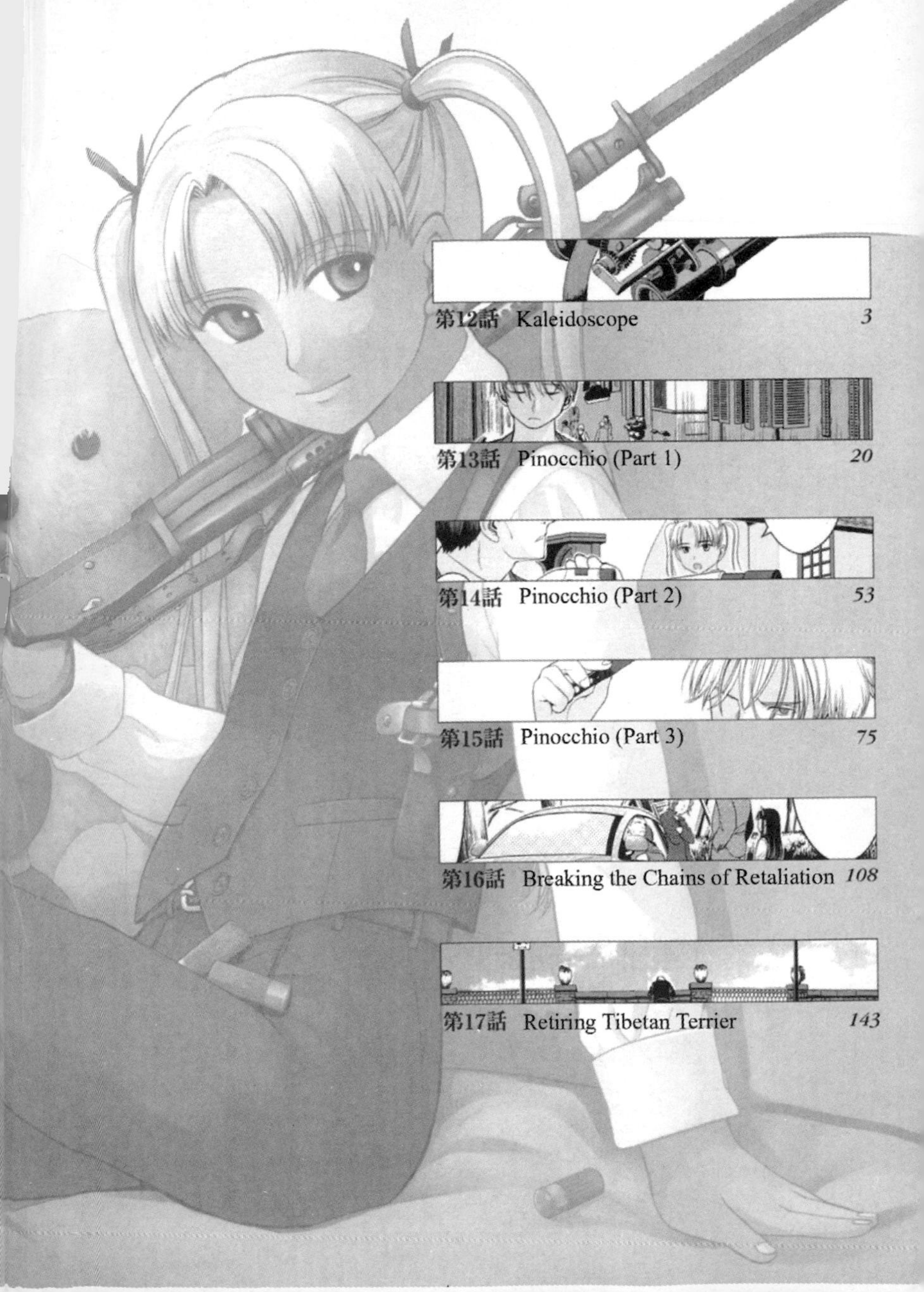

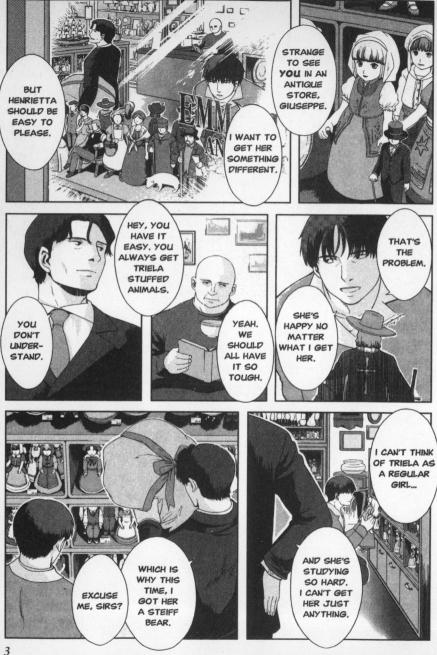

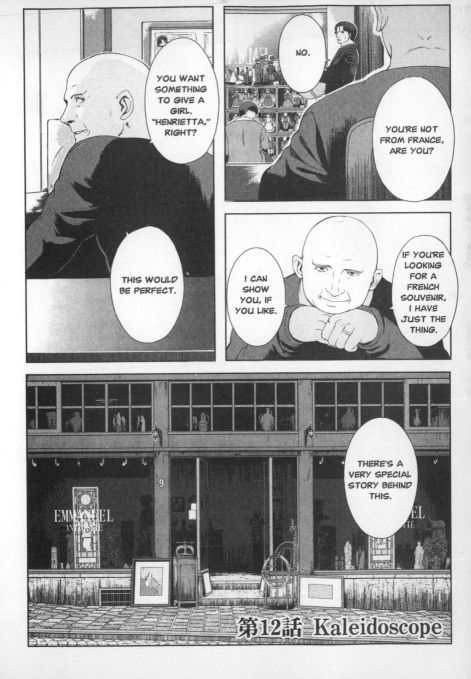

第12話 Kaleidoscope

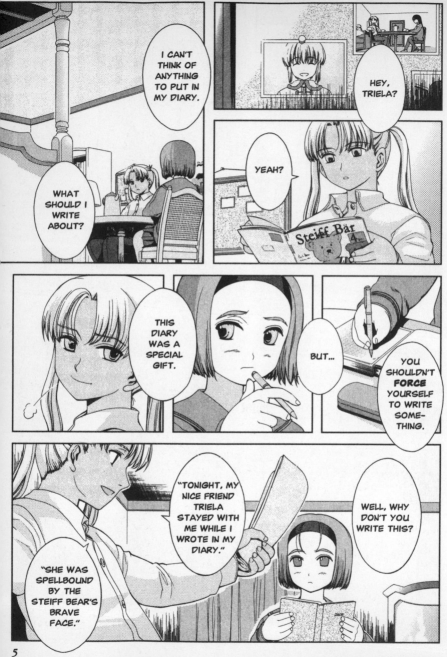

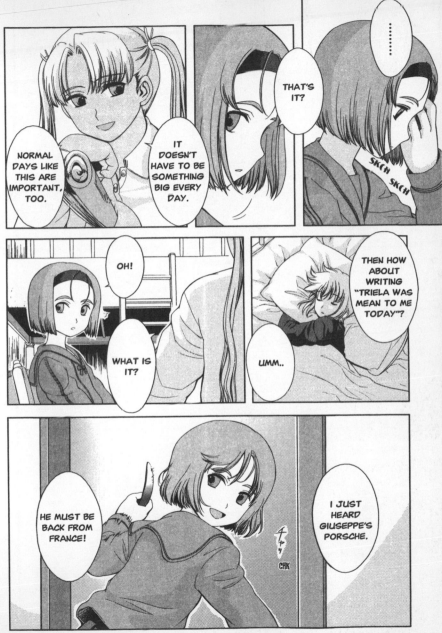

6

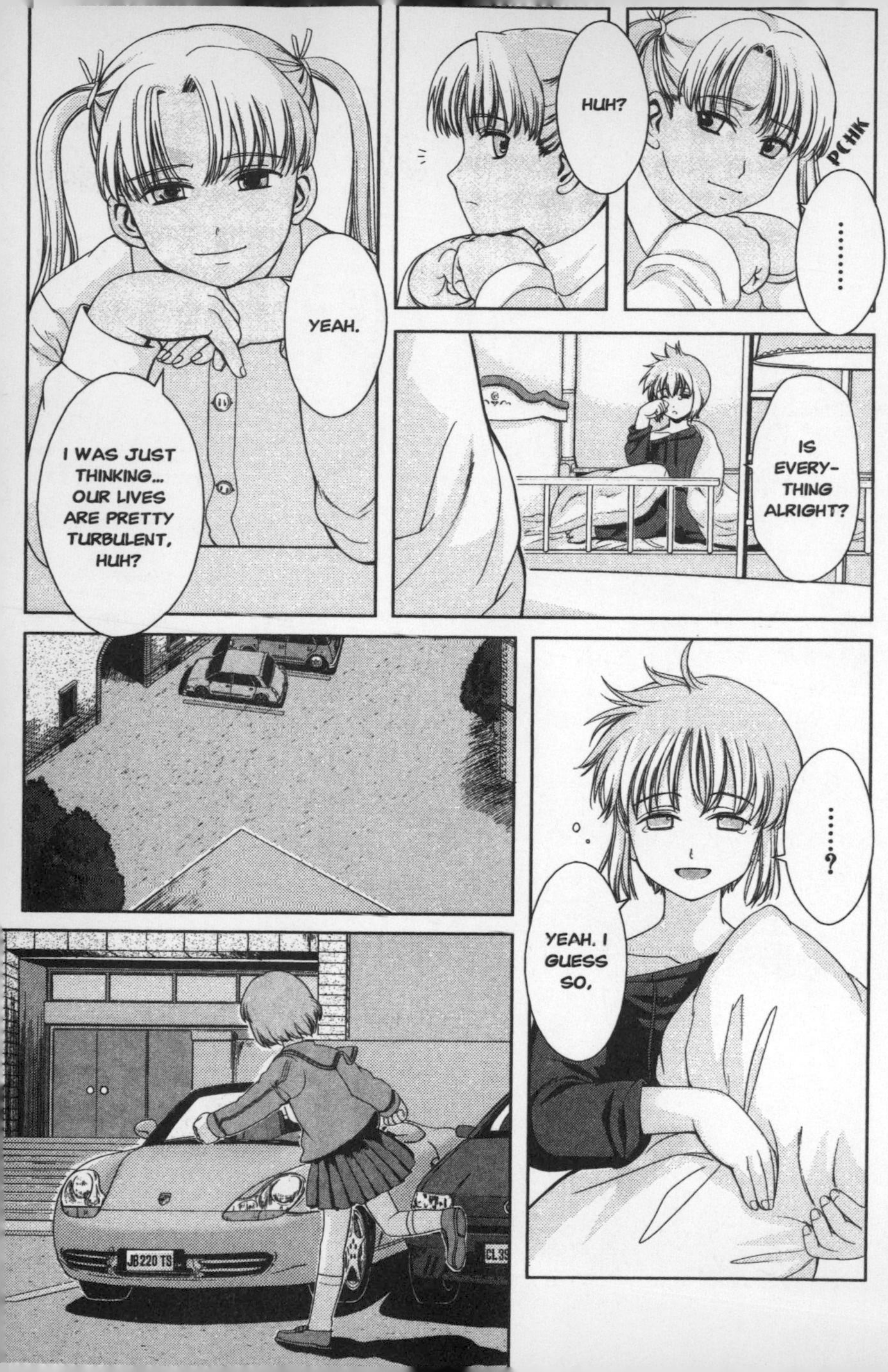
PCHK
......
HUH?
IS EVERY-THING ALRIGHT?
YEAH.
I WAS JUST THINKING... OUR LIVES ARE PRETTY TURBULENT, HUH?
......?
YEAH. I GUESS SO,
JB220 TS

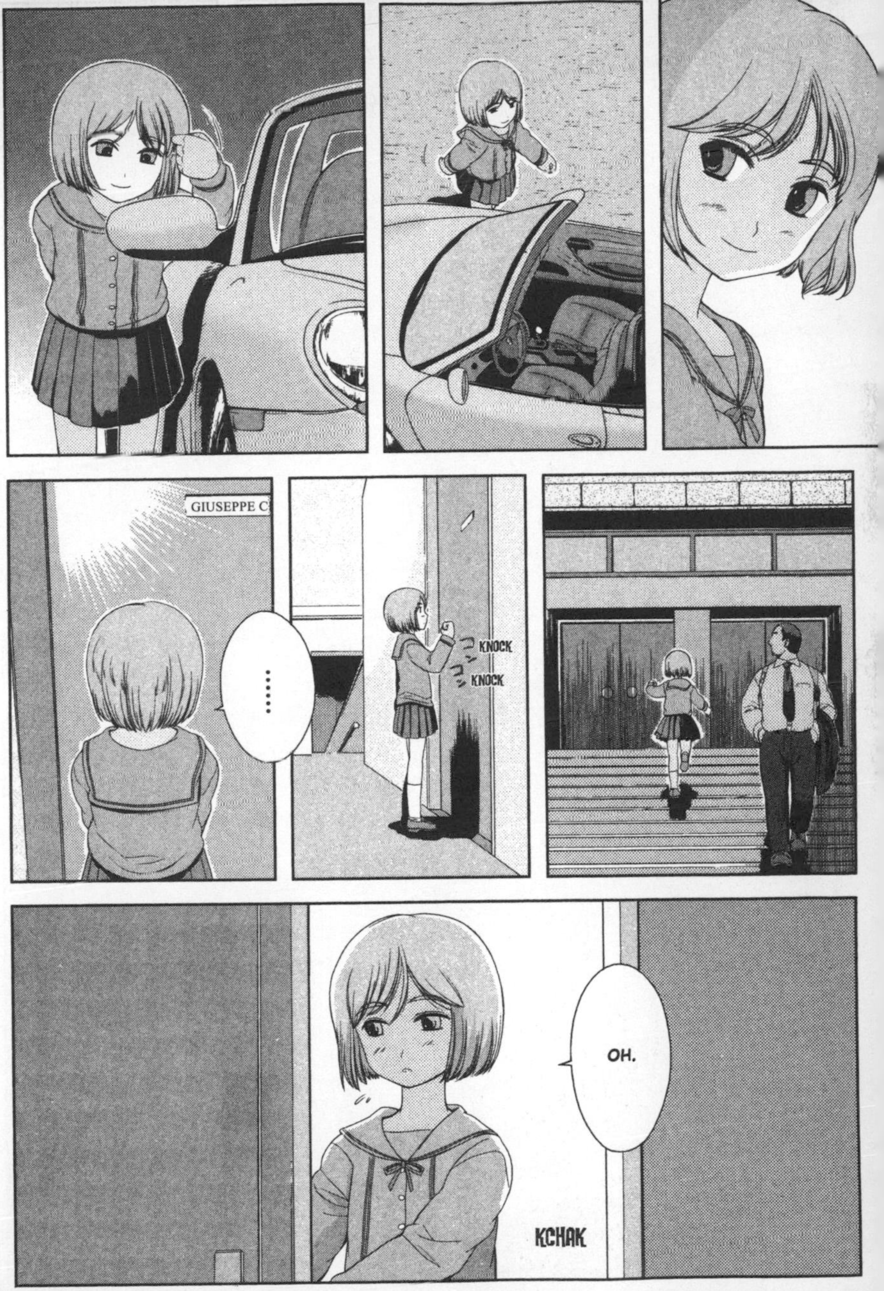
KNOCK
KNOCK
GIUSEPPE C
......
OH.
KCHAK

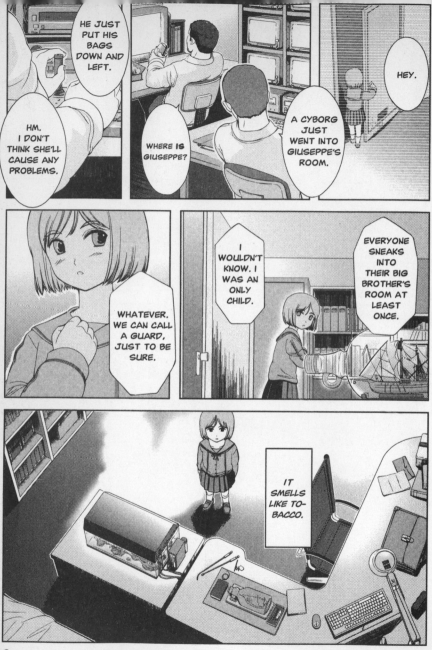

9

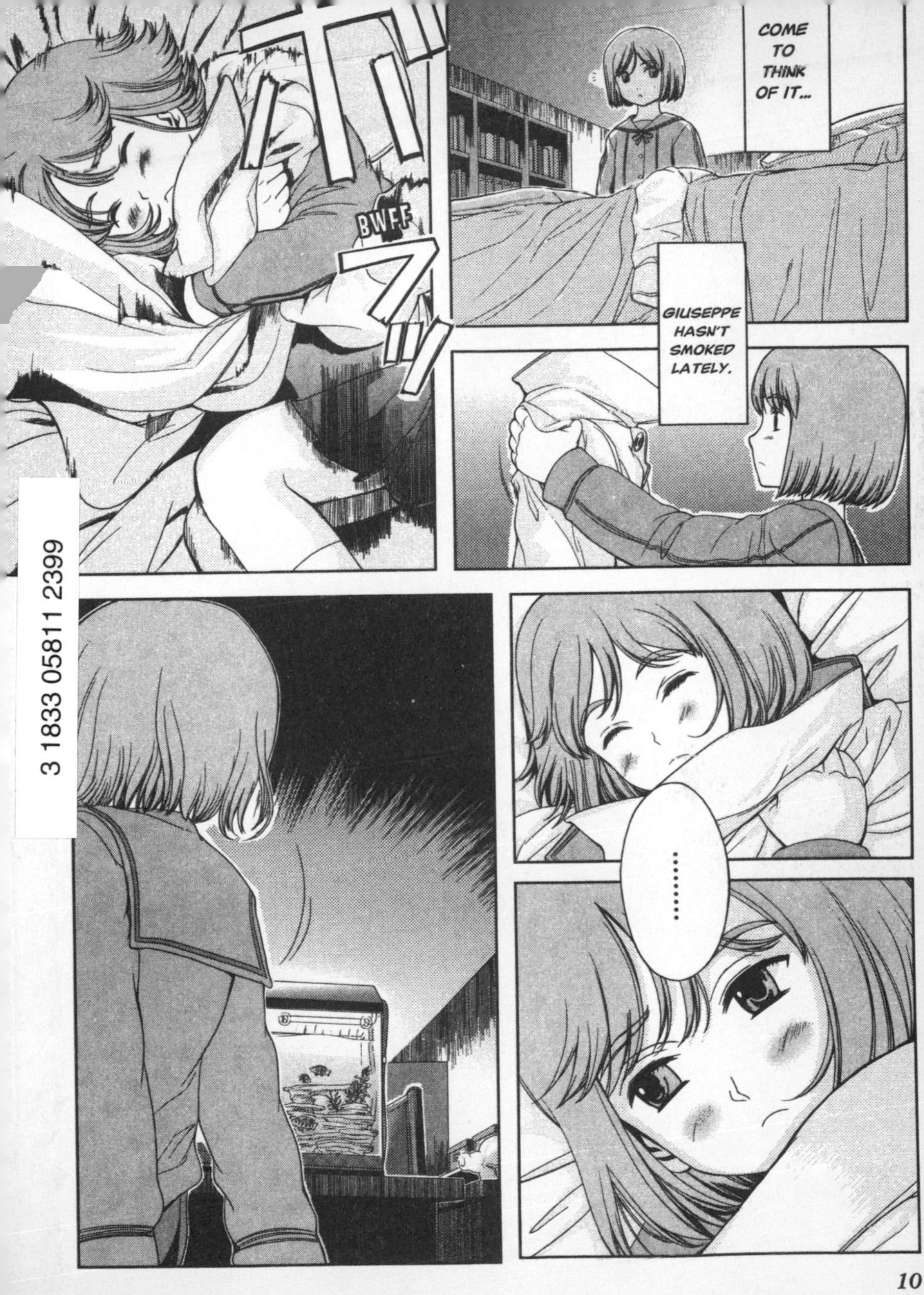
COME TO THINK OF IT...
GIUSEPPE HASN'T SMOKED LATELY.
BWFF
......

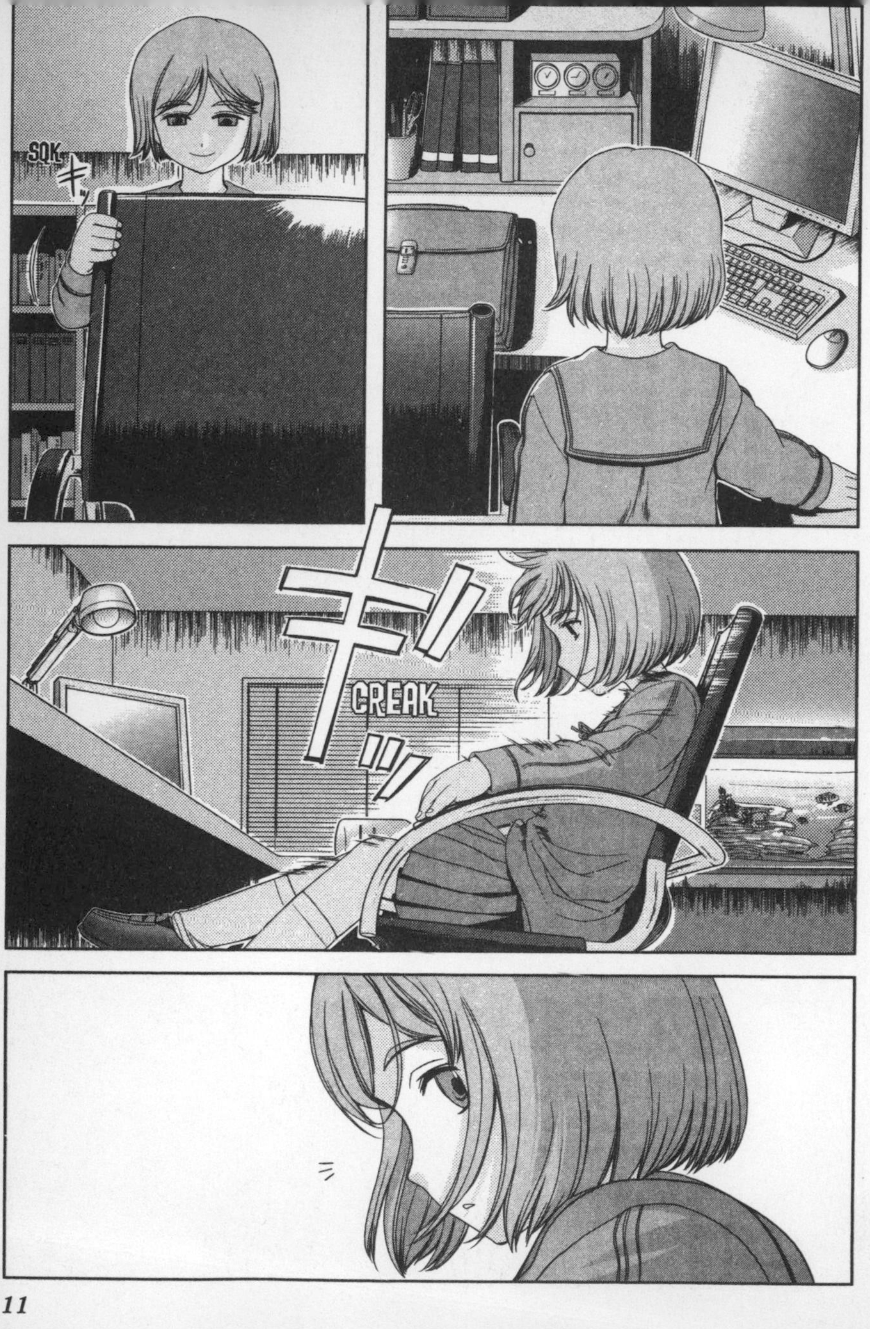
SQK
キ
CREAK

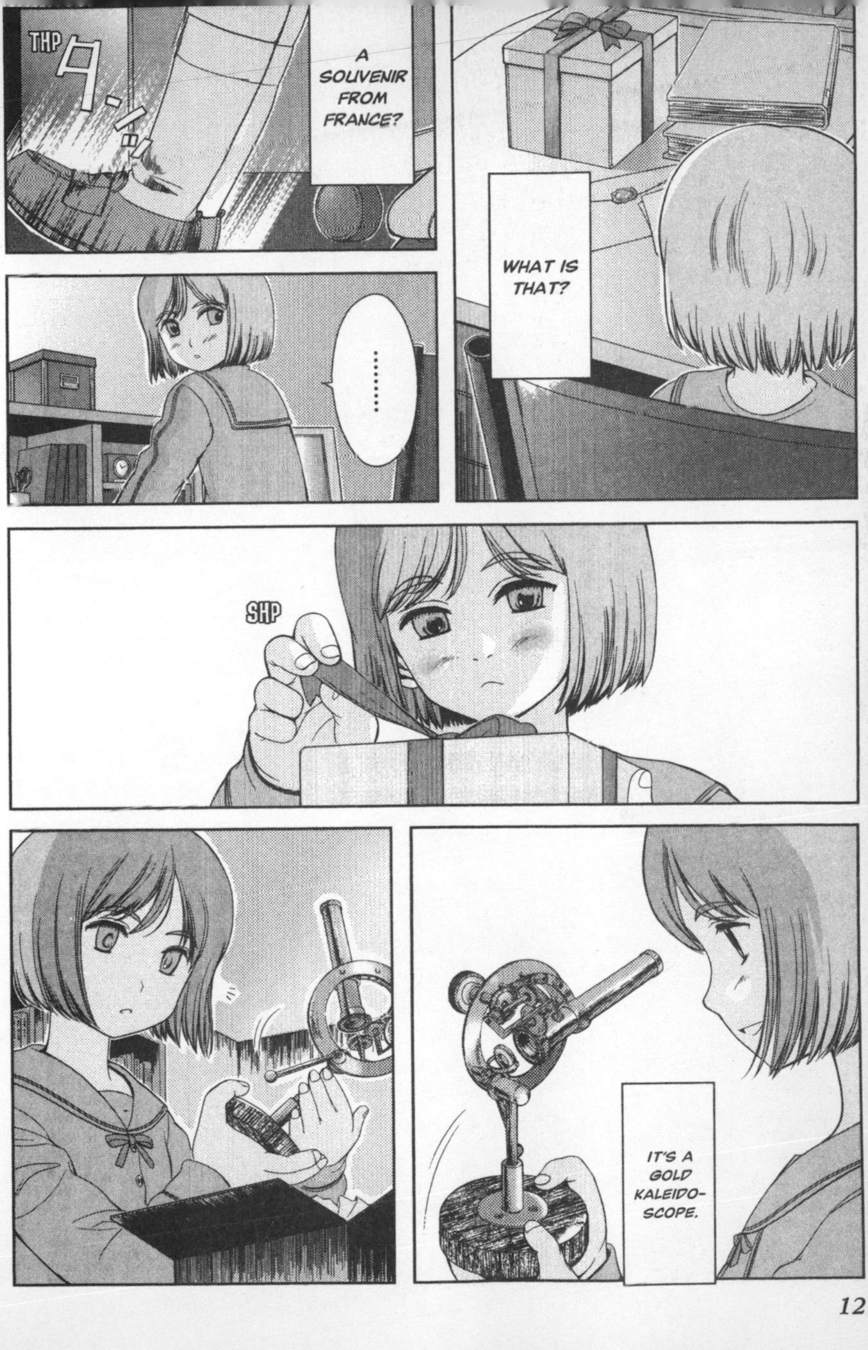
WHAT IS THAT?
THP
A SOUVENIR FROM FRANCE?
....
SHP
IT'S A GOLD KALEIDO-SCOPE.

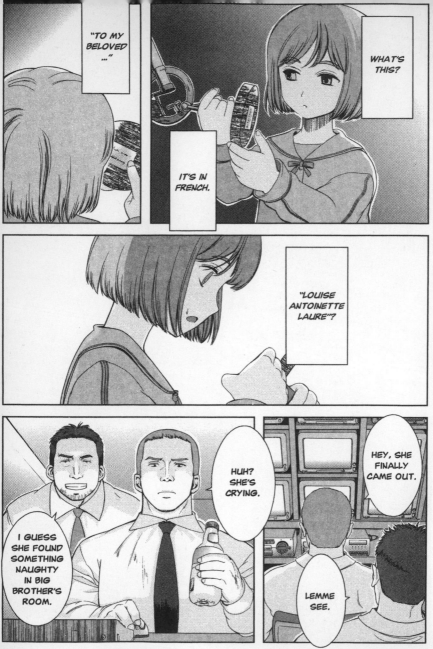

13

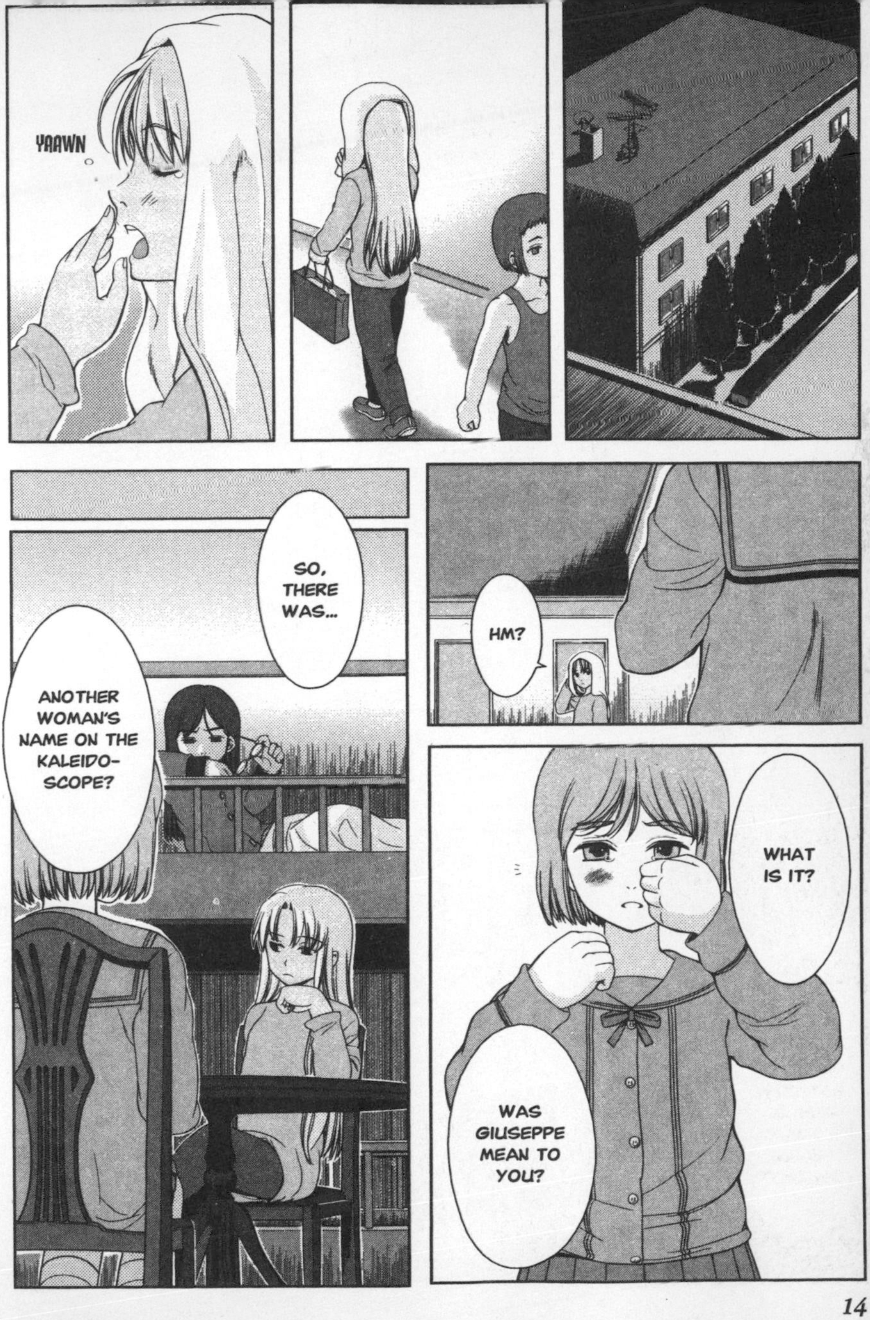
YAAWN
HM?
WHAT IS IT?
WAS GIUSEPPE MEAN TO YOU?
SO, THERE WAS...
ANOTHER WOMAN'S NAME ON THE KALEIDO-SCOPE?

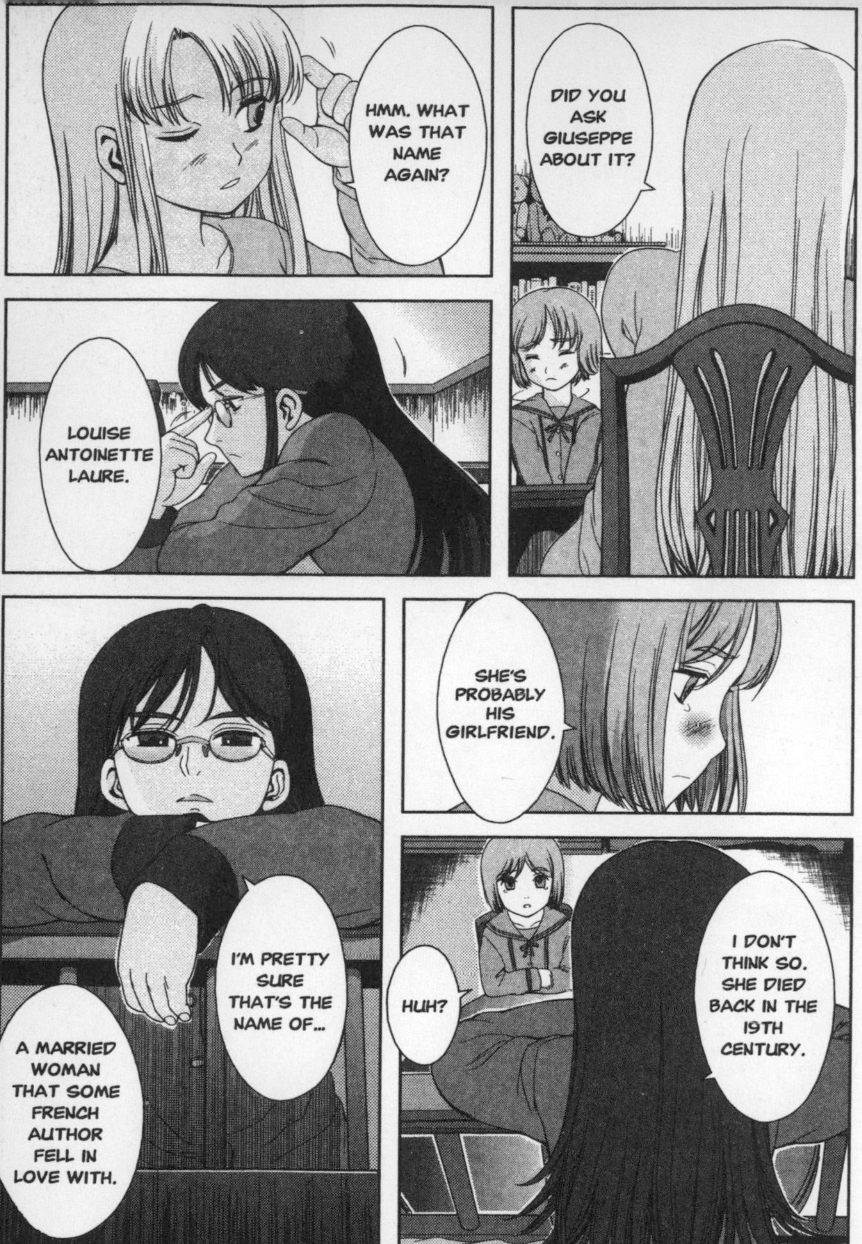
DID YOU ASK GIUSEPPE ABOUT IT?
HMM. WHAT WAS THAT NAME AGAIN?
LOUISE ANTOINETTE LAURE.
SHE'S PROBABLY HIS GIRLFRIEND.
I DON'T THINK SO. SHE DIED BACK IN THE 19TH CENTURY.
HUH?
I'M PRETTY SURE THAT'S THE NAME OF...
A MARRIED WOMAN THAT SOME FRENCH AUTHOR FELL IN LOVE WITH.

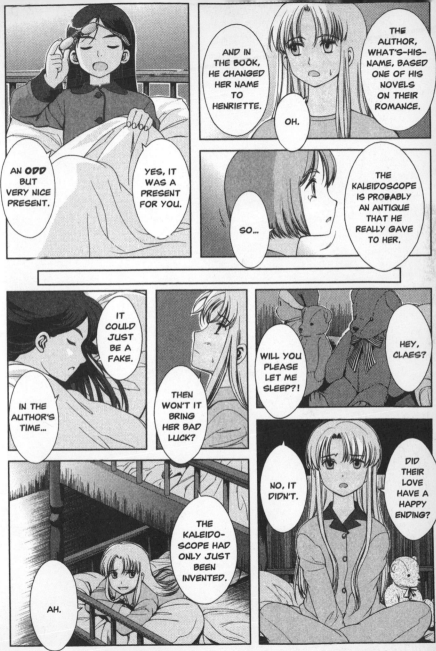

AND IN THE BOOK, HE CHANGED HER NAME TO HENRIETTE.

THE AUTHOR, WHAT'S-HIS-NAME, BASED ONE OF HIS NOVELS ON THEIR ROMANCE.

OH.

AN ODD BUT VERY NICE PRESENT.

YES, IT WAS A PRESENT FOR YOU.

SO...

THE KALEIDOSCOPE IS PROBABLY AN ANTIQUE THAT HE REALLY GAVE TO HER.

IT COULD JUST BE A FAKE.

WILL YOU PLEASE LET ME SLEEP?!

HEY, CLAES?

IN THE AUTHOR'S TIME...

THEN WON'T IT BRING HER BAD LUCK?

NO, IT DIDN'T.

DID THEIR LOVE HAVE A HAPPY ENDING?

THE KALEIDO-SCOPE HAD ONLY JUST BEEN INVENTED.

AH.

16

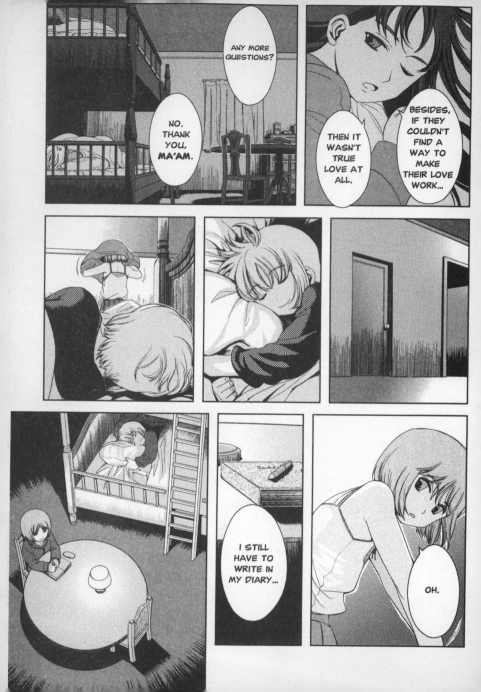

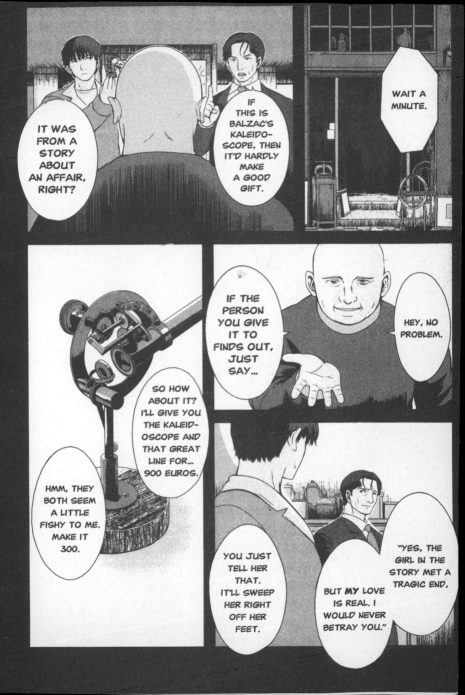

GUNSLINGERGIRL.

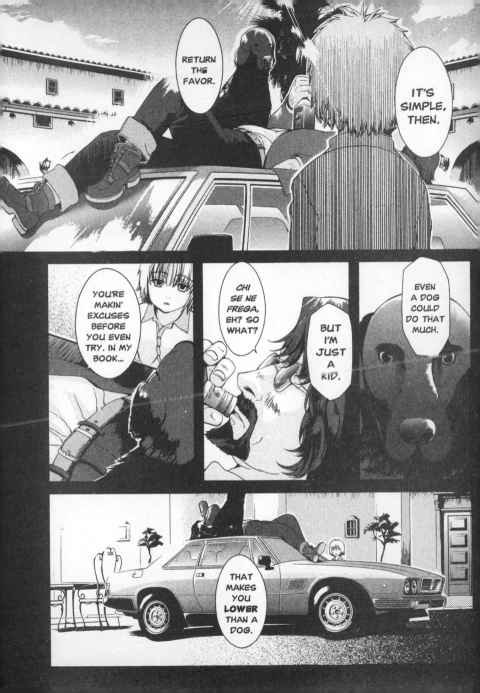

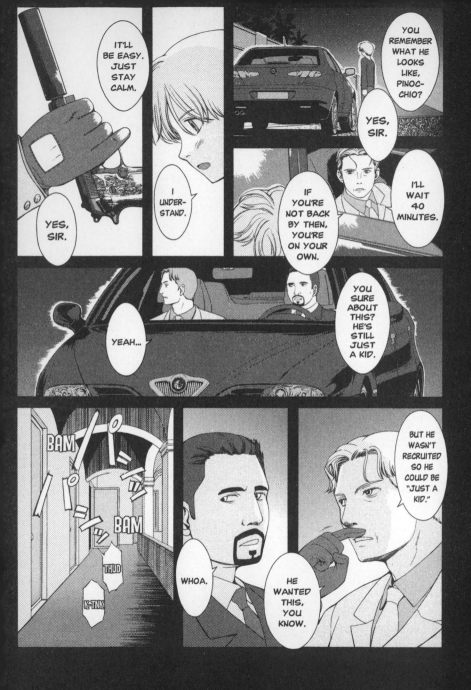

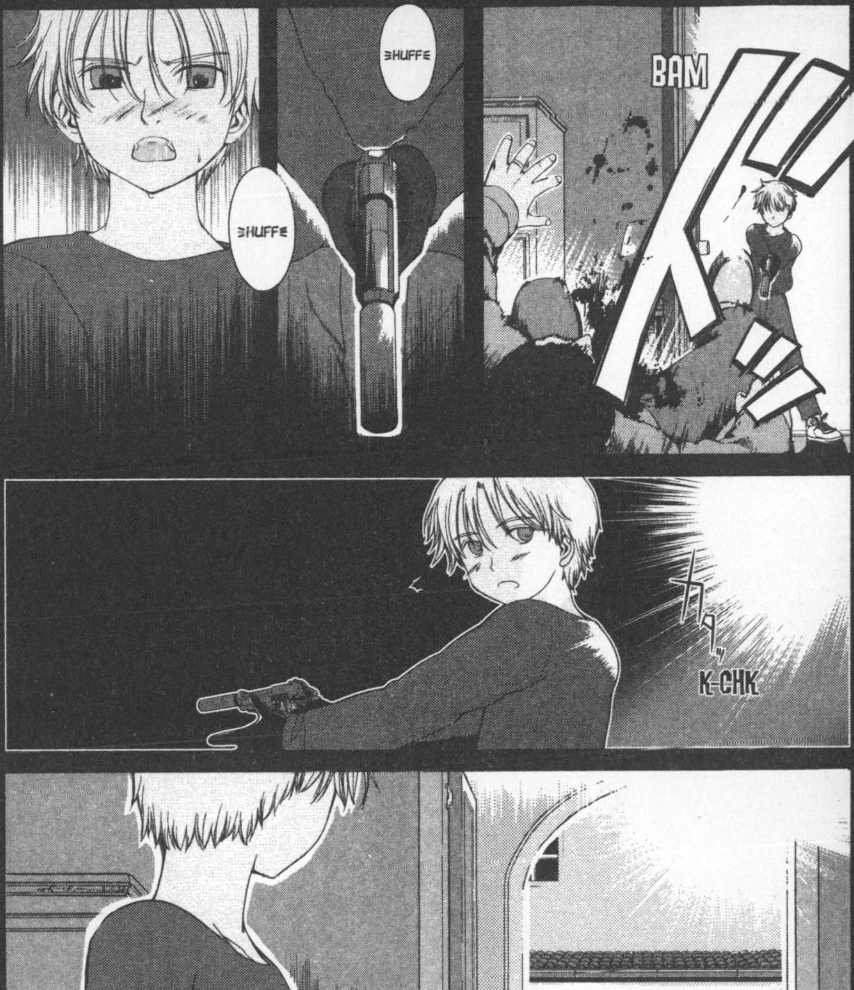
BAM
HUFF
HUFF
K-CHK
FATHER?

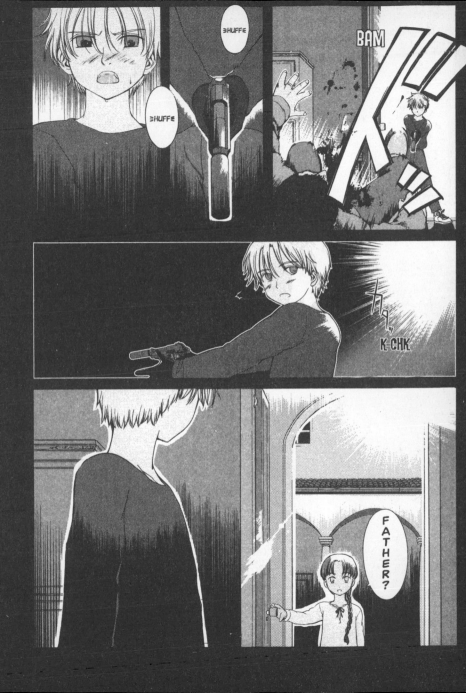

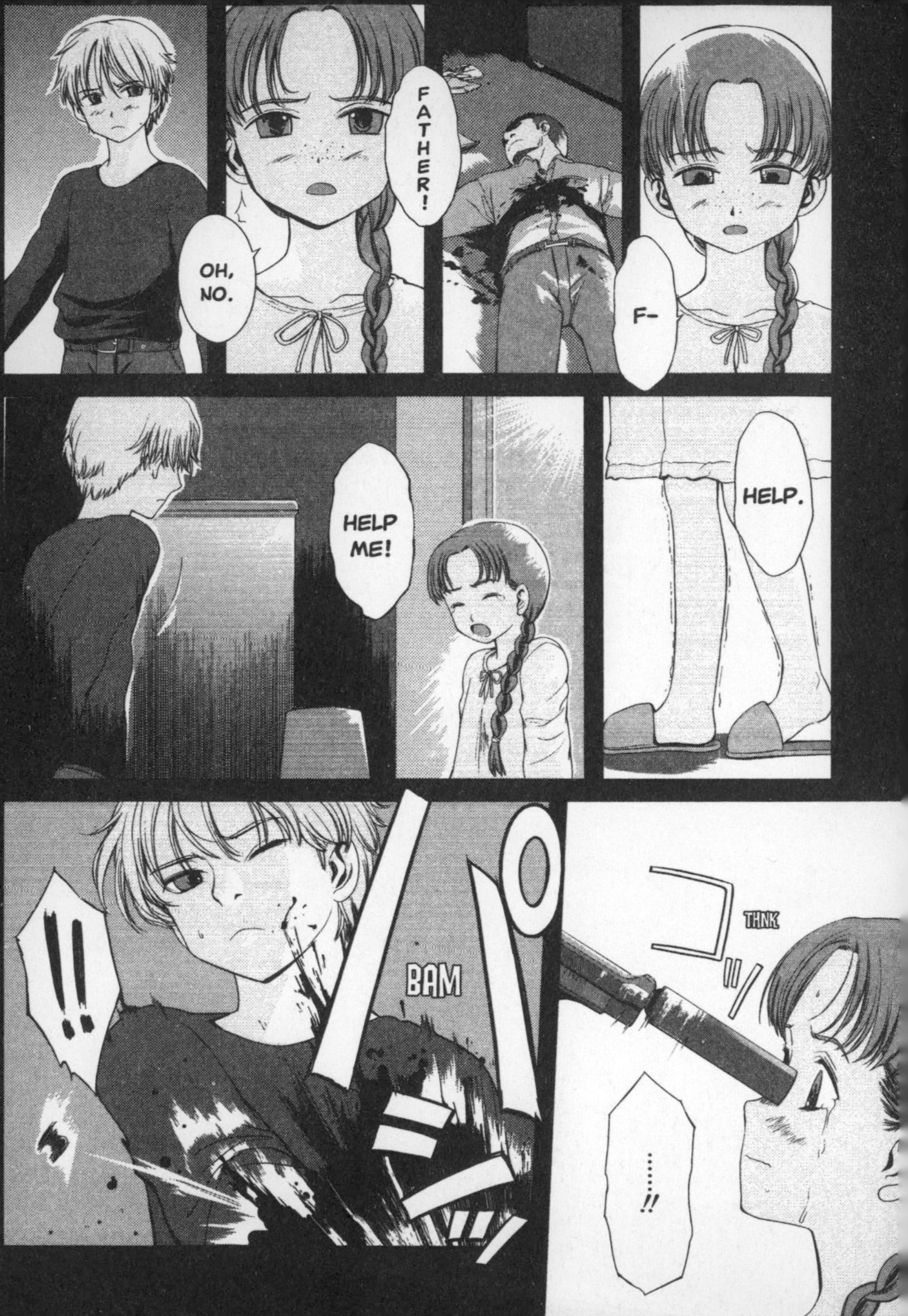
F-
FATHER!
OH, NO.
HELP.
HELP ME!
THNK
……!!
BAM
!!

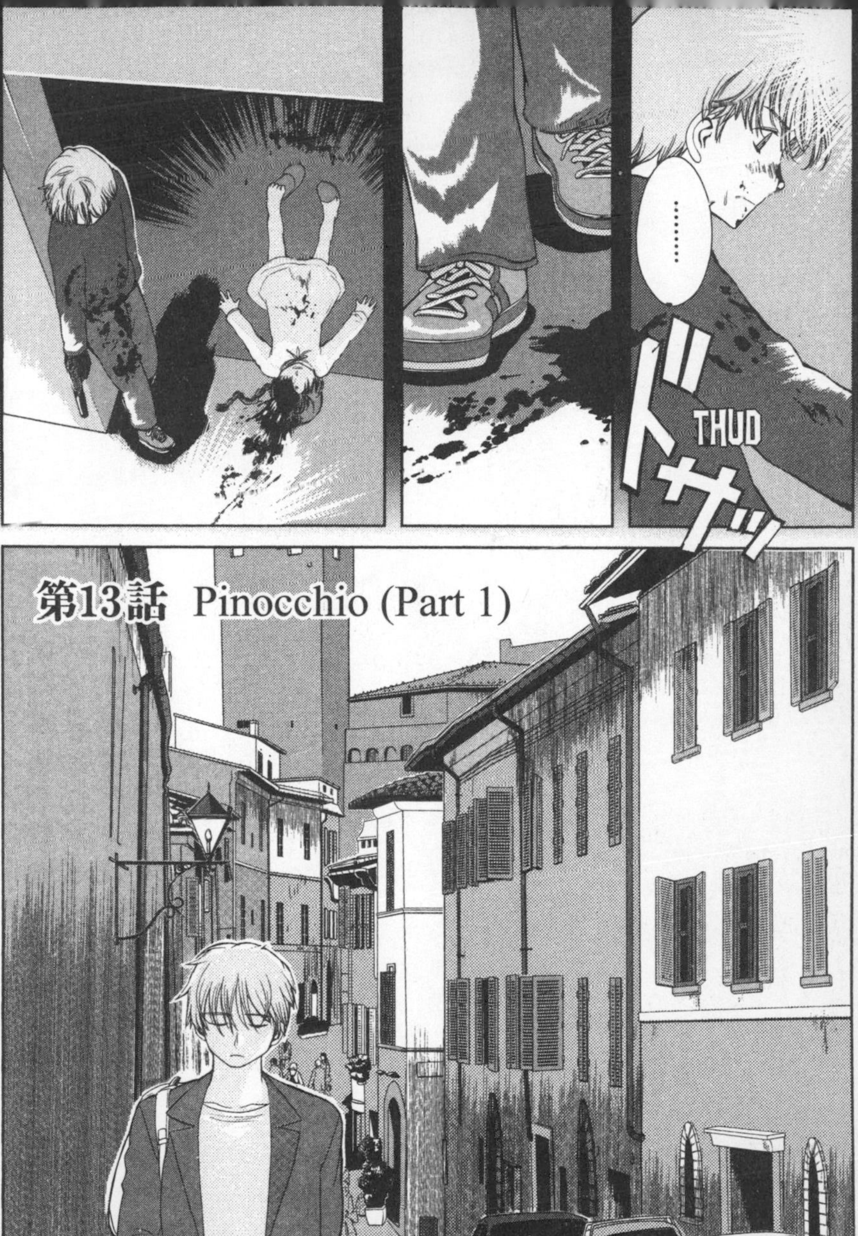
……
ドサッ
THUD
第13話 Pinocchio (Part 1)

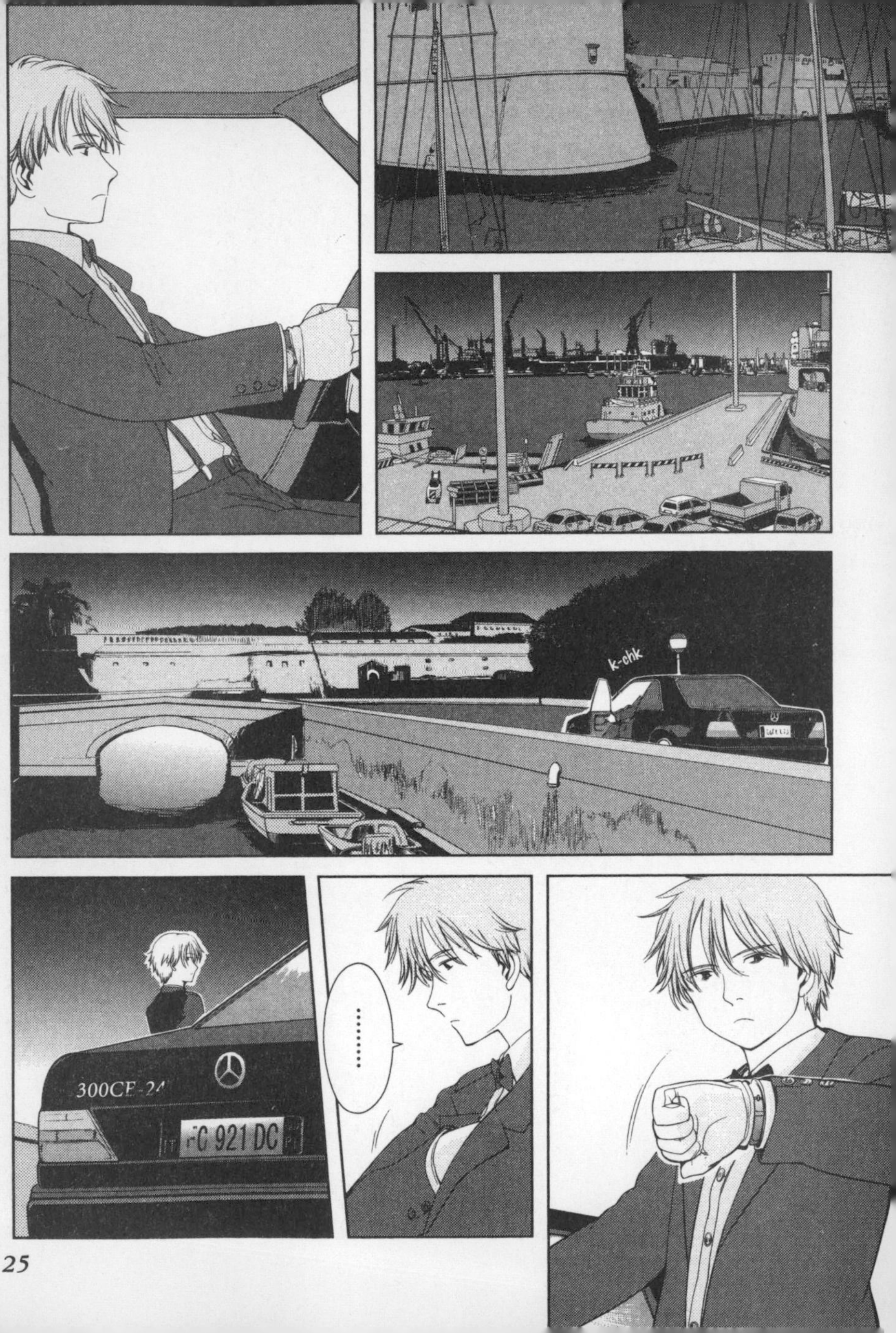
k-chk
....
300CE-24
C 921 DC

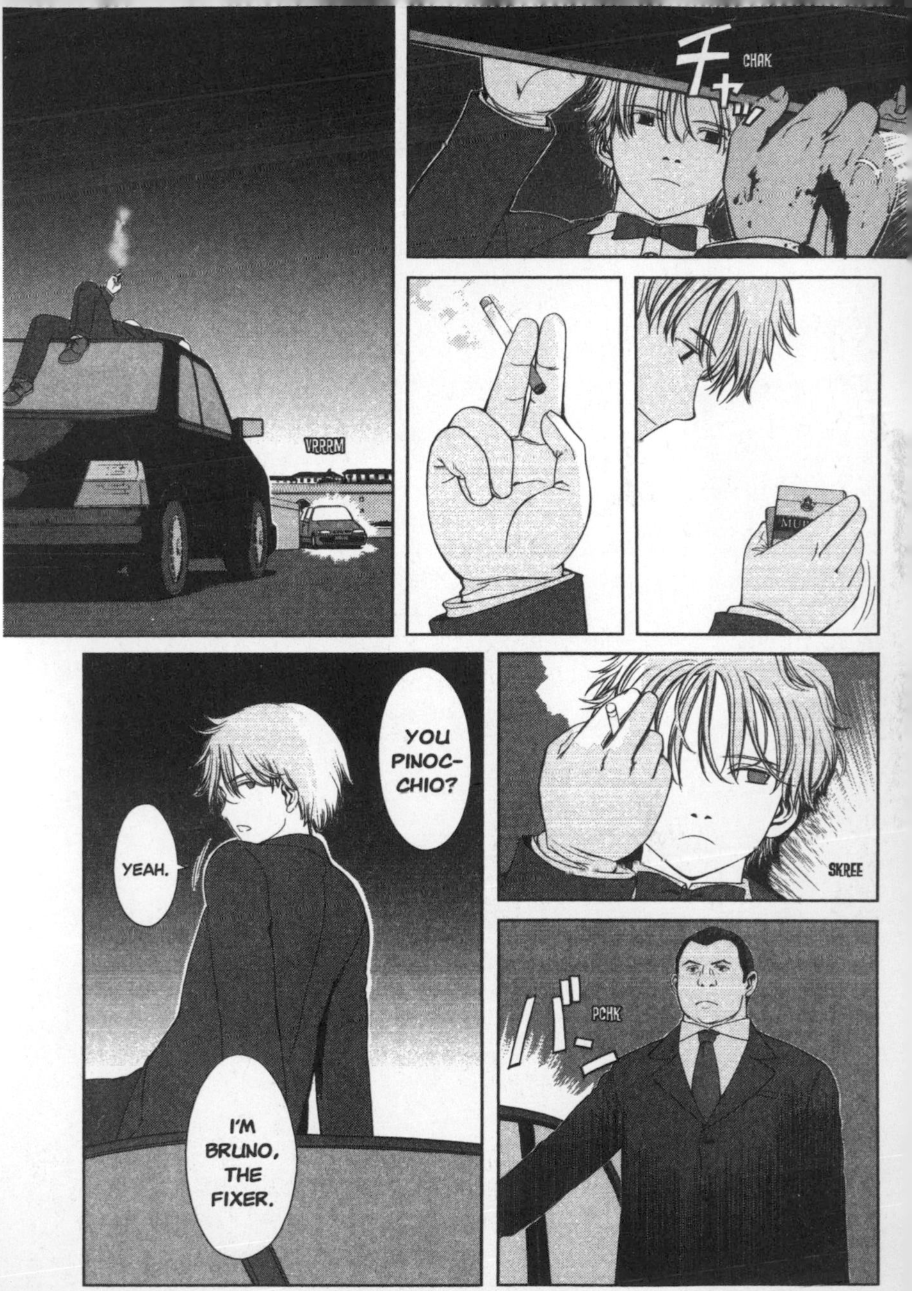
チャッ
CHAK
SKREE
バーー
PCHK
VRRRM
YOU PINOC-CHIO?
YEAH.
I'M BRUNO, THE FIXER.

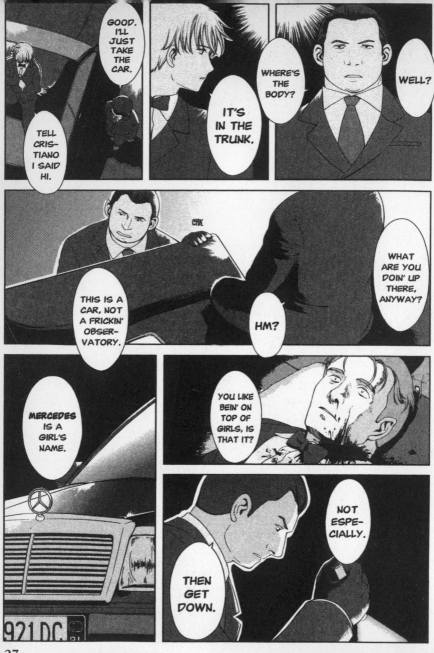

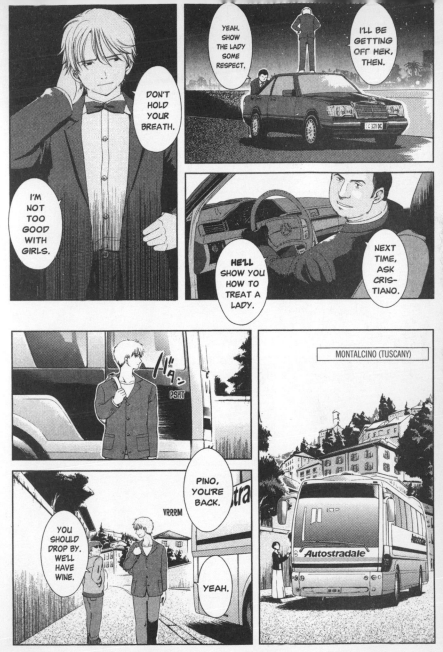

28

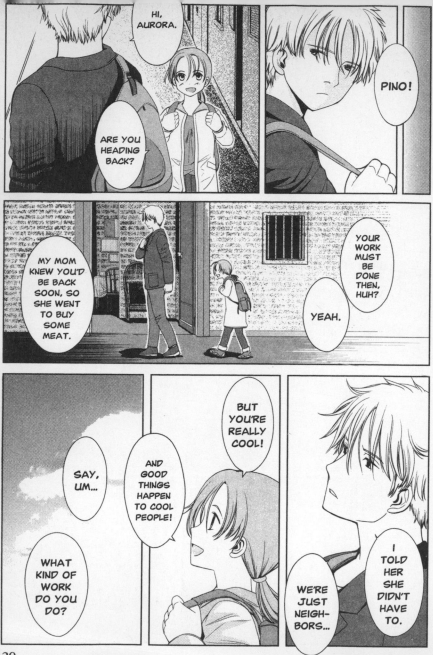

29

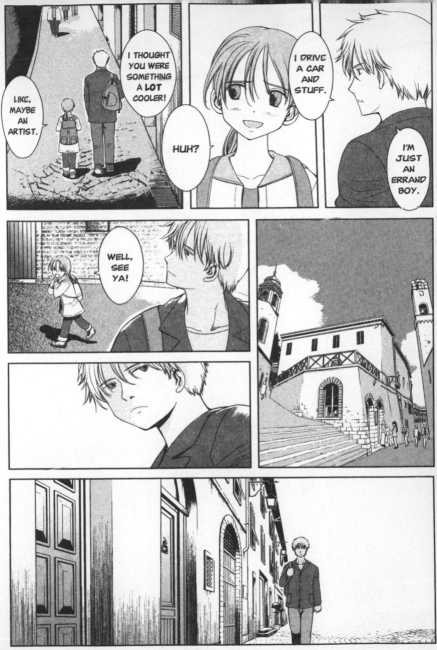

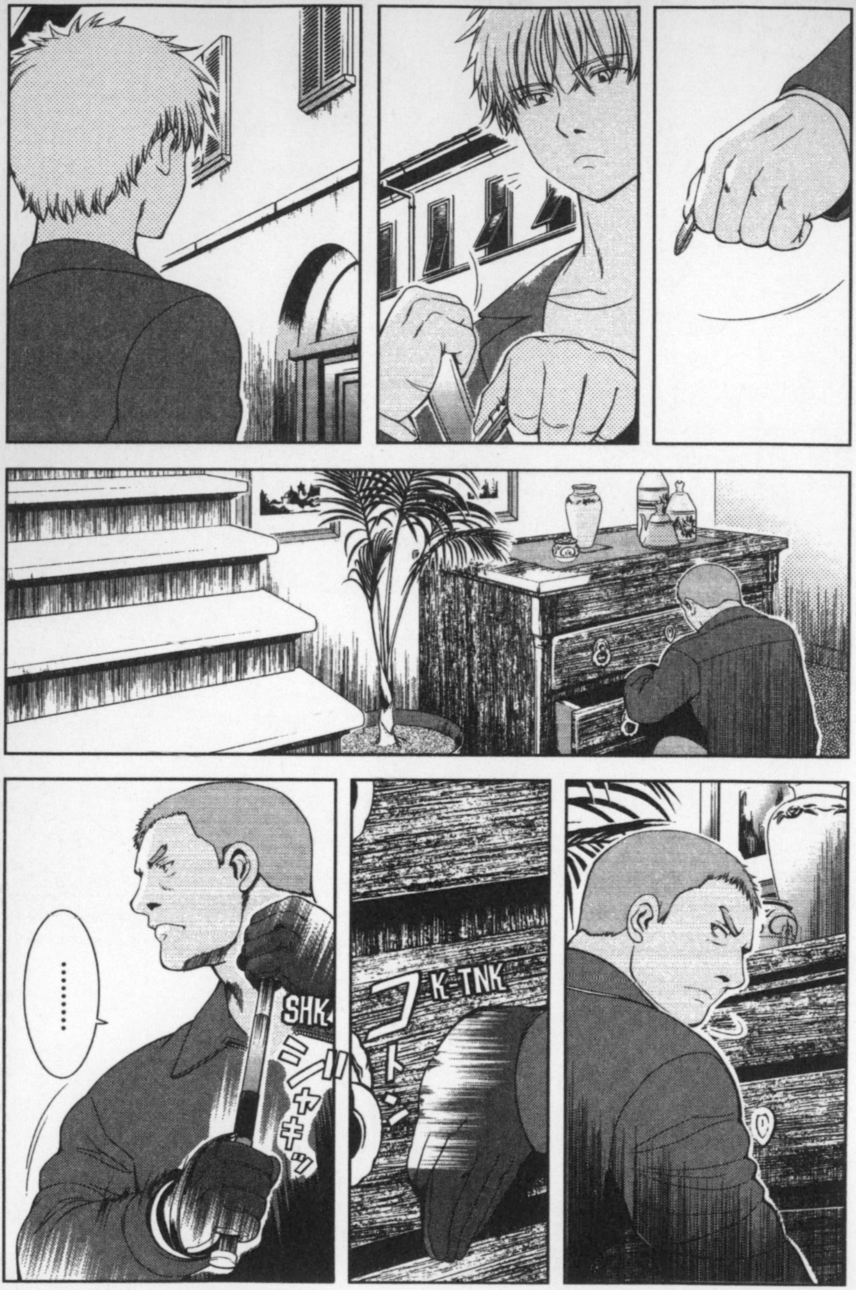
K-TNK
コトン
SHK
シャキッ
……

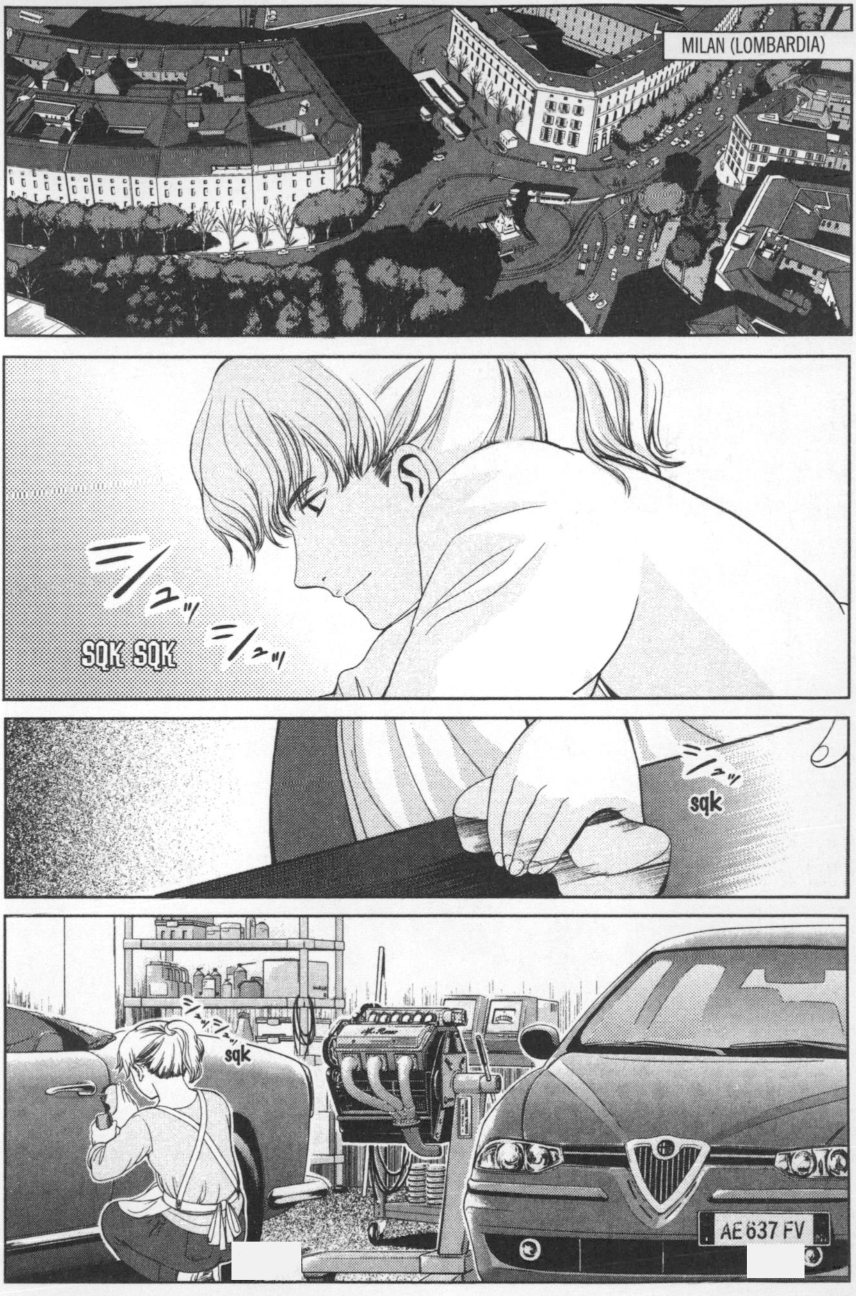
MILAN (LOMBARDIA)
SQK SQK
sqk
sqk
AE 637 FV

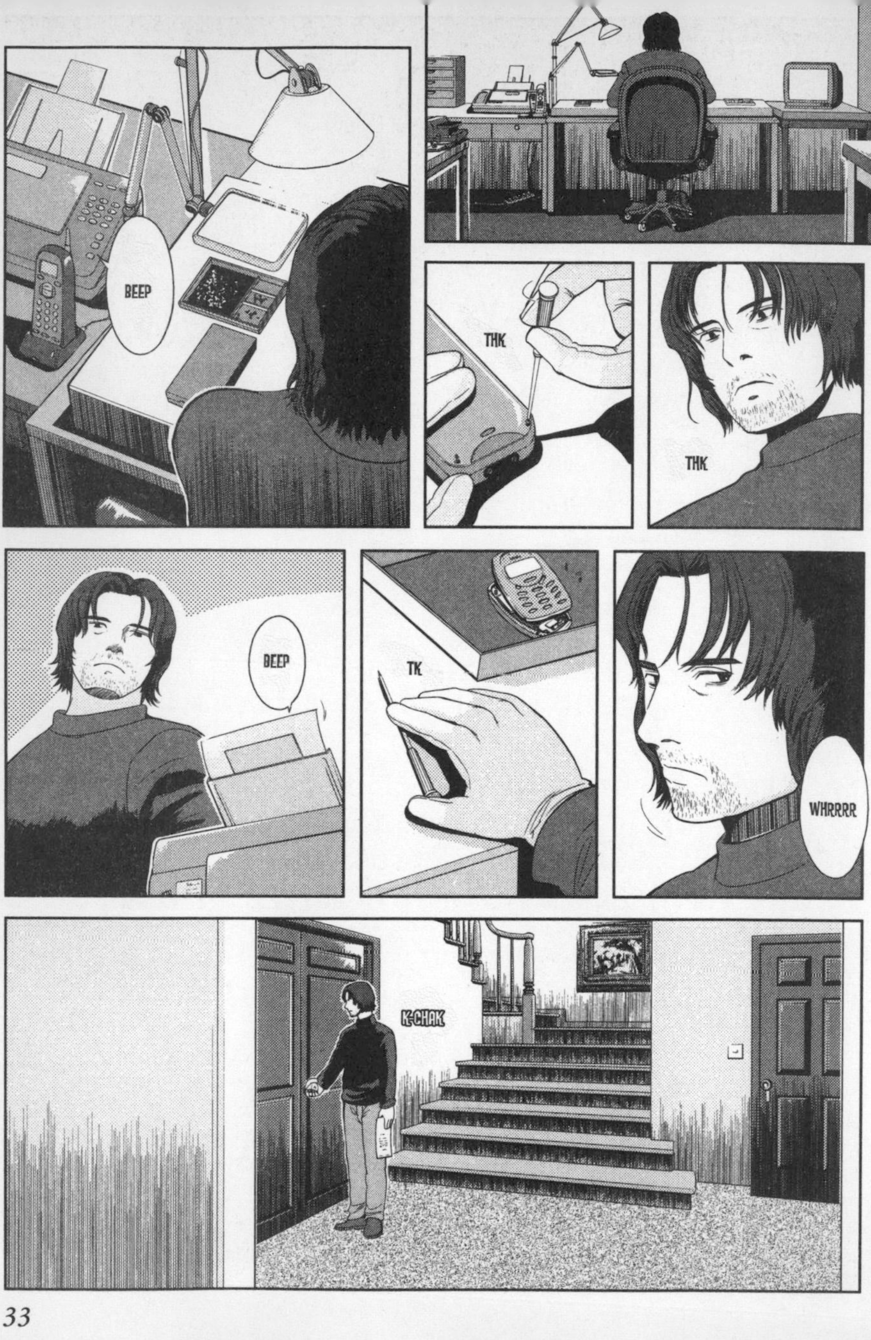
THK
THK
BEEP
WHRRRR
TK
BEEP
K-CHAK

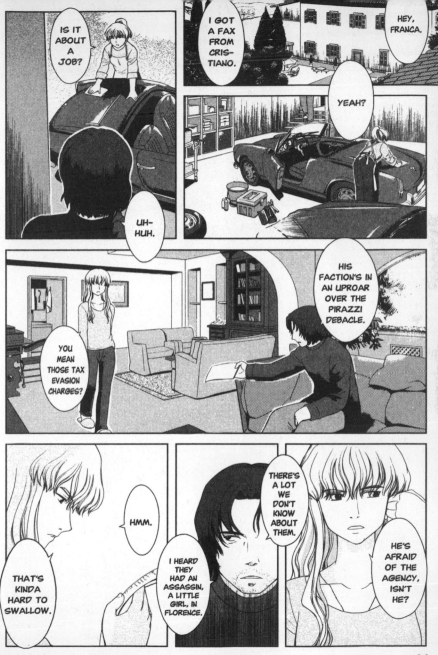

34

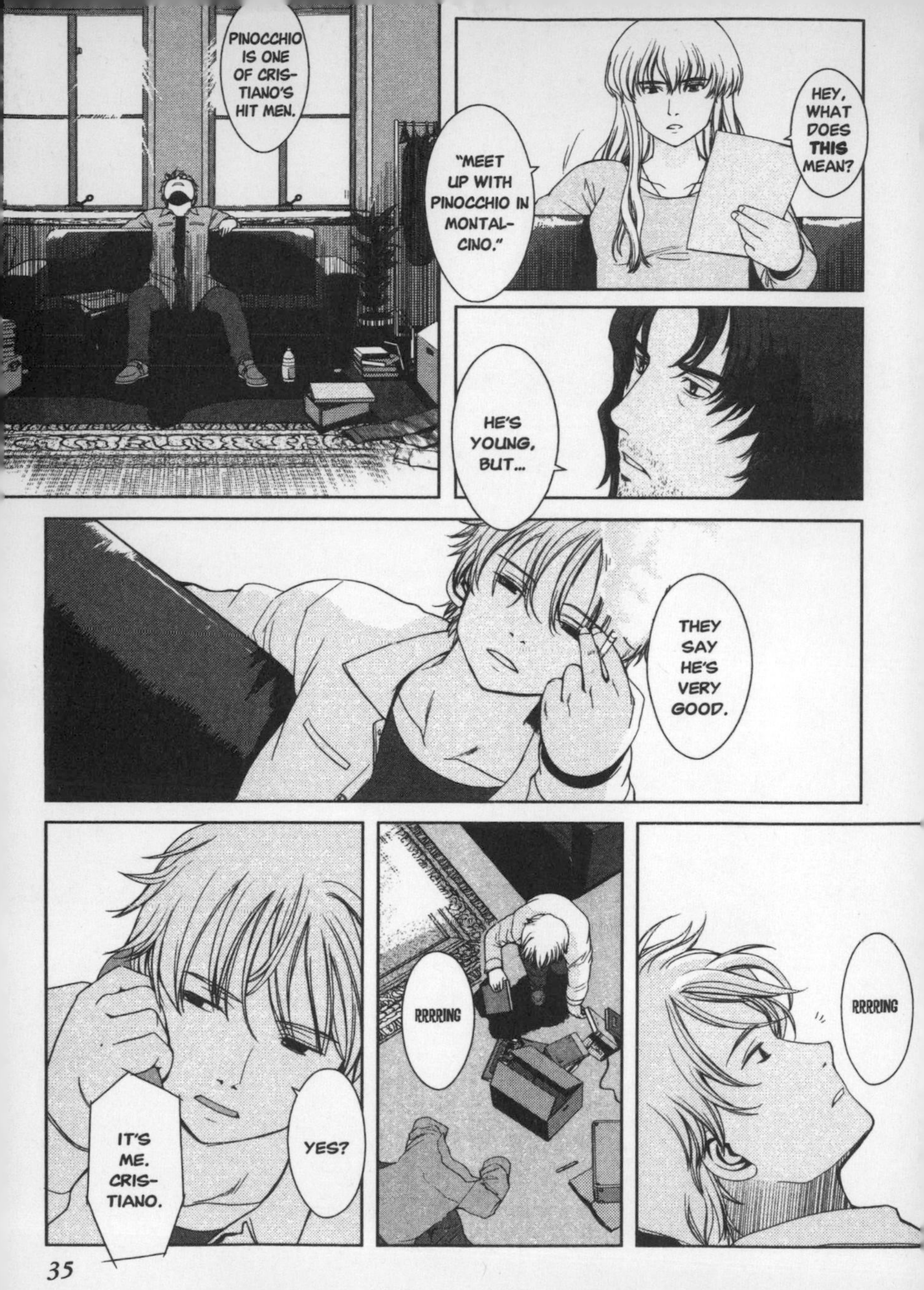
HEY, WHAT DOES THIS MEAN?
"MEET UP WITH PINOCCHIO IN MONTAL-CINO."
HE'S YOUNG, BUT...
PINOCCHIO IS ONE OF CRIS-TIANO'S HIT MEN.
THEY SAY HE'S VERY GOOD.
RRRRING
RRRRING
YES?
IT'S ME. CRIS-TIANO.

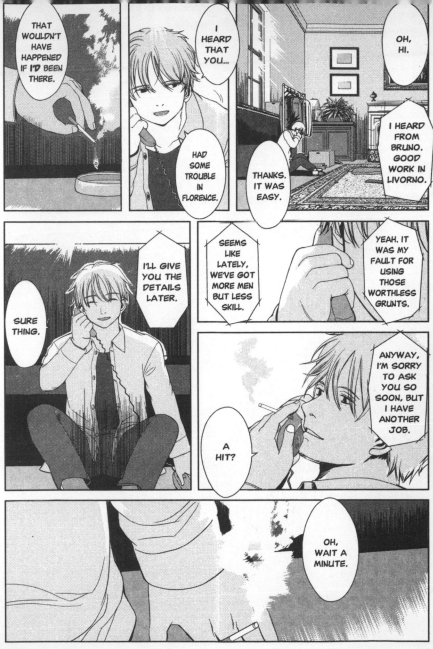

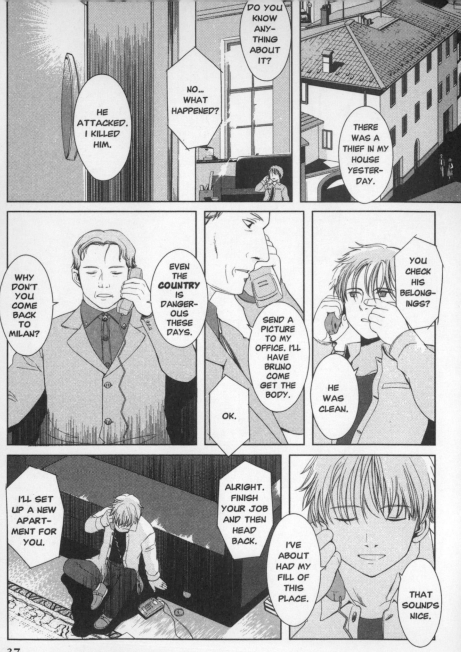

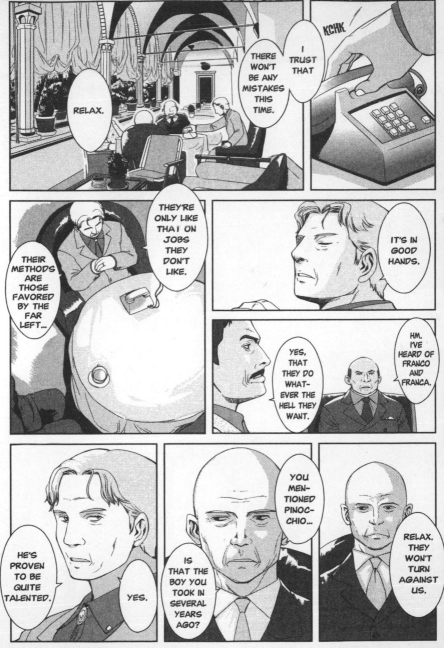

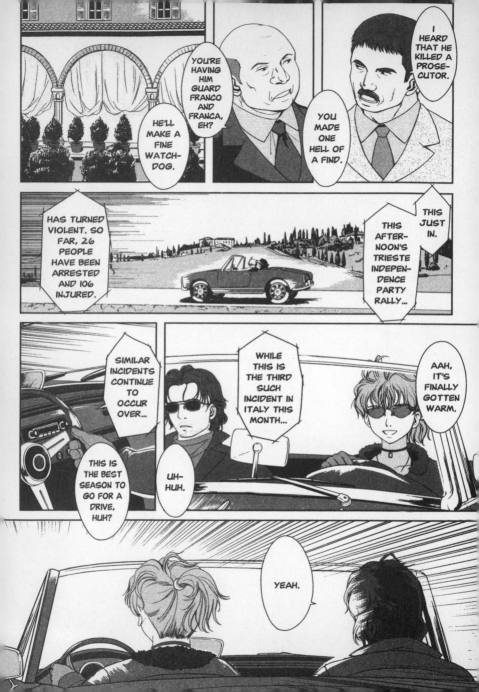

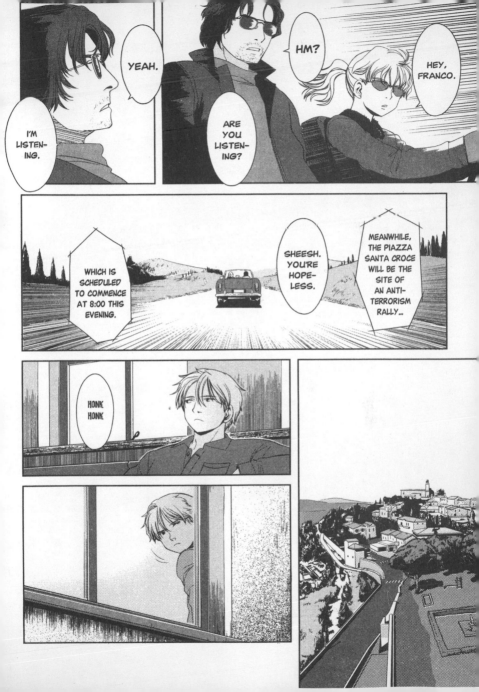

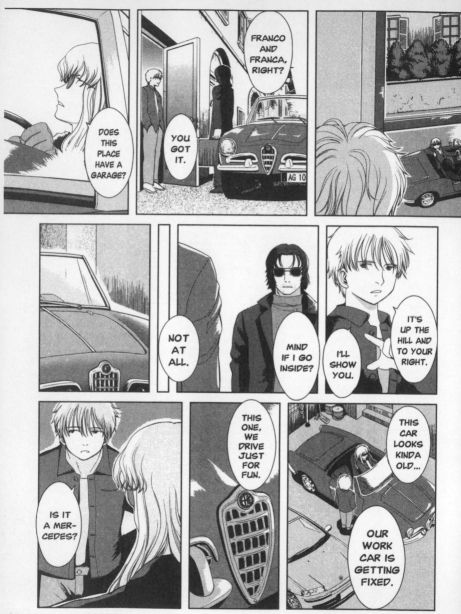

41

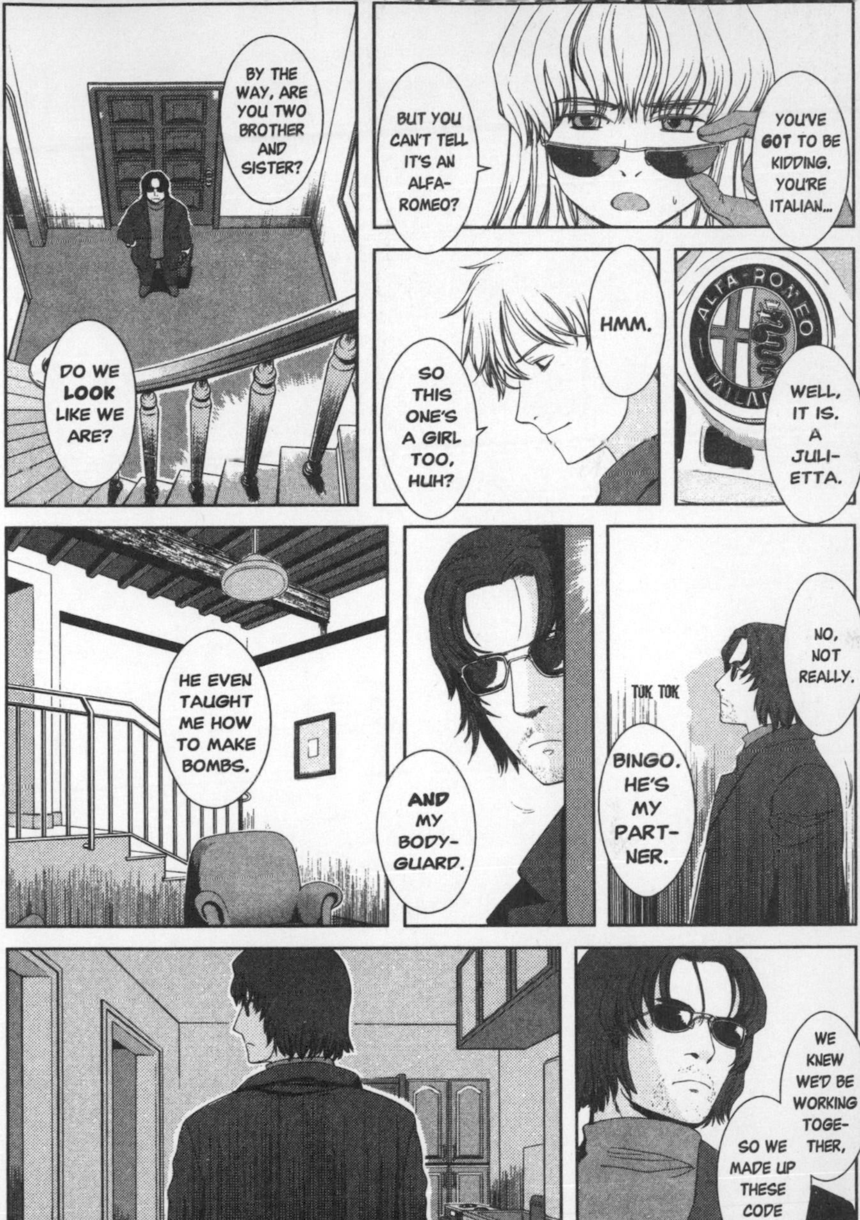
YOU'VE GOT TO BE KIDDING. YOU'RE ITALIAN...
BUT YOU CAN'T TELL IT'S AN ALFA-ROMEO?
ALFA-ROMEO
WELL, IT IS. A JULIETTA.
HMM.
SO THIS ONE'S A GIRL TOO, HUH?
BY THE WAY, ARE YOU TWO BROTHER AND SISTER?
DO WE LOOK LIKE WE ARE?
NO, NOT REALLY.
TOK TOK
BINGO. HE'S MY PARTNER.
AND MY BODYGUARD.
HE EVEN TAUGHT ME HOW TO MAKE BOMBS.
WE KNEW WE'D BE WORKING TOGETHER,
SO WE MADE UP THESE CODE NAMES.

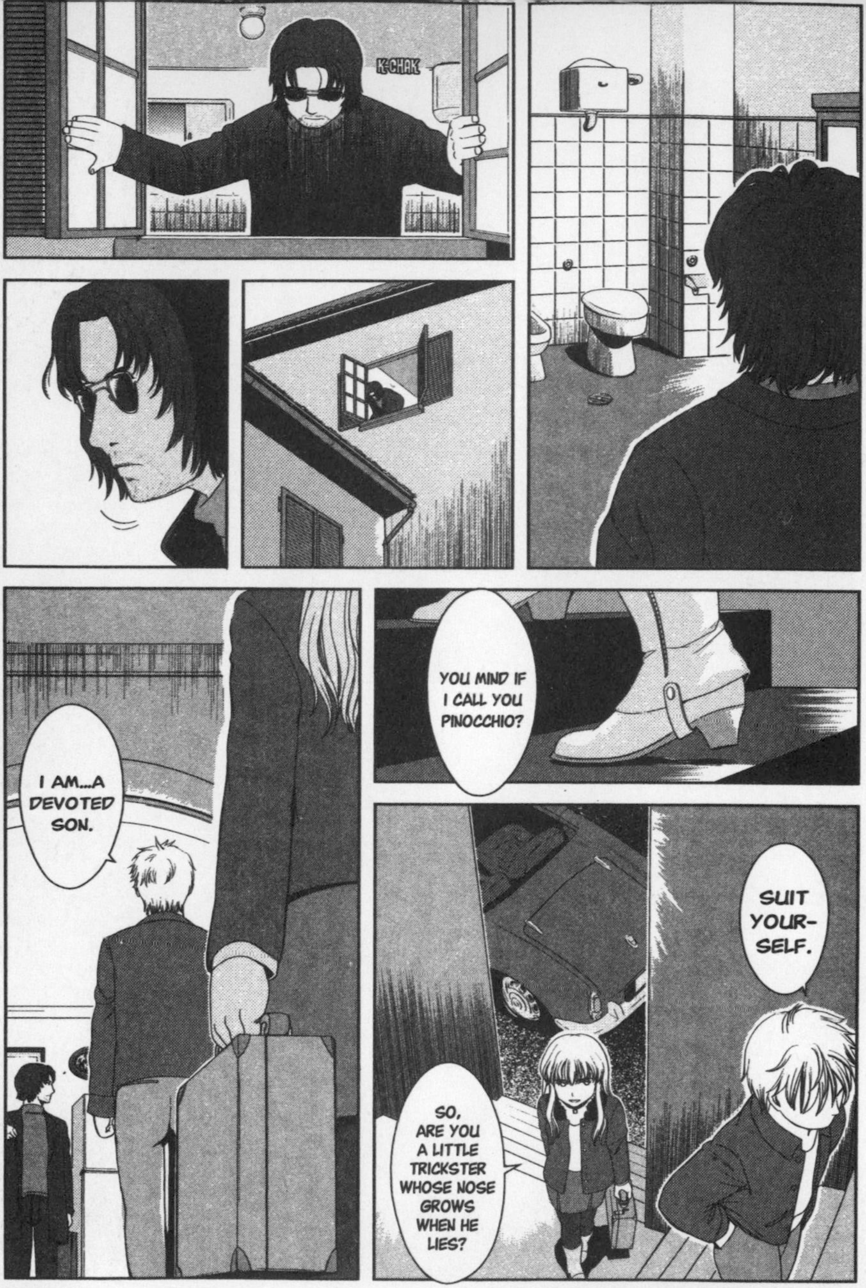
K-CHAK
YOU MIND IF I CALL YOU PINOCCHIO?
SUIT YOURSELF.
SO, ARE YOU A LITTLE TRICKSTER WHOSE NOSE GROWS WHEN HE LIES?
I AM...A DEVOTED SON.

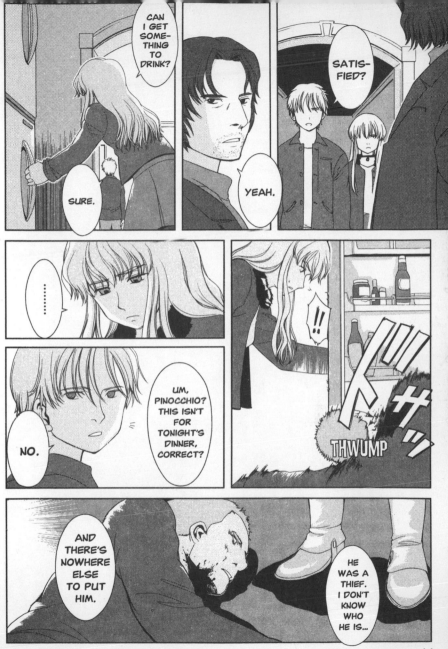

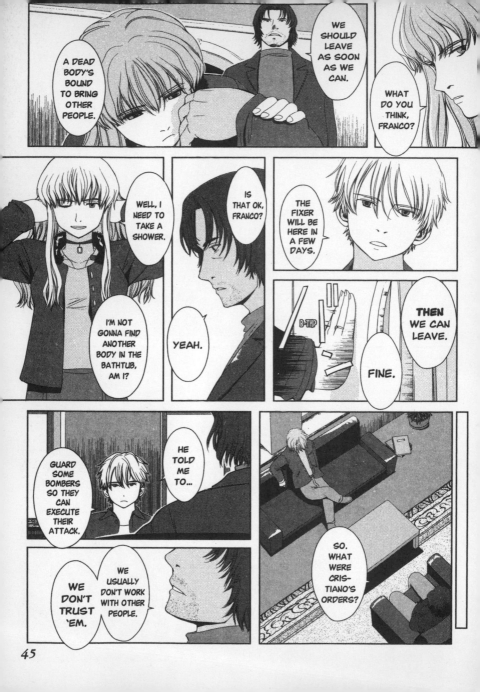

A DEAD BODY'S BOUND TO BRING OTHER PEOPLE.

WE SHOULD LEAVE AS SOON AS WE CAN.

WHAT DO YOU THINK, FRANCO?

WELL, I NEED TO TAKE A SHOWER.

IS THAT OK, FRANCO?

THE FIXER WILL BE HERE IN A FEW DAYS.

I'M NOT GONNA FIND ANOTHER BODY IN THE BATHTUB, AM I?

YEAH.

B-THP

THEN WE CAN LEAVE.

FINE.

GUARD SOME BOMBERS SO THEY CAN EXECUTE THEIR ATTACK.

HE TOLD ME TO...

WE DON'T TRUST 'EM.

WE USUALLY DON'T WORK WITH OTHER PEOPLE.

SO. WHAT WERE CRISTIANO'S ORDERS?

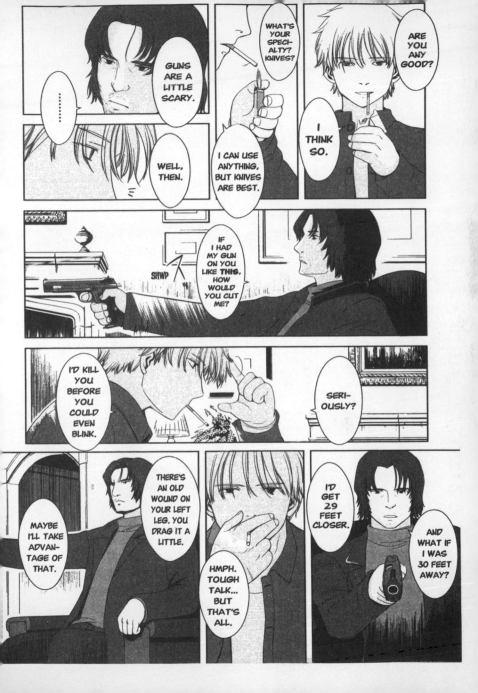

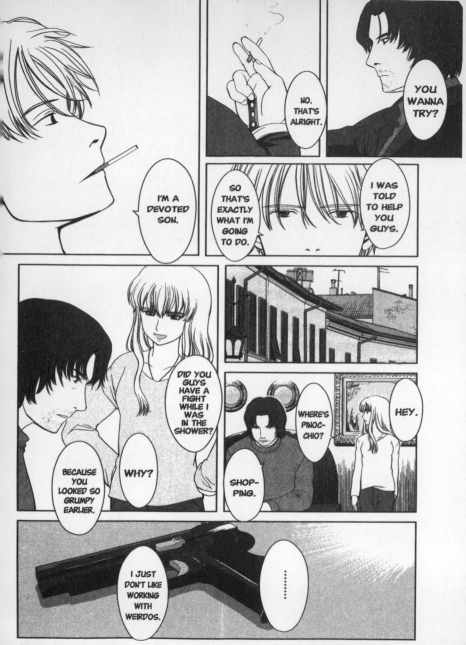

47

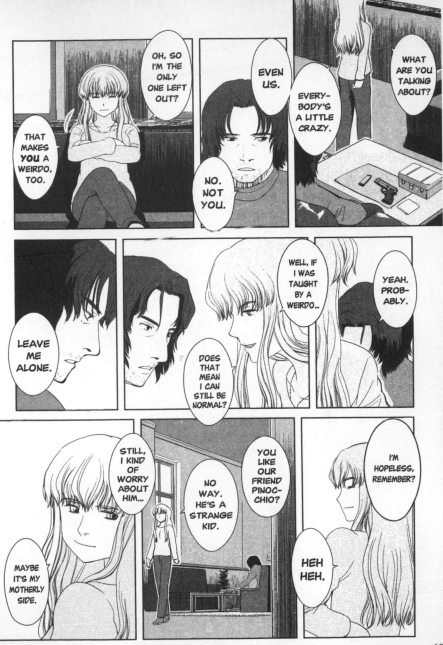

48

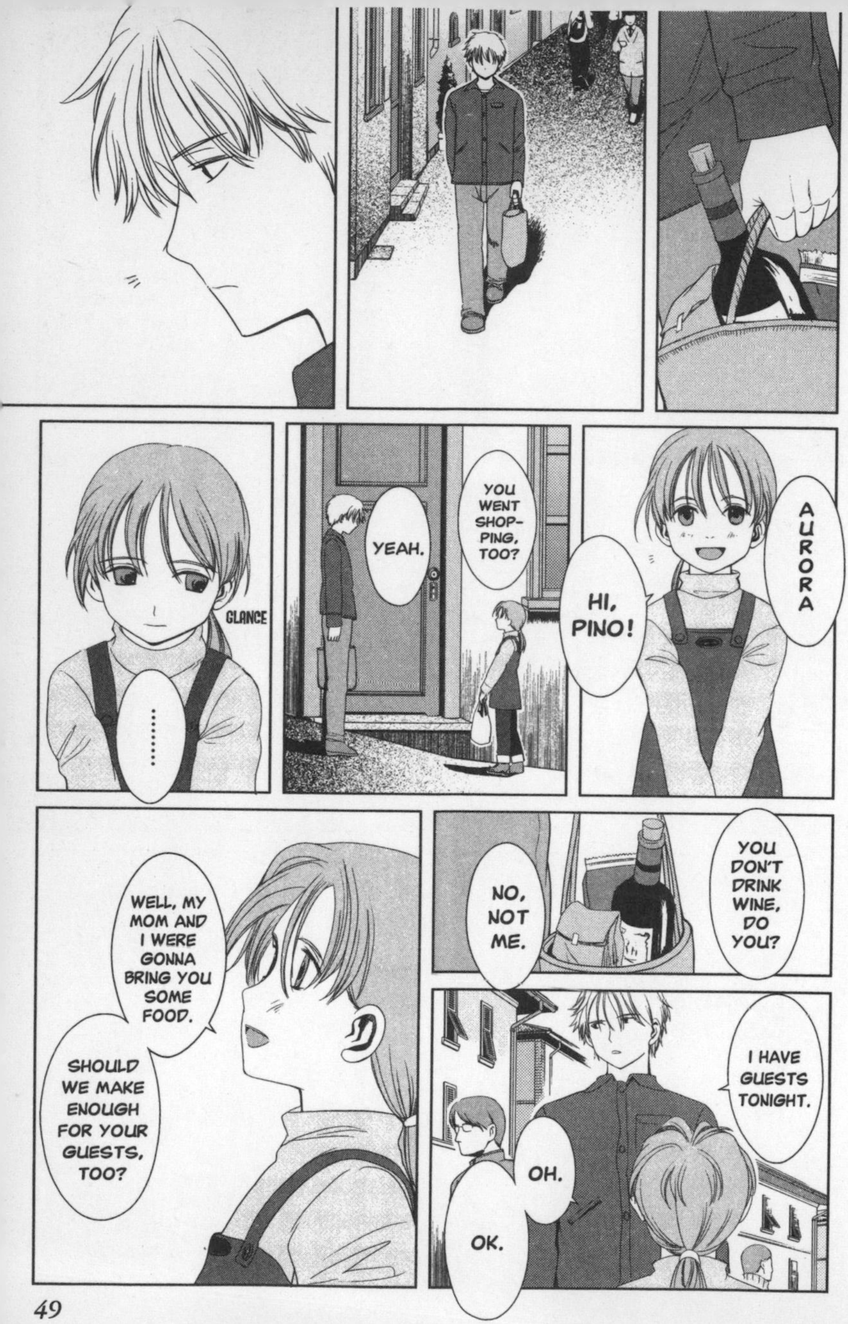
AURORA
HI, PINO!
YOU WENT SHOPPING, TOO?
YEAH.
GLANCE
......
YOU DON'T DRINK WINE, DO YOU?
NO, NOT ME.
I HAVE GUESTS TONIGHT.
OH.
OK.
WELL, MY MOM AND I WERE GONNA BRING YOU SOME FOOD.
SHOULD WE MAKE ENOUGH FOR YOUR GUESTS, TOO?

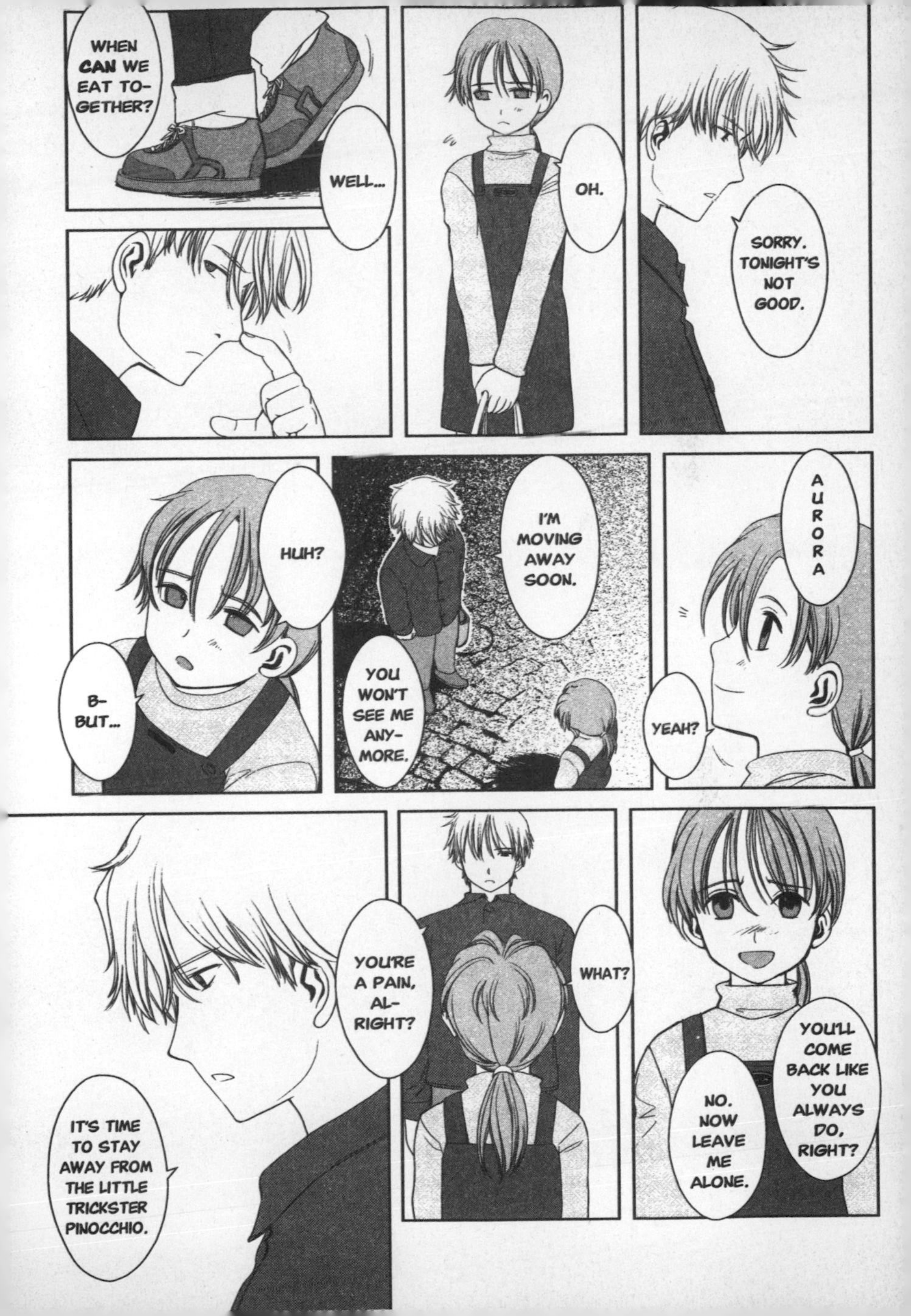
SORRY. TONIGHT'S NOT GOOD.
OH.
WHEN CAN WE EAT TOGETHER?
WELL...
AURORA
YEAH?
I'M MOVING AWAY SOON.
YOU WON'T SEE ME ANYMORE.
HUH?
B-BUT...
YOU'LL COME BACK LIKE YOU ALWAYS DO, RIGHT?
NO. NOW LEAVE ME ALONE.
WHAT?
YOU'RE A PAIN, ALRIGHT?
IT'S TIME TO STAY AWAY FROM THE LITTLE TRICKSTER PINOCCHIO.

GUNSLINGERGIRL,

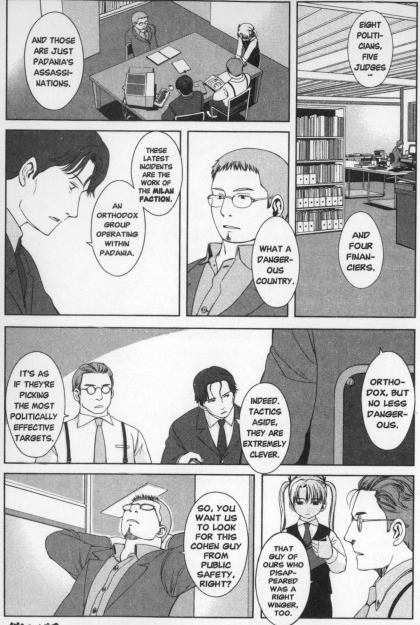

第14話 Pinocchio (Part 2)

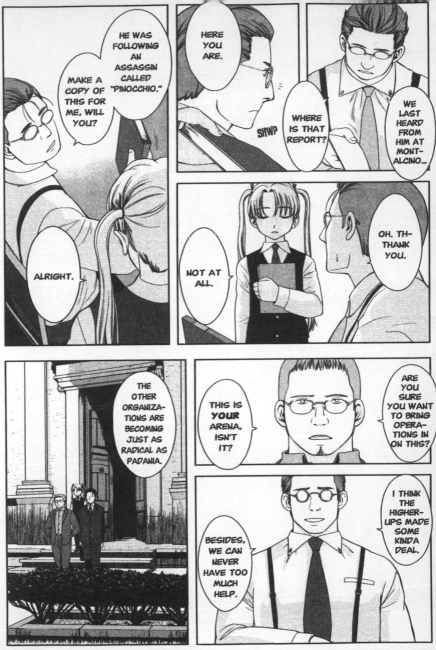

54

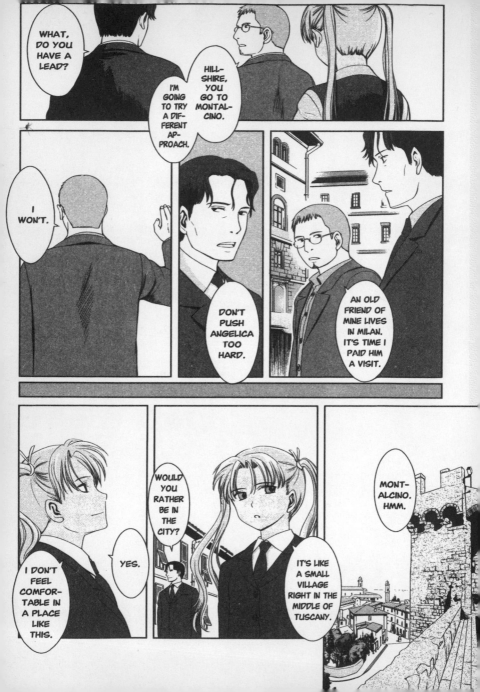

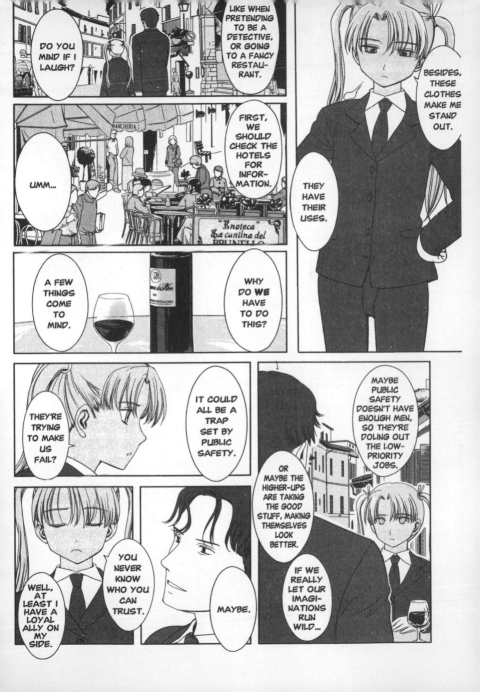

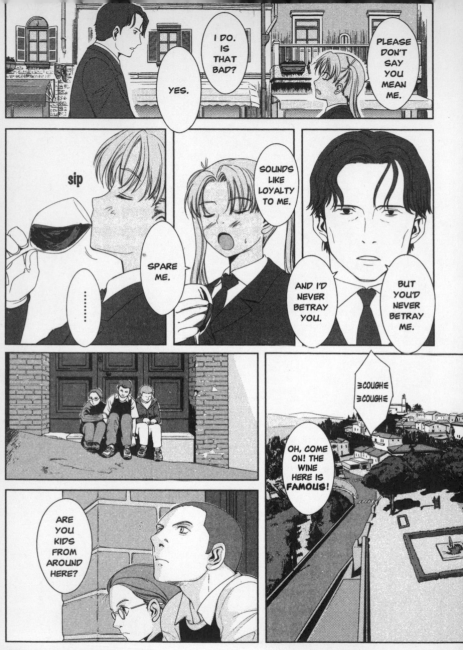

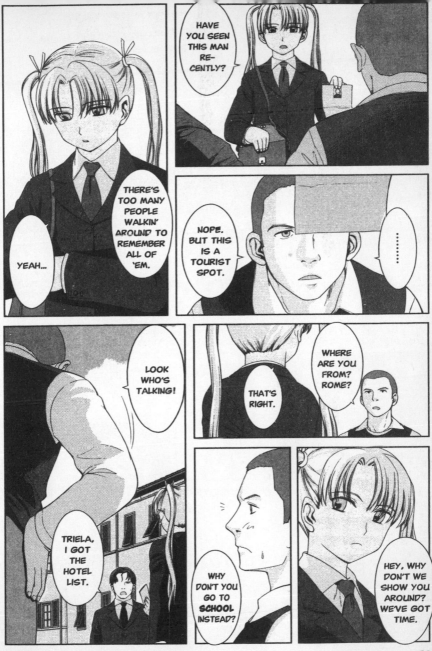

58

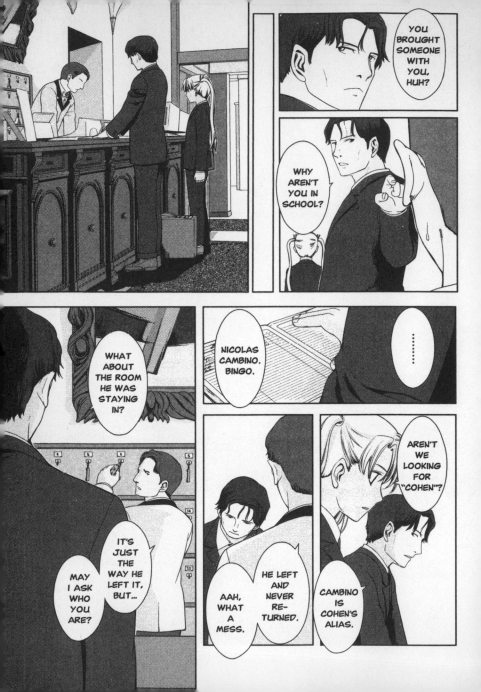

YOU BROUGHT SOMEONE WITH YOU, HUH?

WHY AREN'T YOU IN SCHOOL?

WHAT ABOUT THE ROOM HE WAS STAYING IN?

NICOLAS CAMBINO. BINGO.

· · · · · · · · ·

MAY I ASK WHO YOU ARE?

IT'S JUST THE WAY HE LEFT IT, BUT...

AAH, WHAT A MESS.

HE LEFT AND NEVER RE-TURNED.

AREN'T WE LOOKING FOR "COHEN"?

CAMBINO IS COHEN'S ALIAS.

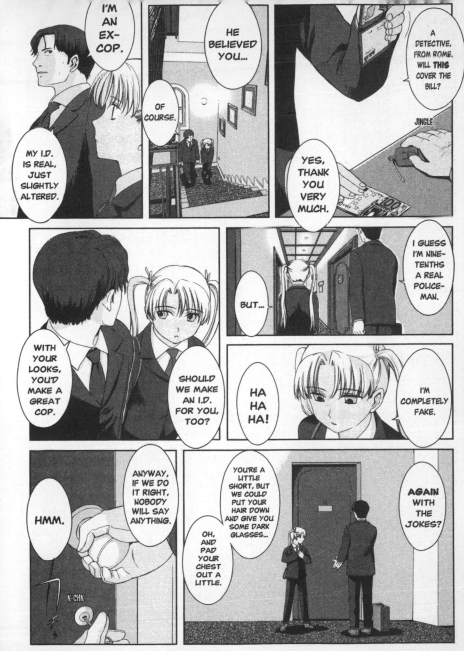

60

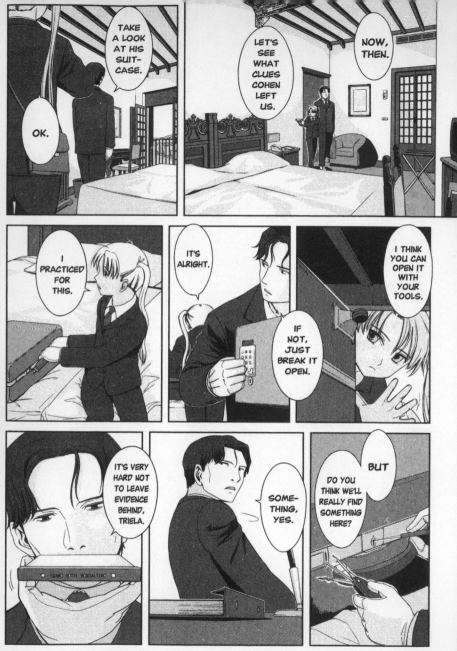

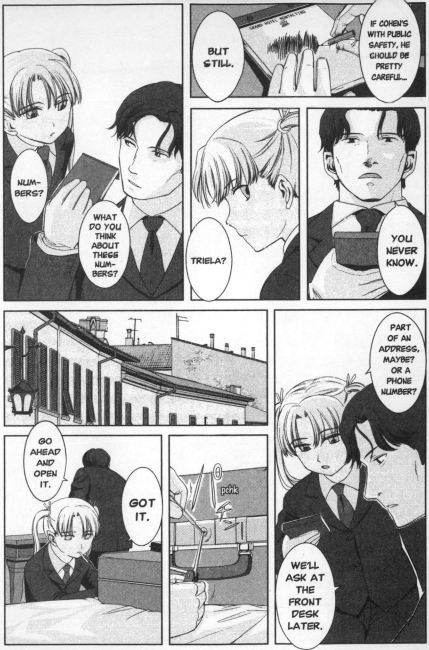

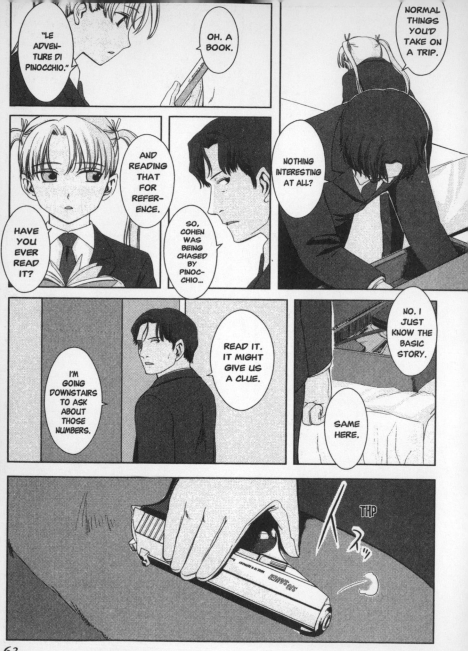

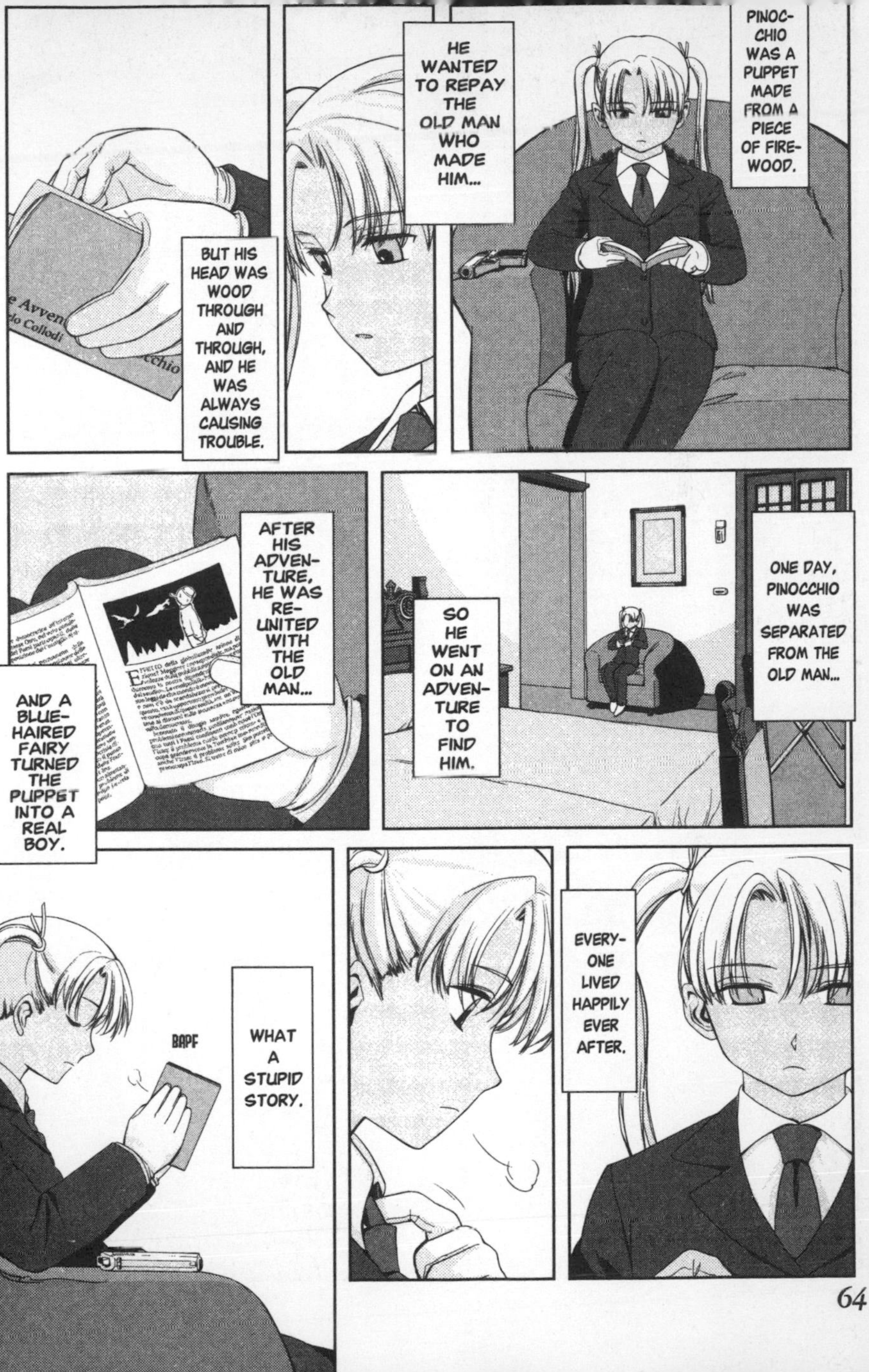
PINOCCHIO WAS A PUPPET MADE FROM A PIECE OF FIRE-WOOD.
HE WANTED TO REPAY THE OLD MAN WHO MADE HIM...
BUT HIS HEAD WAS WOOD THROUGH AND THROUGH, AND HE WAS ALWAYS CAUSING TROUBLE.
ONE DAY, PINOCCHIO WAS SEPARATED FROM THE OLD MAN...
SO HE WENT ON AN ADVENTURE TO FIND HIM.
AFTER HIS ADVENTURE, HE WAS RE-UNITED WITH THE OLD MAN...
AND A BLUE-HAIRED FAIRY TURNED THE PUPPET INTO A REAL BOY.
EVERY-ONE LIVED HAPPILY EVER AFTER.
WHAT A STUPID STORY.
BAPF

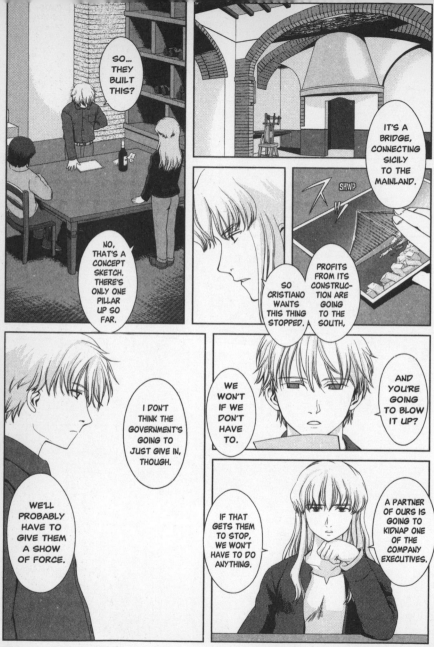

SO... THEY BUILT THIS?

IT'S A BRIDGE, CONNECTING SICILY TO THE MAINLAND.

NO, THAT'S A CONCEPT SKETCH. THERE'S ONLY ONE PILLAR UP SO FAR.

SHWP

PROFITS FROM ITS CONSTRUCTION ARE GOING TO THE SOUTH,

SO CRISTIANO WANTS THIS THING STOPPED.

I DON'T THINK THE GOVERNMENT'S GOING TO JUST GIVE IN, THOUGH.

WE WON'T IF WE DON'T HAVE TO.

AND YOU'RE GOING TO BLOW IT UP?

WE'LL PROBABLY HAVE TO GIVE THEM A SHOW OF FORCE.

IF THAT GETS THEM TO STOP, WE WON'T HAVE TO DO ANYTHING.

A PARTNER OF OURS IS GOING TO KIDNAP ONE OF THE COMPANY EXECUTIVES.

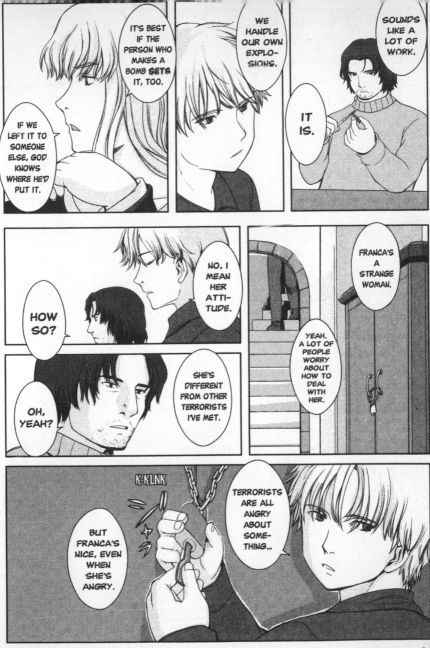

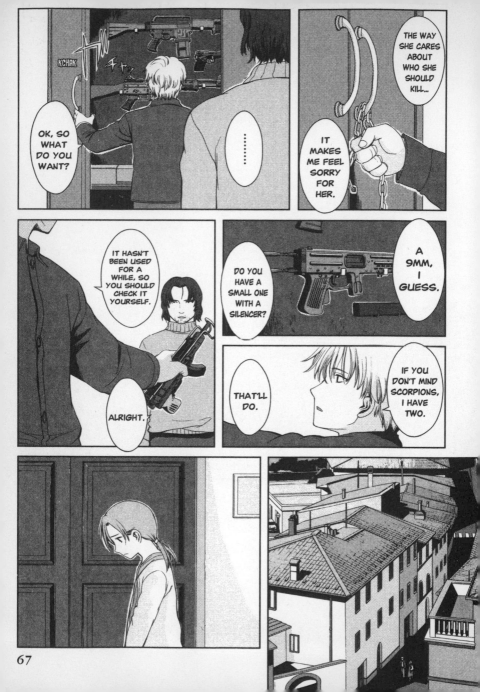

KCHAK

OK, SO WHAT DO YOU WANT?

......

THE WAY SHE CARES ABOUT WHO SHE SHOULD KILL...

IT MAKES ME FEEL SORRY FOR HER.

IT HASN'T BEEN USED FOR A WHILE, SO YOU SHOULD CHECK IT YOURSELF.

ALRIGHT.

DO YOU HAVE A SMALL ONE WITH A SILENCER?

A 9MM, I GUESS.

THAT'LL DO.

IF YOU DON'T MIND SCORPIONS, I HAVE TWO.

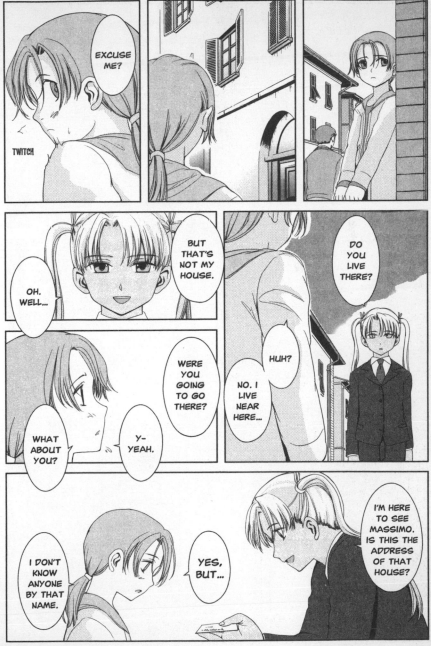

68

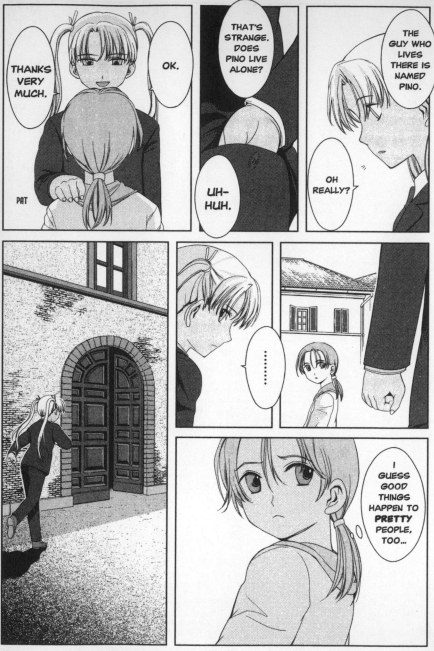

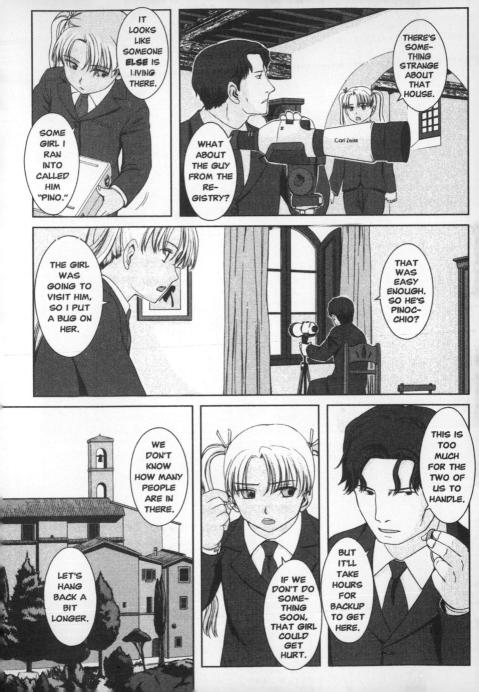

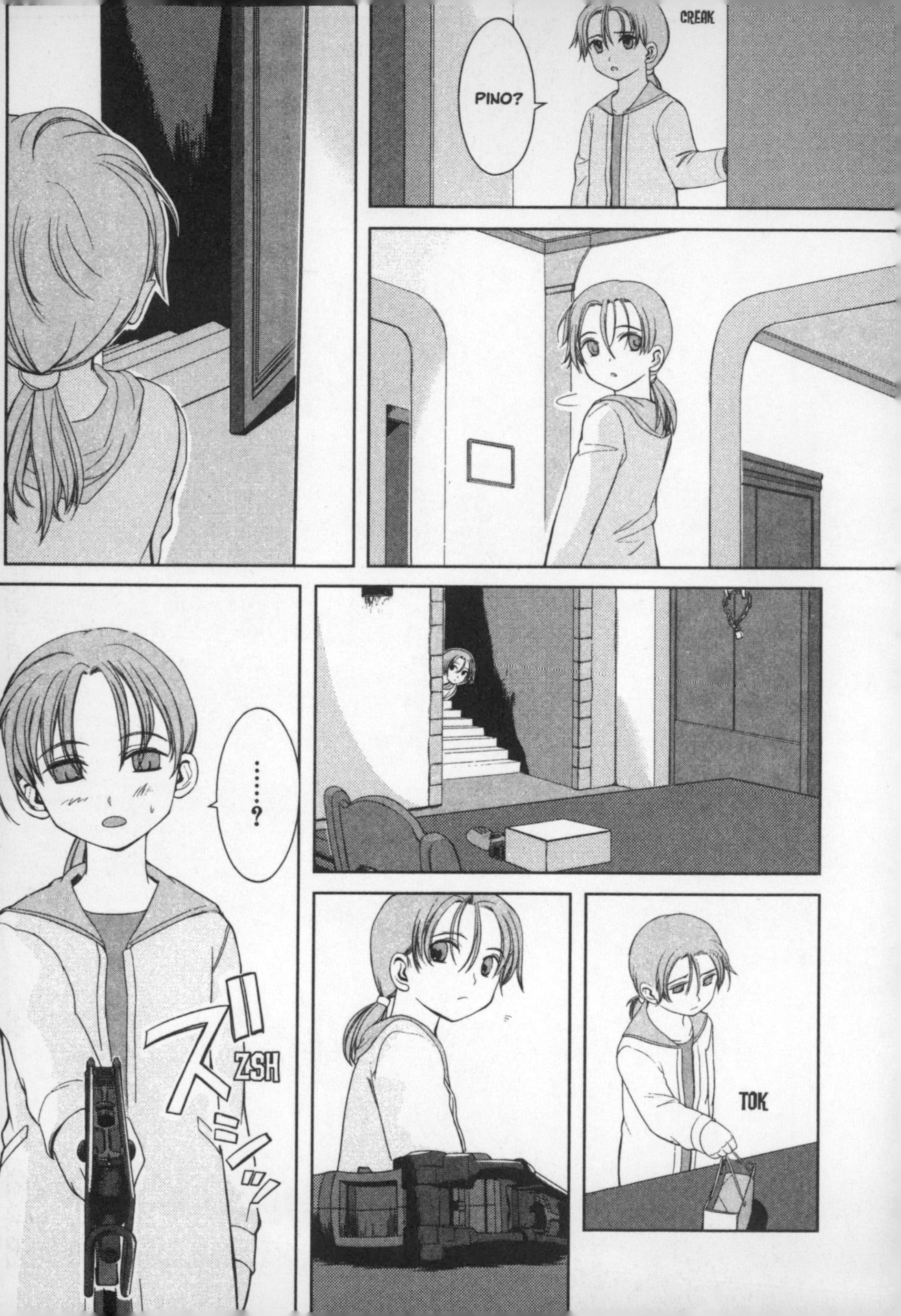
CREAK
PINO?
TOK
......?
ZSH

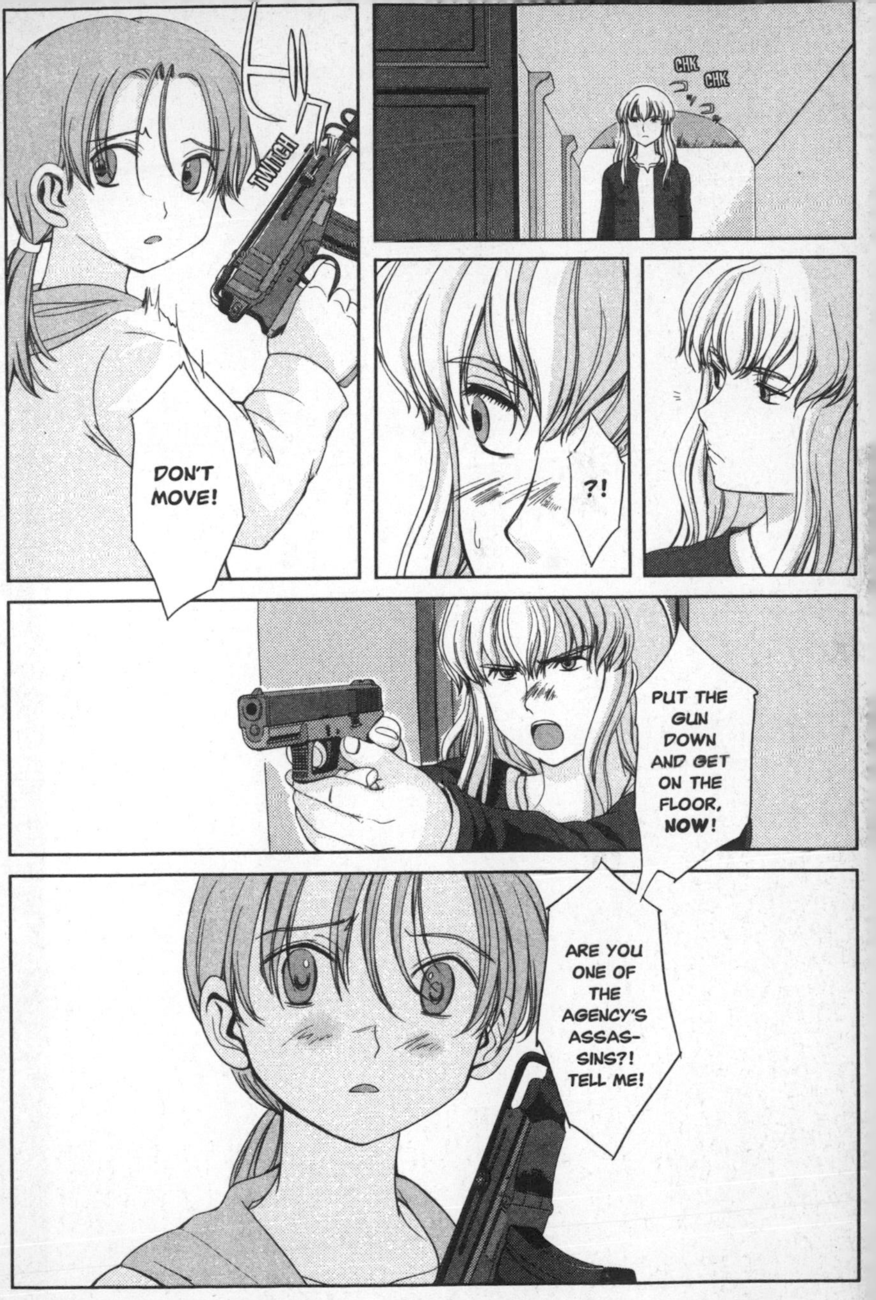
CHK CHK
?!
TWITCH
DON'T MOVE!
PUT THE GUN DOWN AND GET ON THE FLOOR, NOW!
ARE YOU ONE OF THE AGENCY'S ASSAS-SINS?! TELL ME!

GUNSLINGERGIRL.

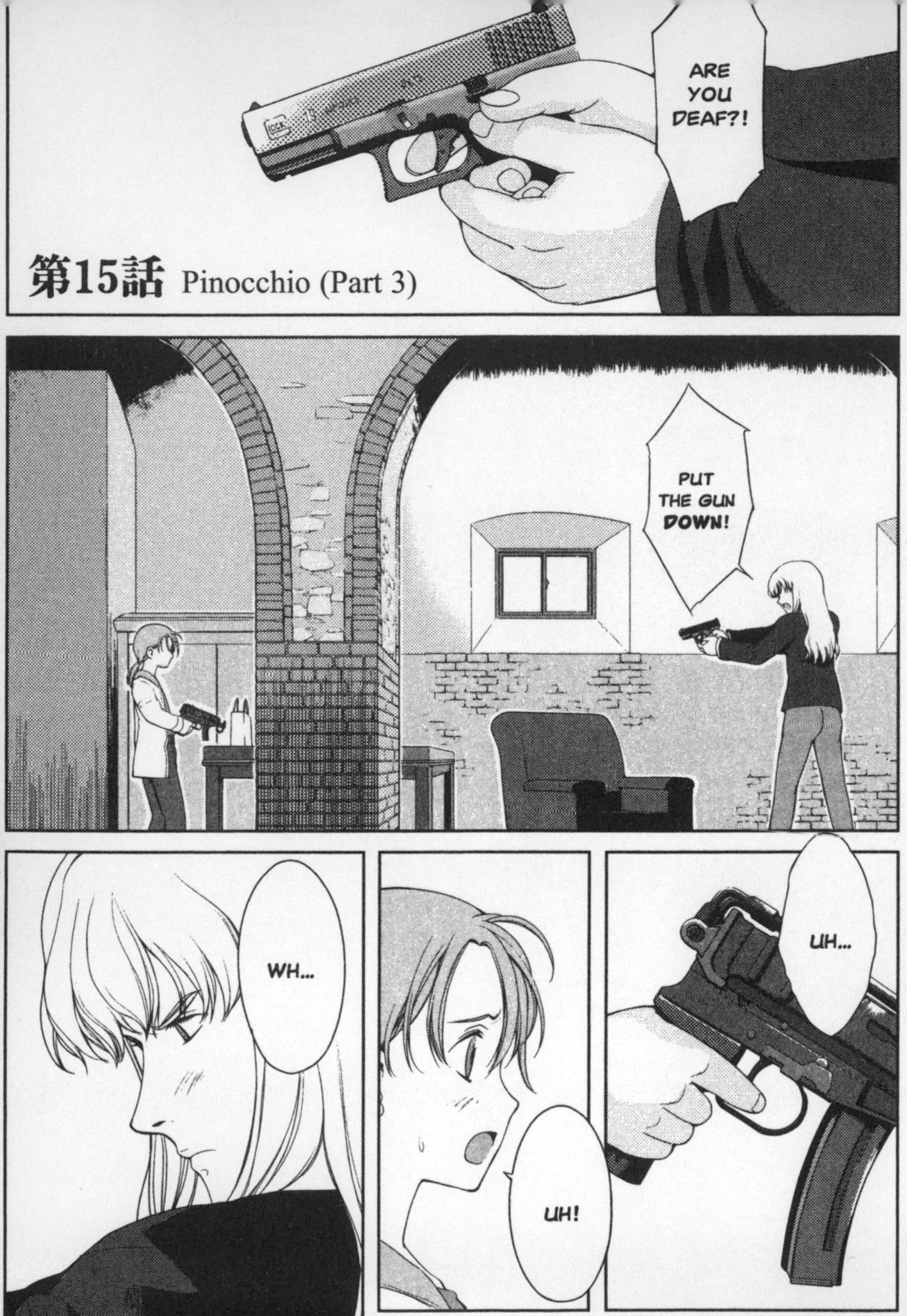
ARE YOU DEAF?!
第15話 Pinocchio (Part 3)
PUT THE GUN DOWN!
UH...
UH!
WH...

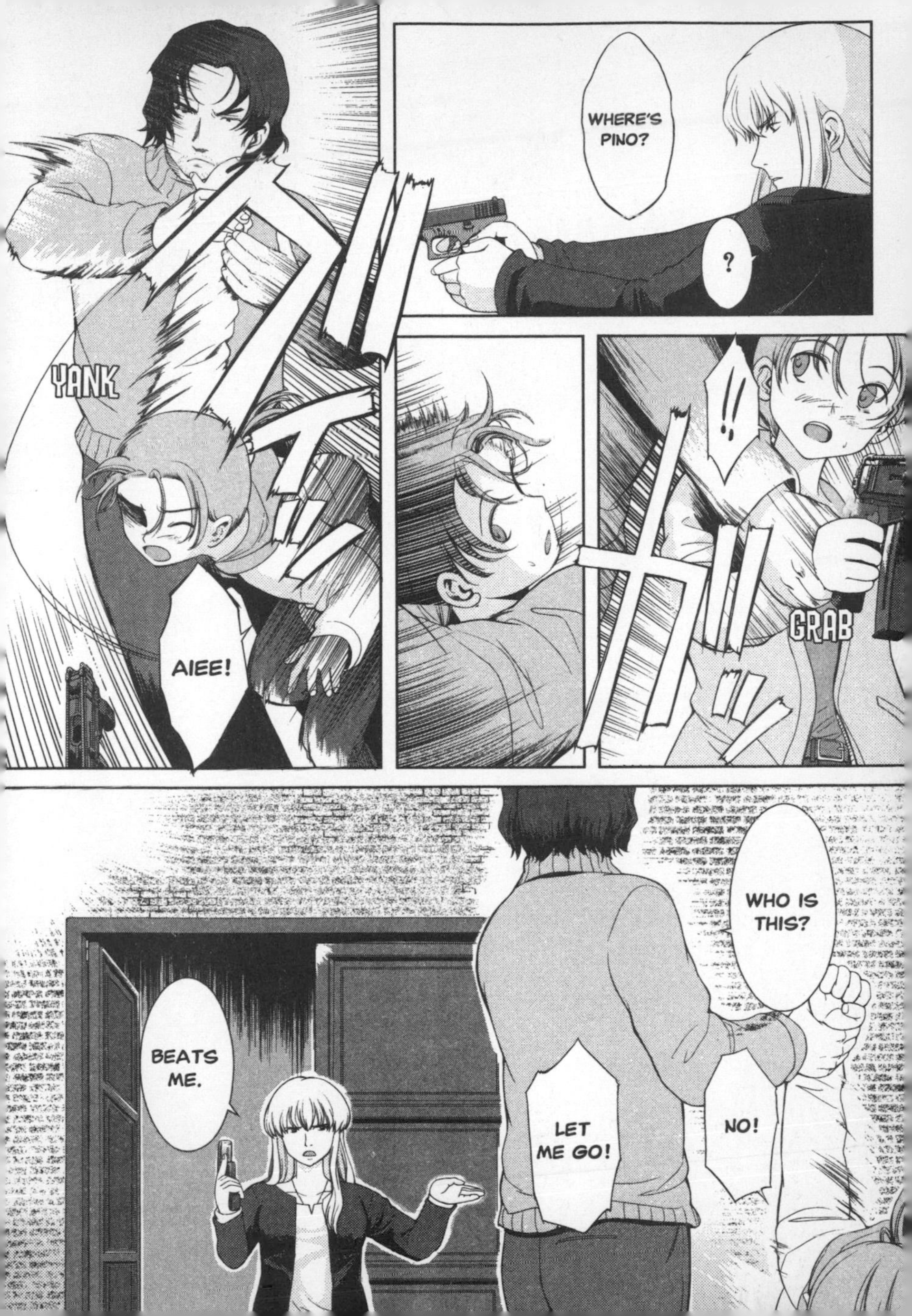
WHERE'S PINO?
?
!!
GRAB
YANK
AIEE!
WHO IS THIS?
NO!
LET ME GO!
BEATS ME.

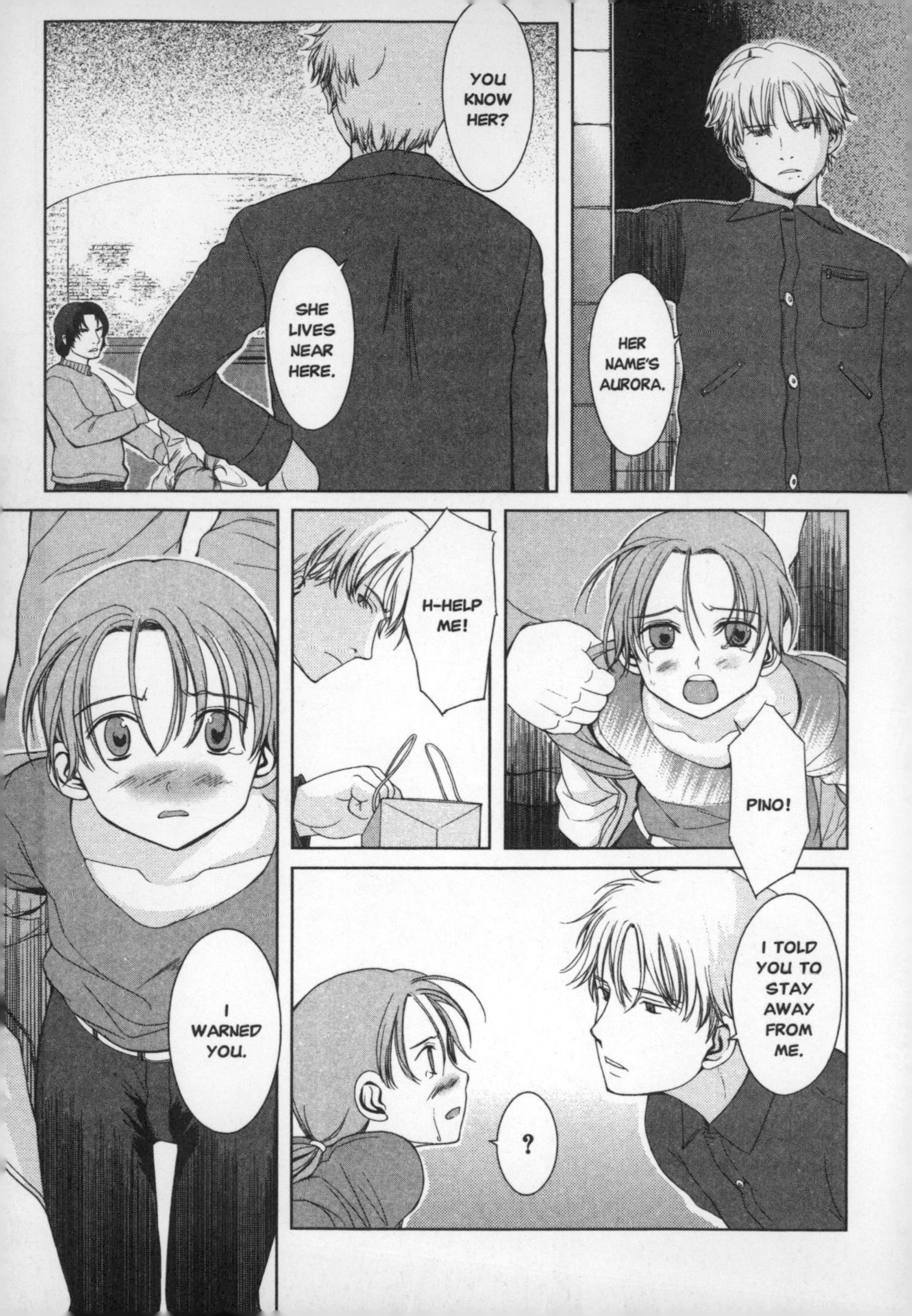
HER NAME'S AURORA.
YOU KNOW HER?
SHE LIVES NEAR HERE.
PINO!
H-HELP ME!
I TOLD YOU TO STAY AWAY FROM ME.
?
I WARNED YOU.

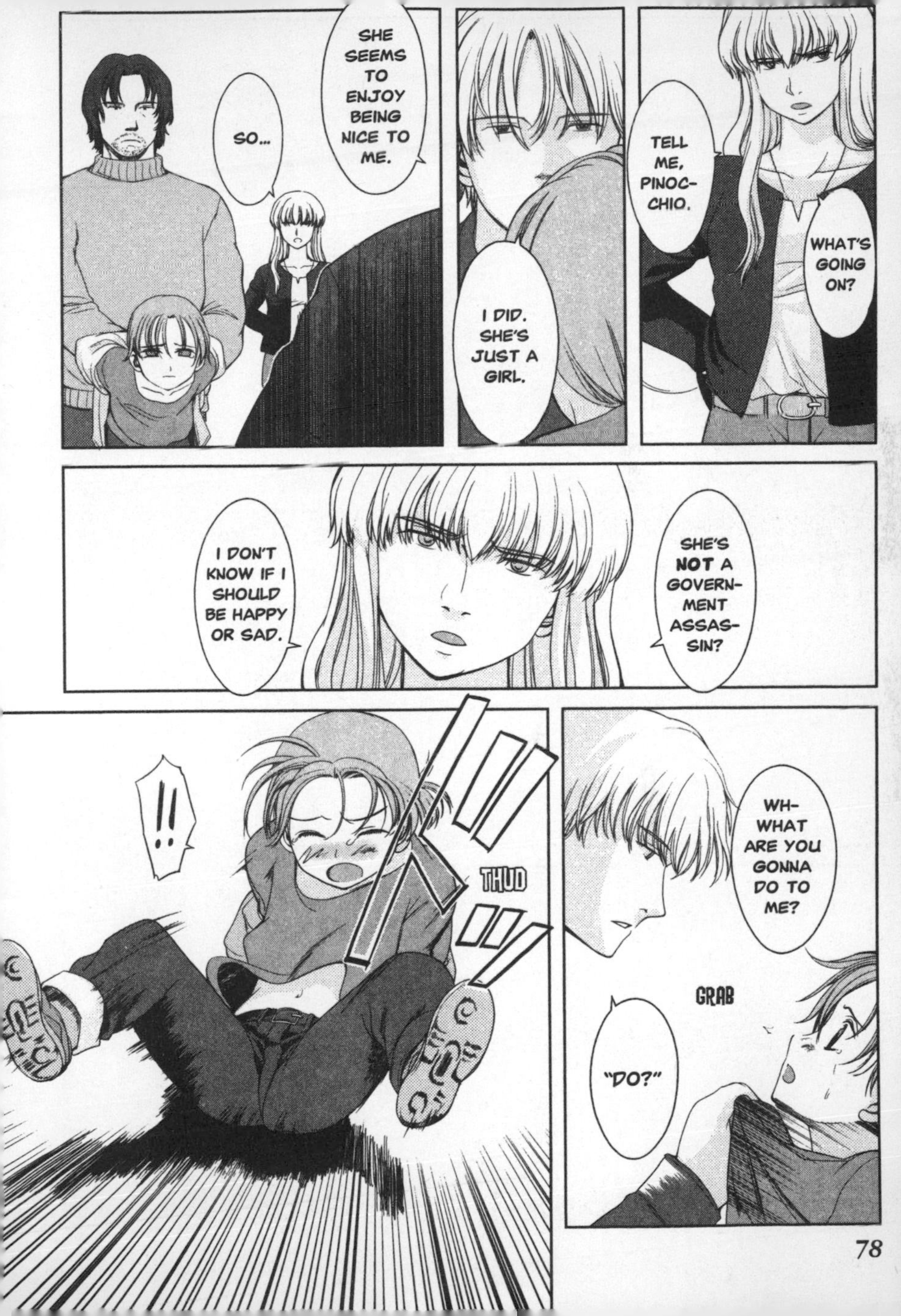
TELL ME, PINOCCHIO.
WHAT'S GOING ON?
I DID. SHE'S JUST A GIRL.
SHE SEEMS TO ENJOY BEING NICE TO ME.
SO...
SHE'S **NOT** A GOVERNMENT ASSASSIN?
I DON'T KNOW IF I SHOULD BE HAPPY OR SAD.
WH- WHAT ARE YOU GONNA DO TO ME?
GRAB
"DO?"
THUD
!!

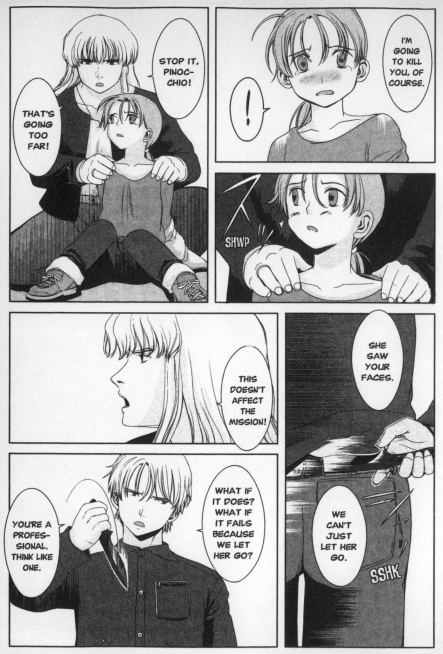

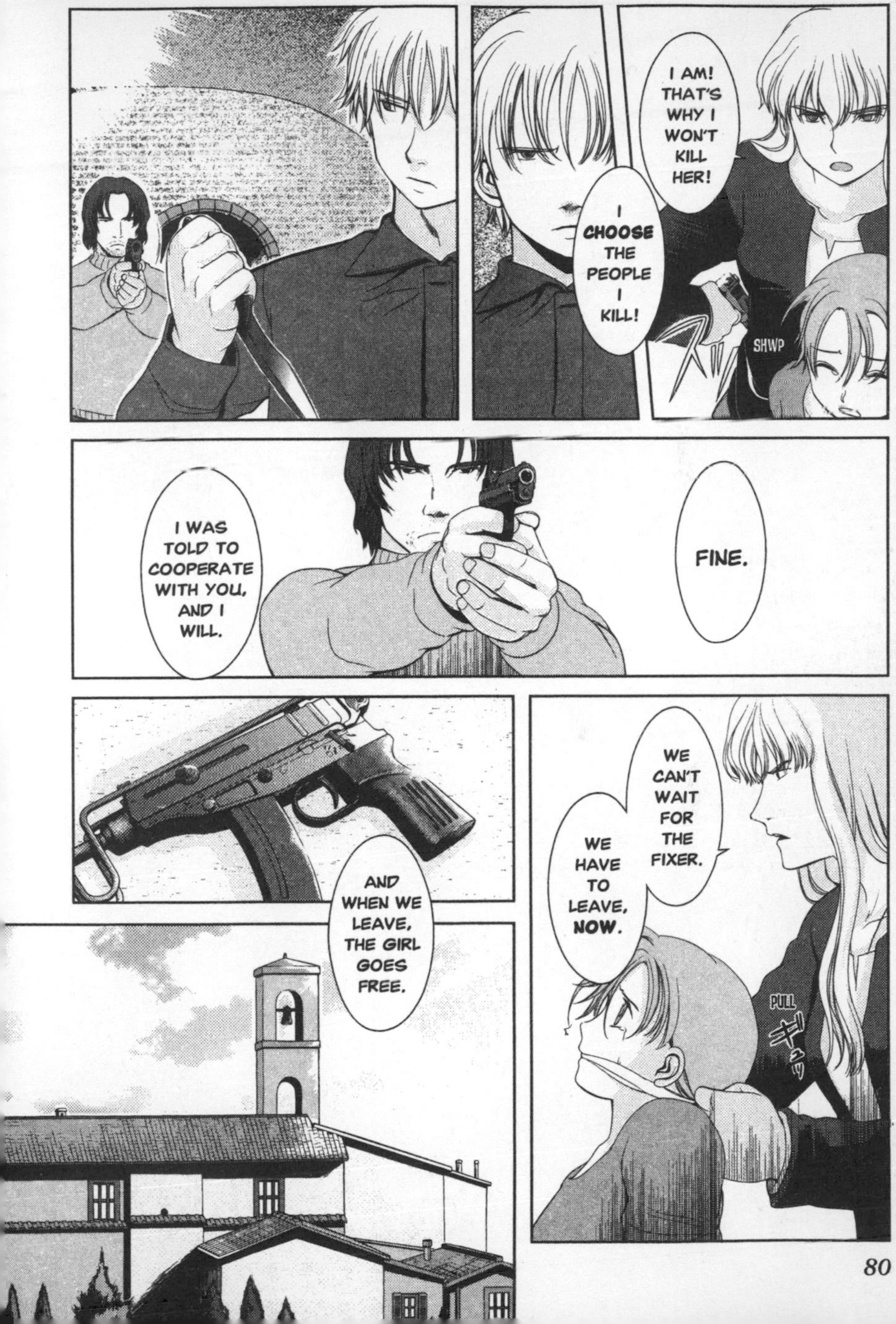
I AM! THAT'S WHY I WON'T KILL HER!
I CHOOSE THE PEOPLE I KILL!
SHWP
FINE.
I WAS TOLD TO COOPERATE WITH YOU, AND I WILL.
WE CAN'T WAIT FOR THE FIXER.
WE HAVE TO LEAVE, NOW.
PULL
AND WHEN WE LEAVE, THE GIRL GOES FREE.

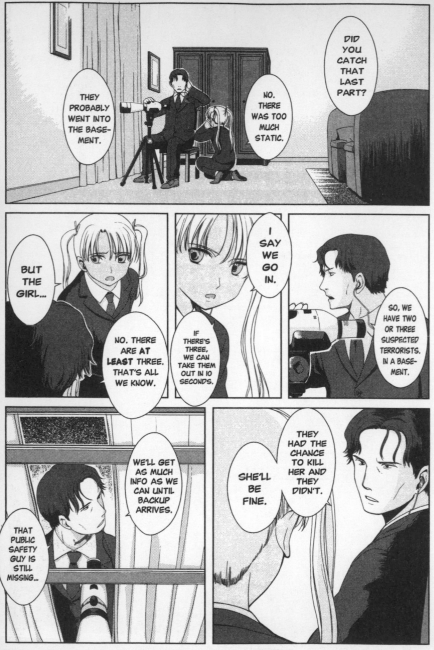

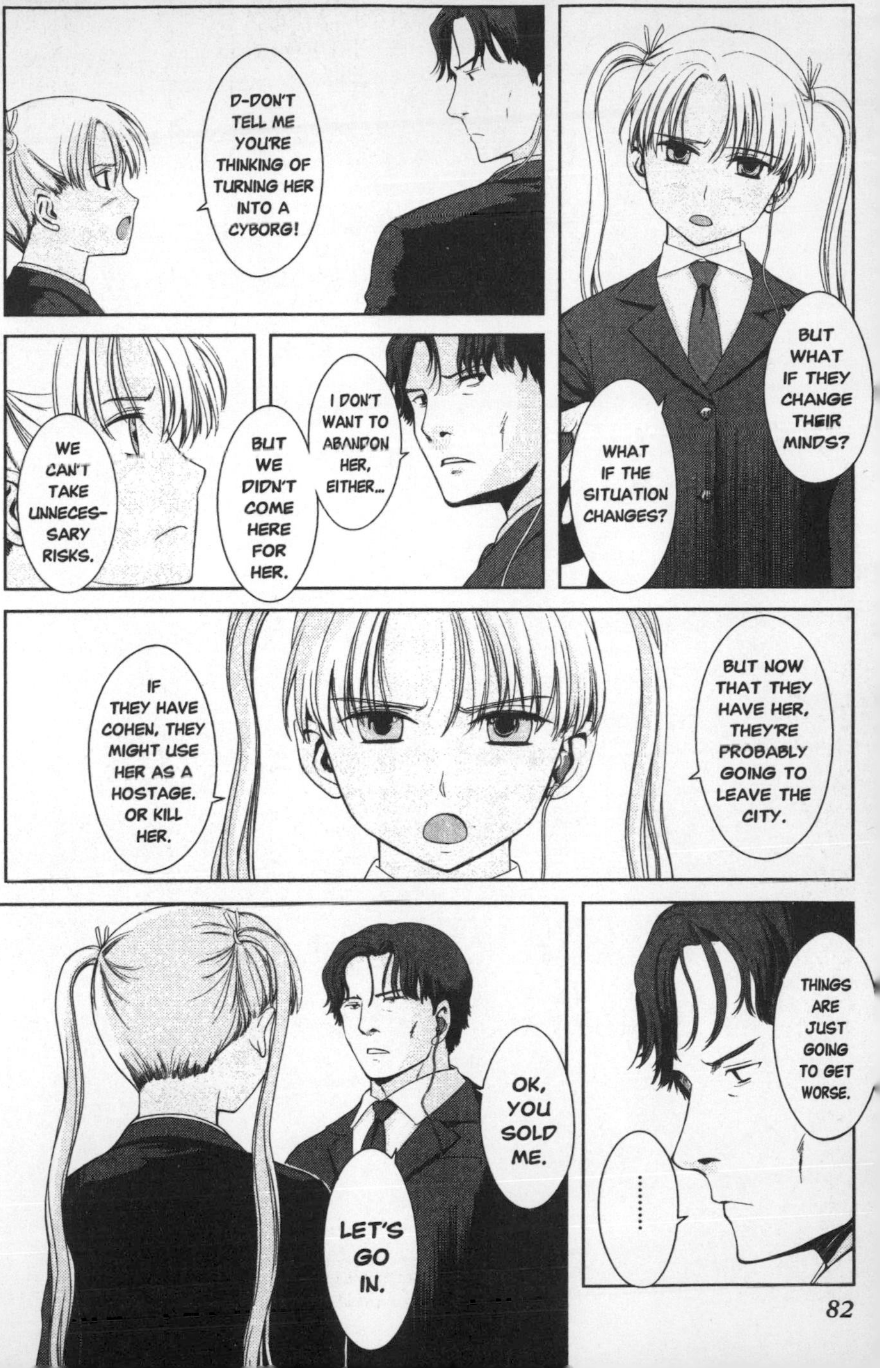
BUT WHAT IF THEY CHANGE THEIR MINDS?
WHAT IF THE SITUATION CHANGES?
D-DON'T TELL ME YOU'RE THINKING OF TURNING HER INTO A CYBORG!
I DON'T WANT TO ABANDON HER, EITHER...
BUT WE DIDN'T COME HERE FOR HER.
WE CAN'T TAKE UNNECES-SARY RISKS.
BUT NOW THAT THEY HAVE HER, THEY'RE PROBABLY GOING TO LEAVE THE CITY.
IF THEY HAVE COHEN, THEY MIGHT USE HER AS A HOSTAGE. OR KILL HER.
THINGS ARE JUST GOING TO GET WORSE.
....
OK, YOU SOLD ME.
LET'S GO IN.

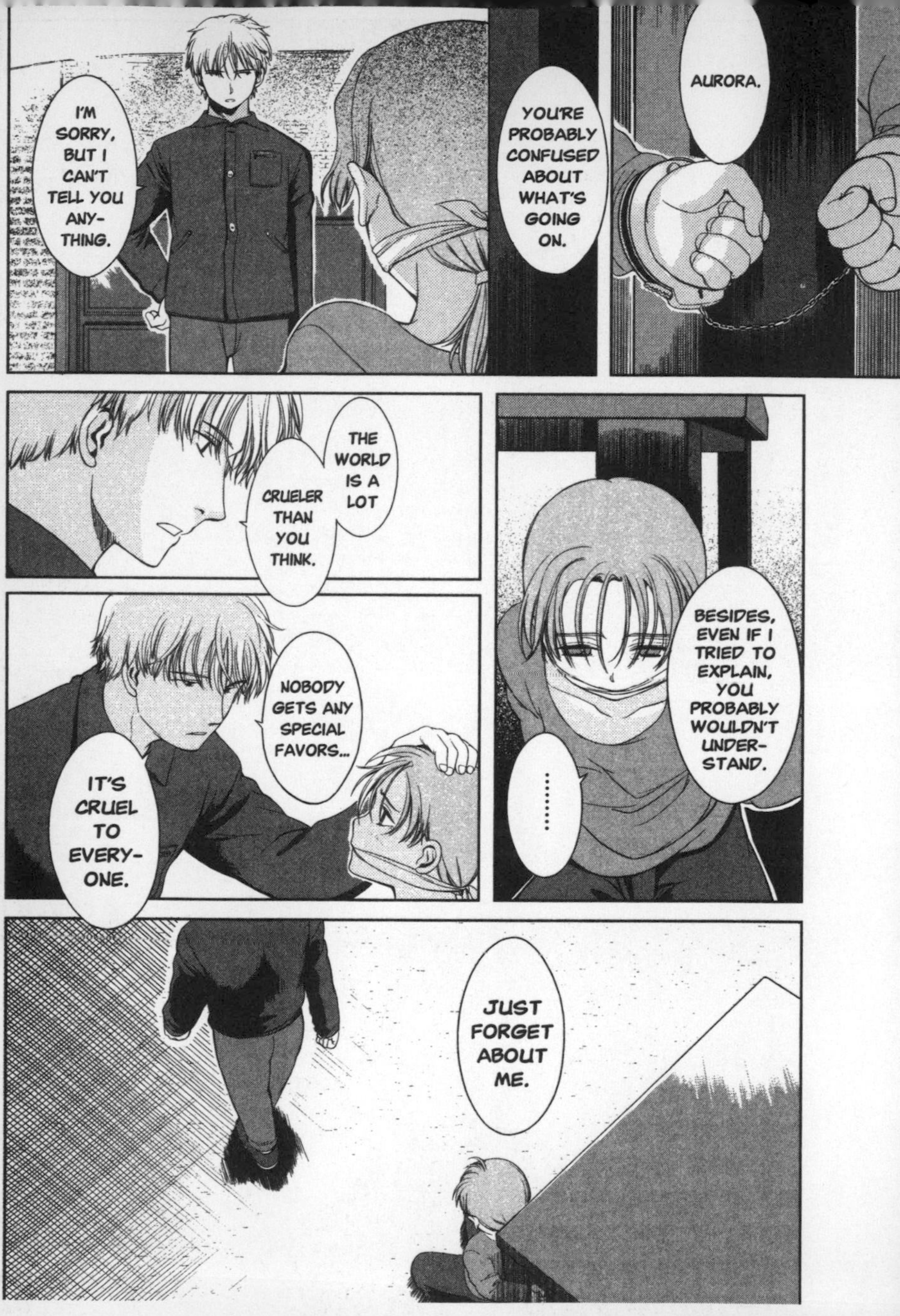
AURORA.
YOU'RE PROBABLY CONFUSED ABOUT WHAT'S GOING ON.
I'M SORRY, BUT I CAN'T TELL YOU ANY-THING.
BESIDES, EVEN IF I TRIED TO EXPLAIN, YOU PROBABLY WOULDN'T UNDER-STAND.
......
THE WORLD IS A LOT
CRUELER THAN YOU THINK.
NOBODY GETS ANY SPECIAL FAVORS...
IT'S CRUEL TO EVERY-ONE.
JUST FORGET ABOUT ME.

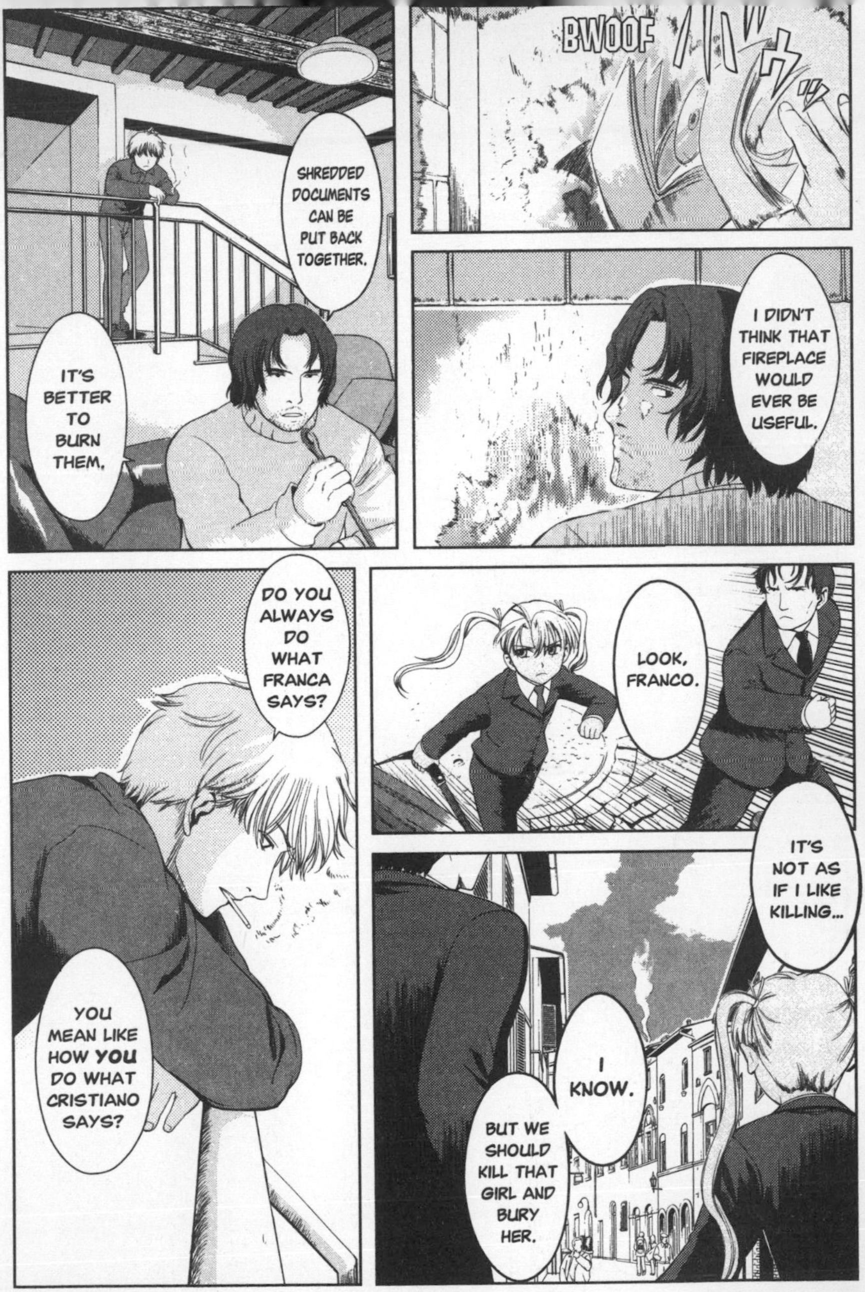
BWOOF
I DIDN'T THINK THAT FIREPLACE WOULD EVER BE USEFUL.
SHREDDED DOCUMENTS CAN BE PUT BACK TOGETHER.
IT'S BETTER TO BURN THEM.
LOOK, FRANCO.
IT'S NOT AS IF I LIKE KILLING...
I KNOW.
BUT WE SHOULD KILL THAT GIRL AND BURY HER.
DO YOU ALWAYS DO WHAT FRANCA SAYS?
YOU MEAN LIKE HOW **YOU** DO WHAT CRISTIANO SAYS?

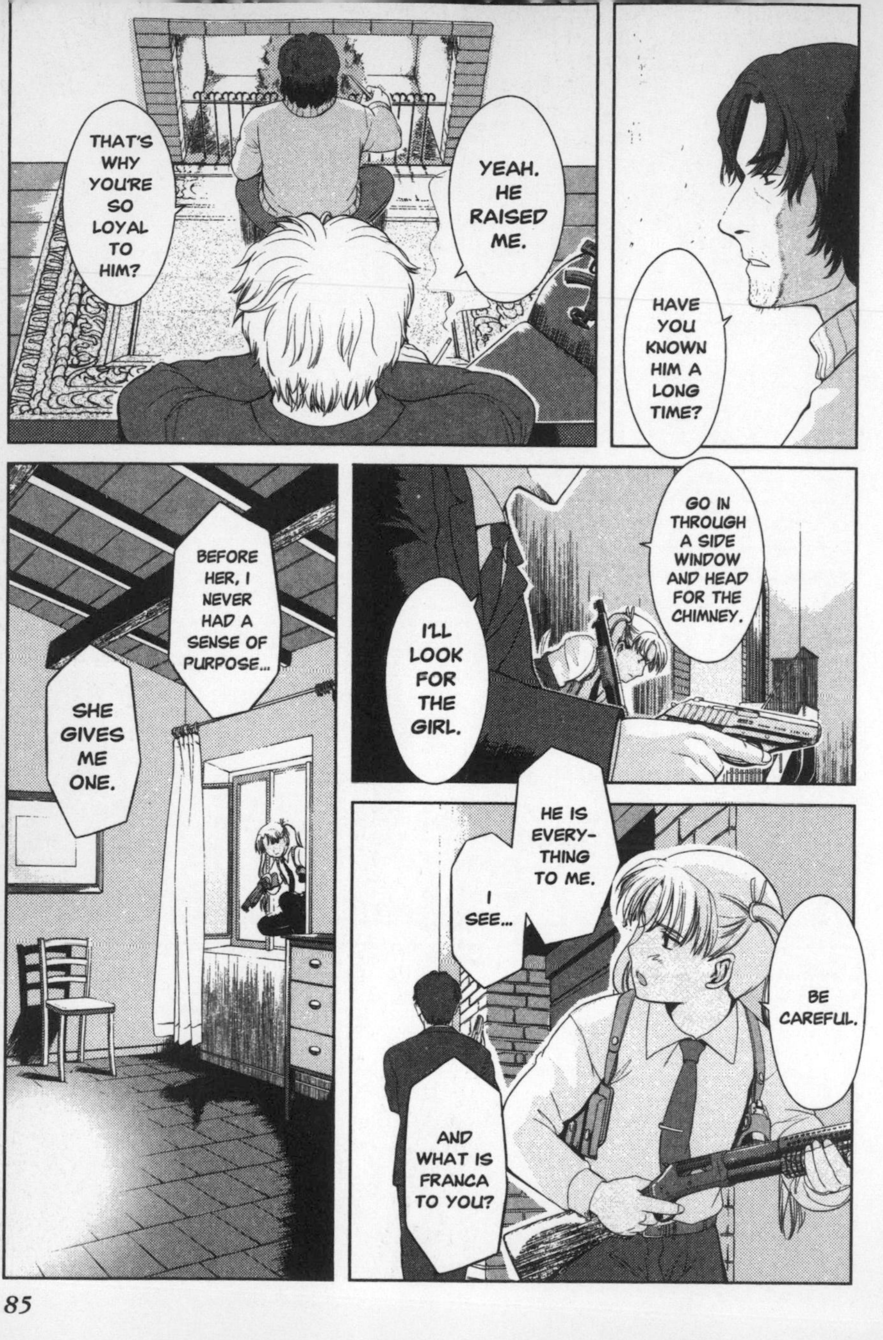
HAVE YOU KNOWN HIM A LONG TIME?
YEAH. HE RAISED ME.
THAT'S WHY YOU'RE SO LOYAL TO HIM?
GO IN THROUGH A SIDE WINDOW AND HEAD FOR THE CHIMNEY.
I'LL LOOK FOR THE GIRL.
BE CAREFUL.
HE IS EVERY-THING TO ME.
I SEE...
AND WHAT IS FRANCA TO YOU?
BEFORE HER, I NEVER HAD A SENSE OF PURPOSE...
SHE GIVES ME ONE.

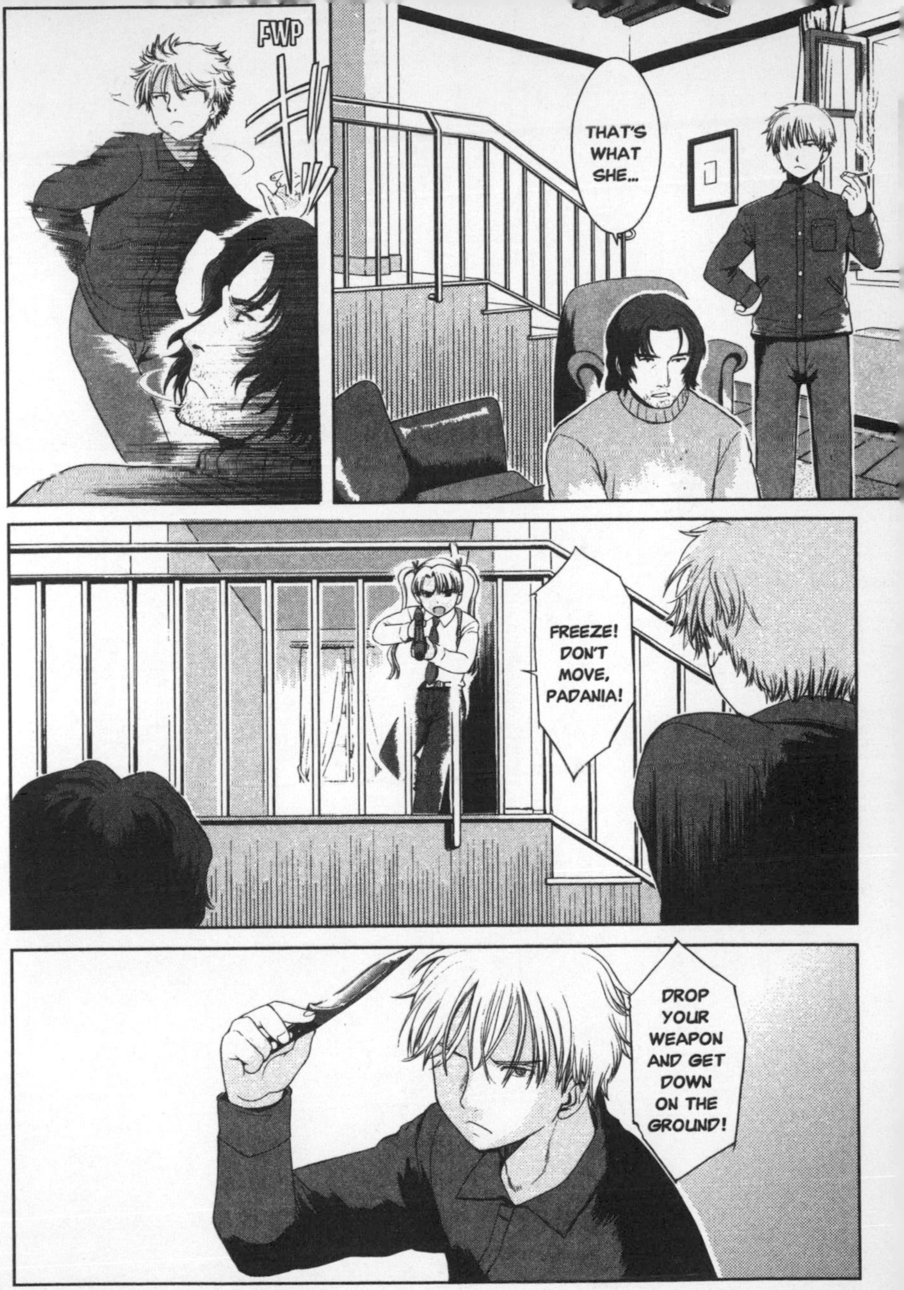
THAT'S WHAT SHE...
FWP
FREEZE! DON'T MOVE, PADANIA!
DROP YOUR WEAPON AND GET DOWN ON THE GROUND!

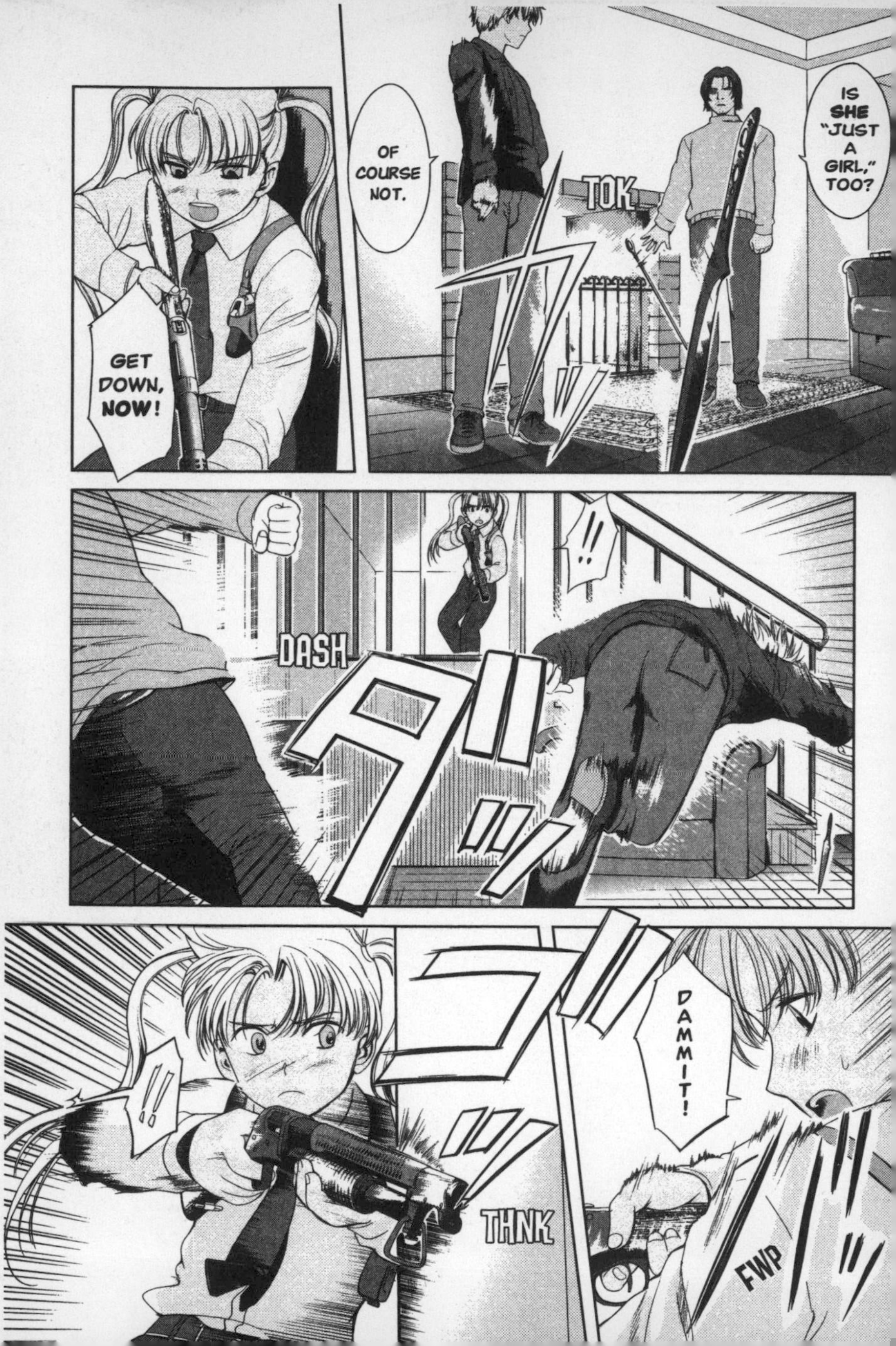
IS SHE "JUST A GIRL," TOO?
OF COURSE NOT.
TOK
GET DOWN, NOW!
!!
DASH
DAMMIT!
FWP
THNK
!!

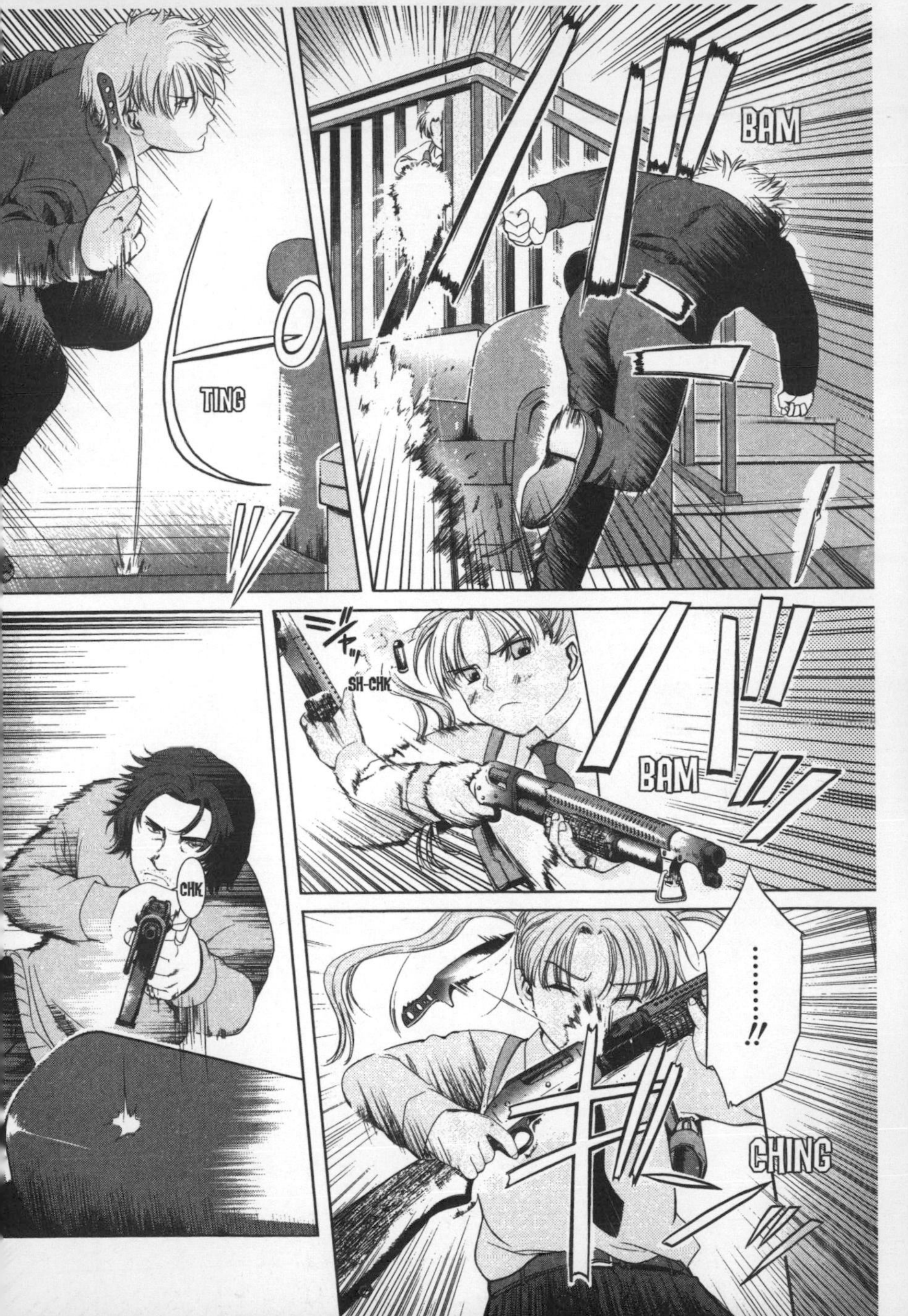
BAM
TING
SH-CHK
BAM
……!!
CHING
CHK

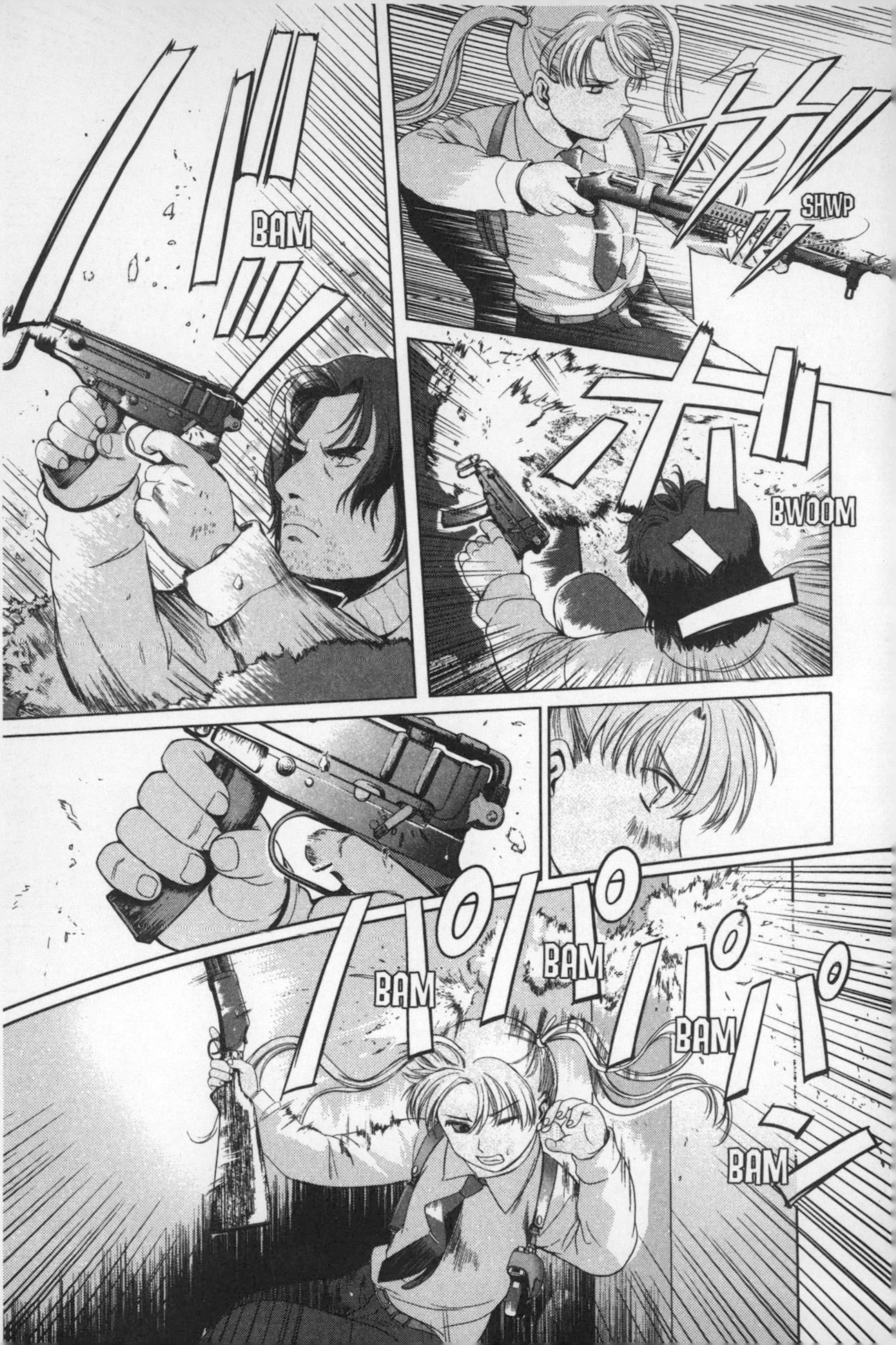
SHWP
BWOOM
BAM
BAM
BAM
BAM
BAM

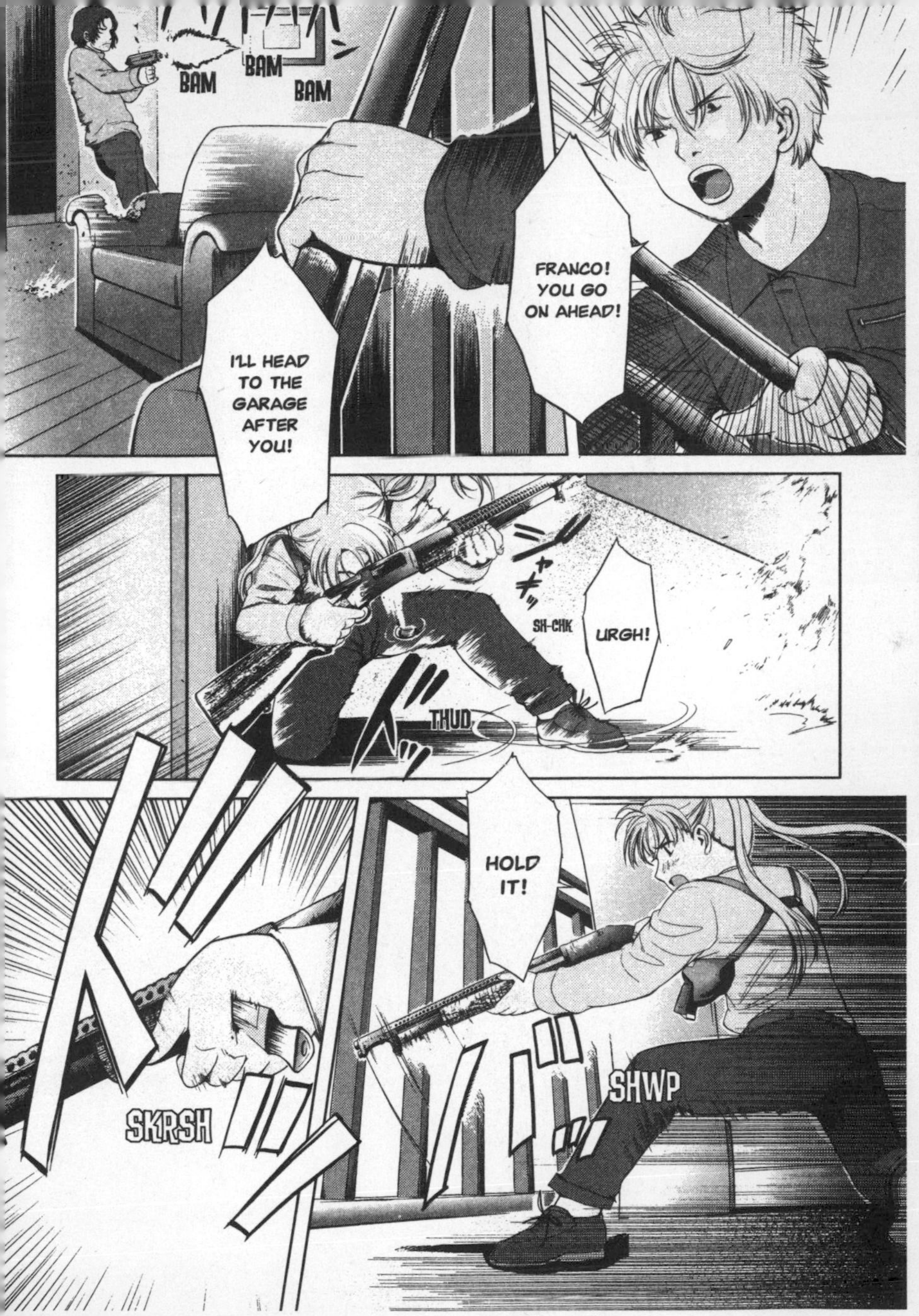
FRANCO! YOU GO ON AHEAD!
I'LL HEAD TO THE GARAGE AFTER YOU!
BAM
BAM
BAM
URGH!
SH-CHK
THUD
HOLD IT!
SHWP
SKRSH

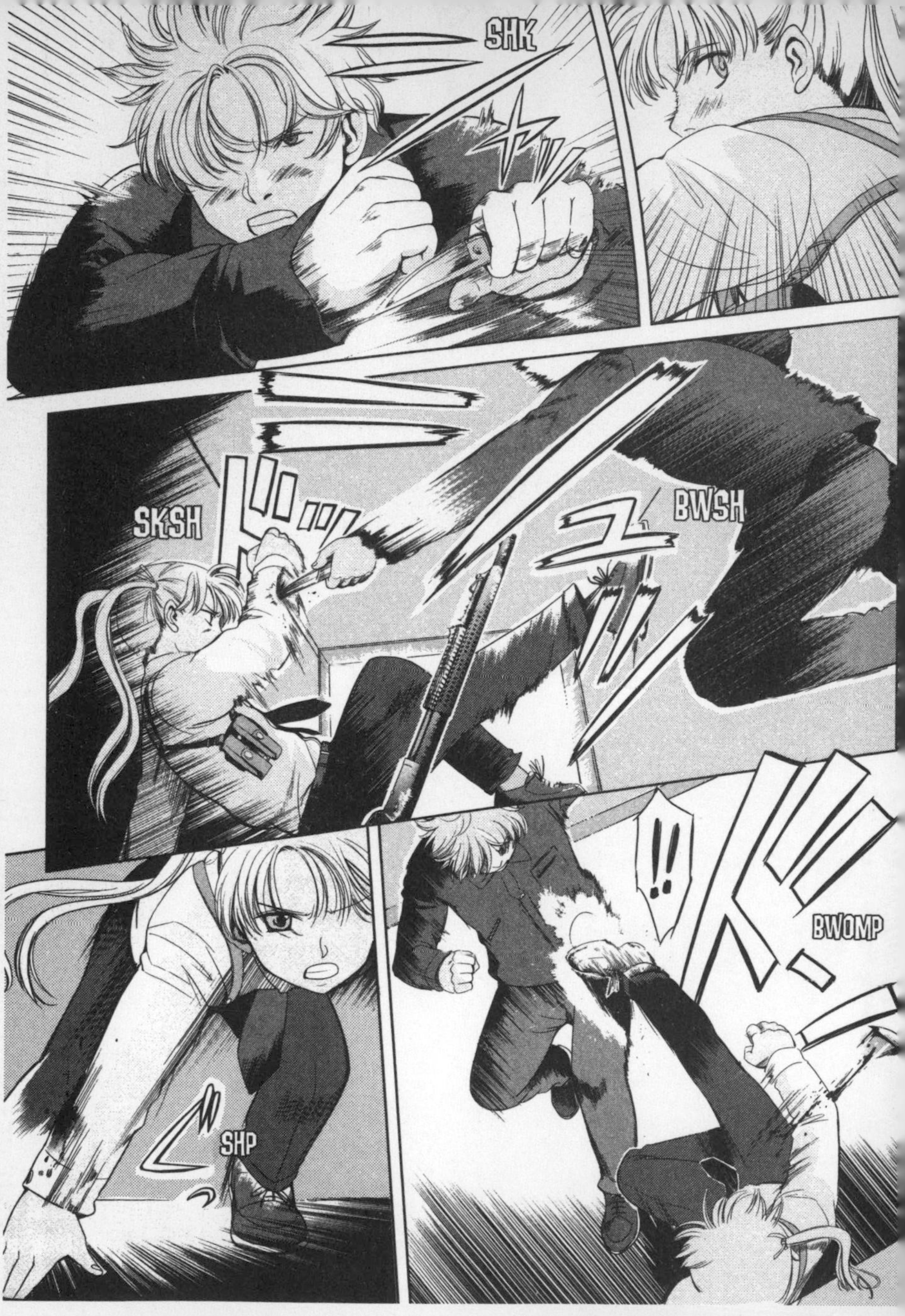
SHK
BWSH
SKSH
!!
BWOMP
SHP

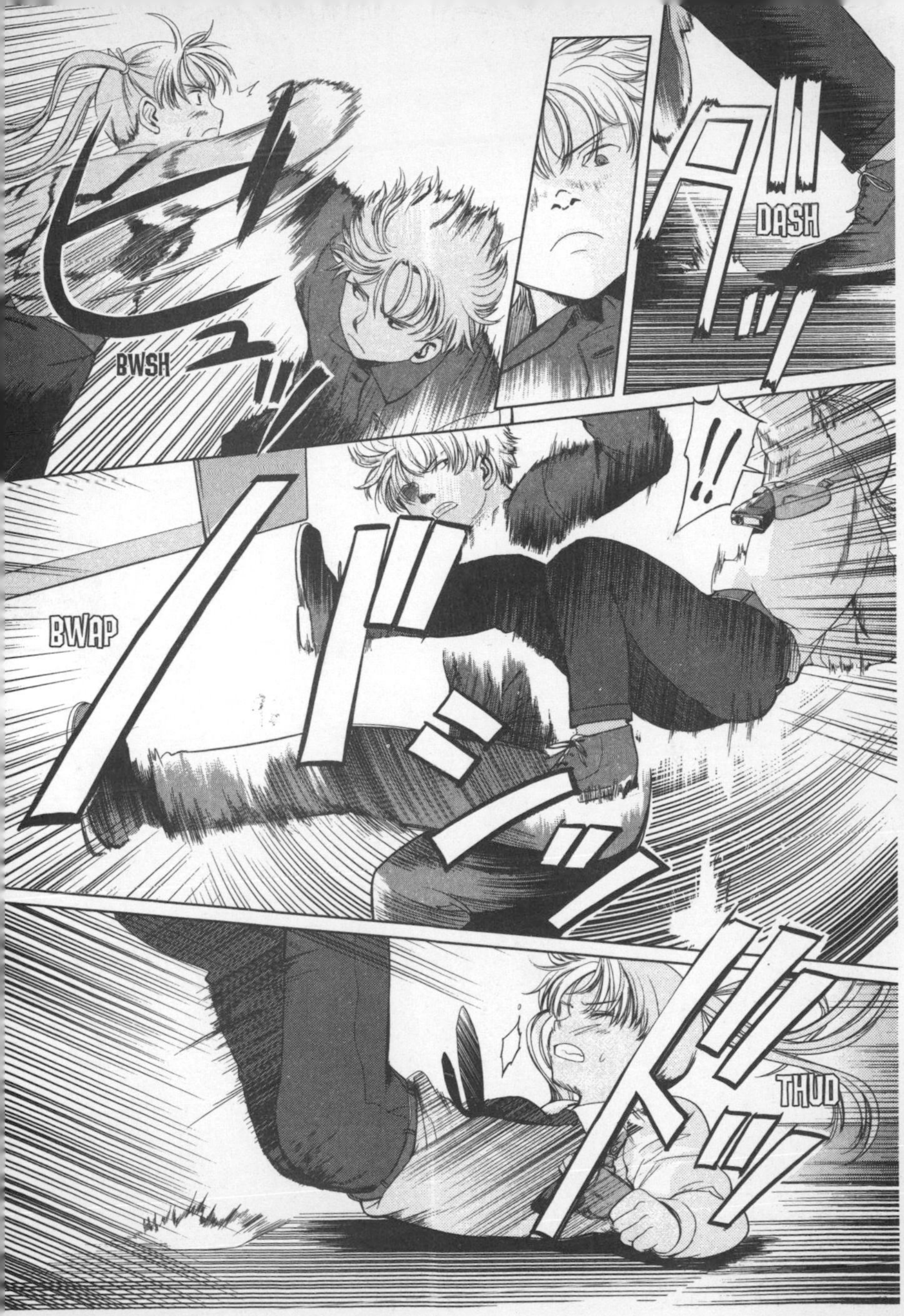
DASH
BWSH
!!
BWAP
THUD

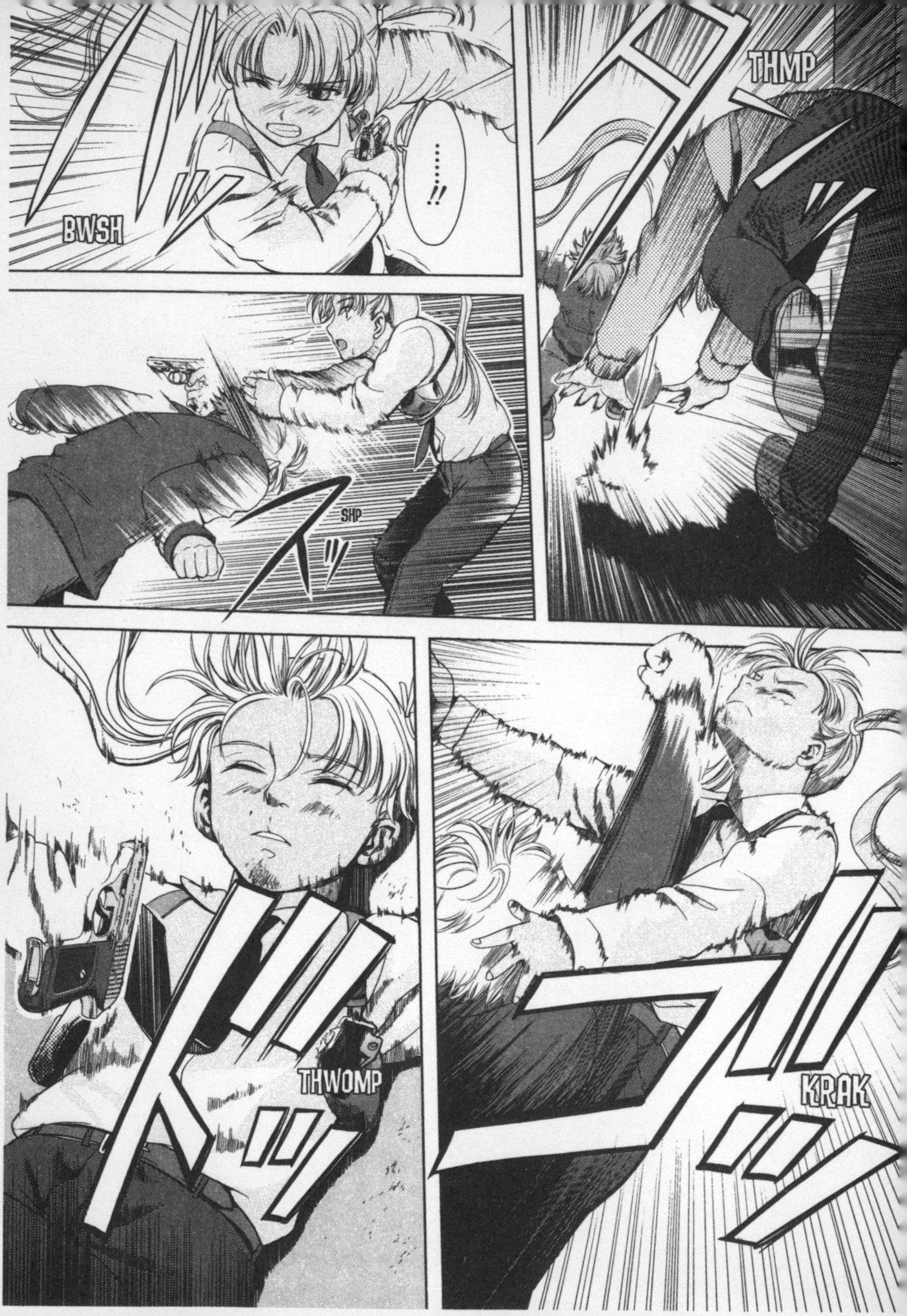
THMP
……!!
BWSH
SHP
KRAK
THWOMP

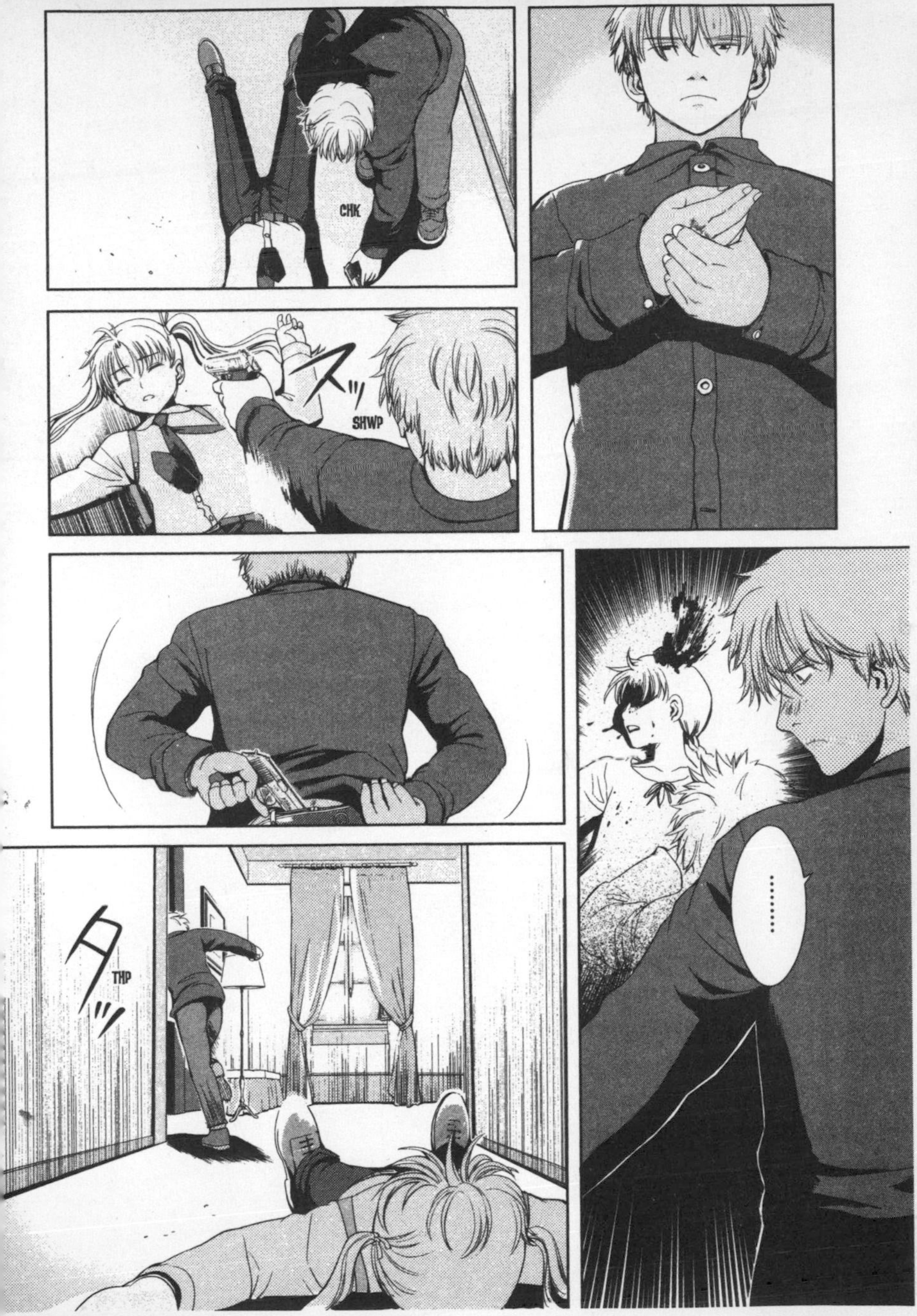
CHK
スッ
SHWP
......
タッ
THP

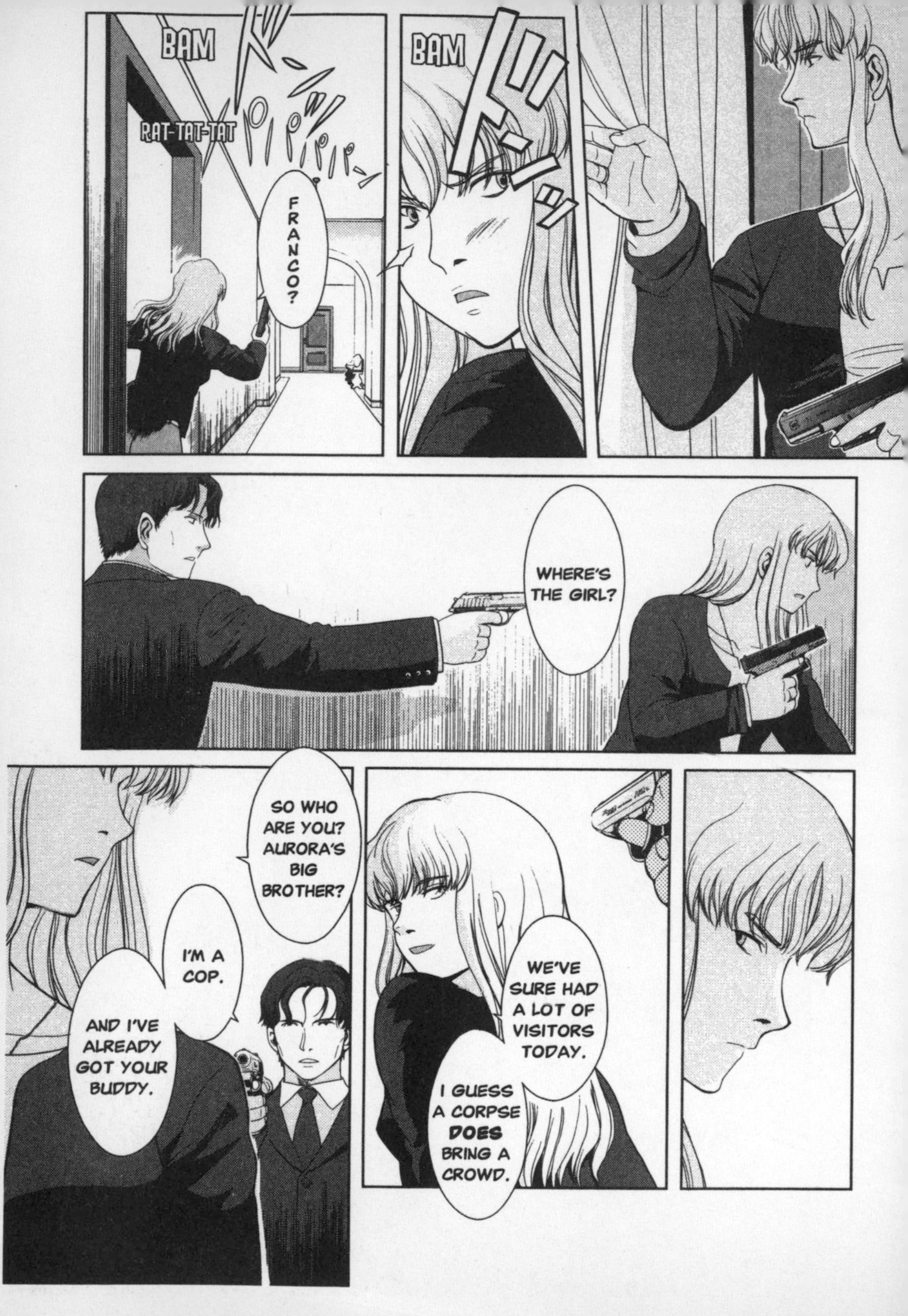
BAM
BAM
RAT-TAT-TAT
FRANCO?
WHERE'S THE GIRL?
WE'VE SURE HAD A LOT OF VISITORS TODAY.
I GUESS A CORPSE DOES BRING A CROWD.
SO WHO ARE YOU? AURORA'S BIG BROTHER?
I'M A COP.
AND I'VE ALREADY GOT YOUR BUDDY.

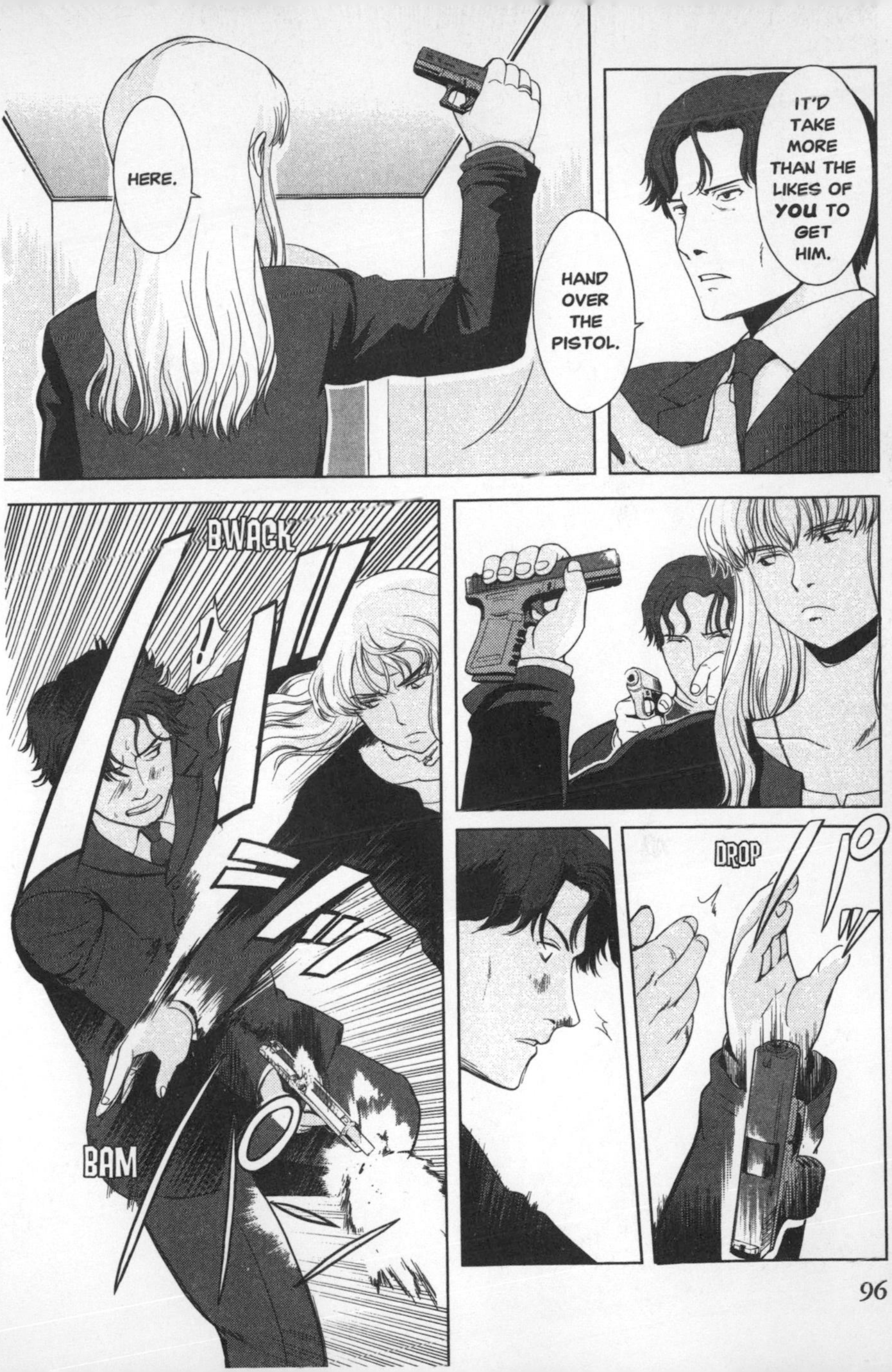
IT'D TAKE MORE THAN THE LIKES OF YOU TO GET HIM.
HAND OVER THE PISTOL.
HERE.
DROP
BWACK
BAM

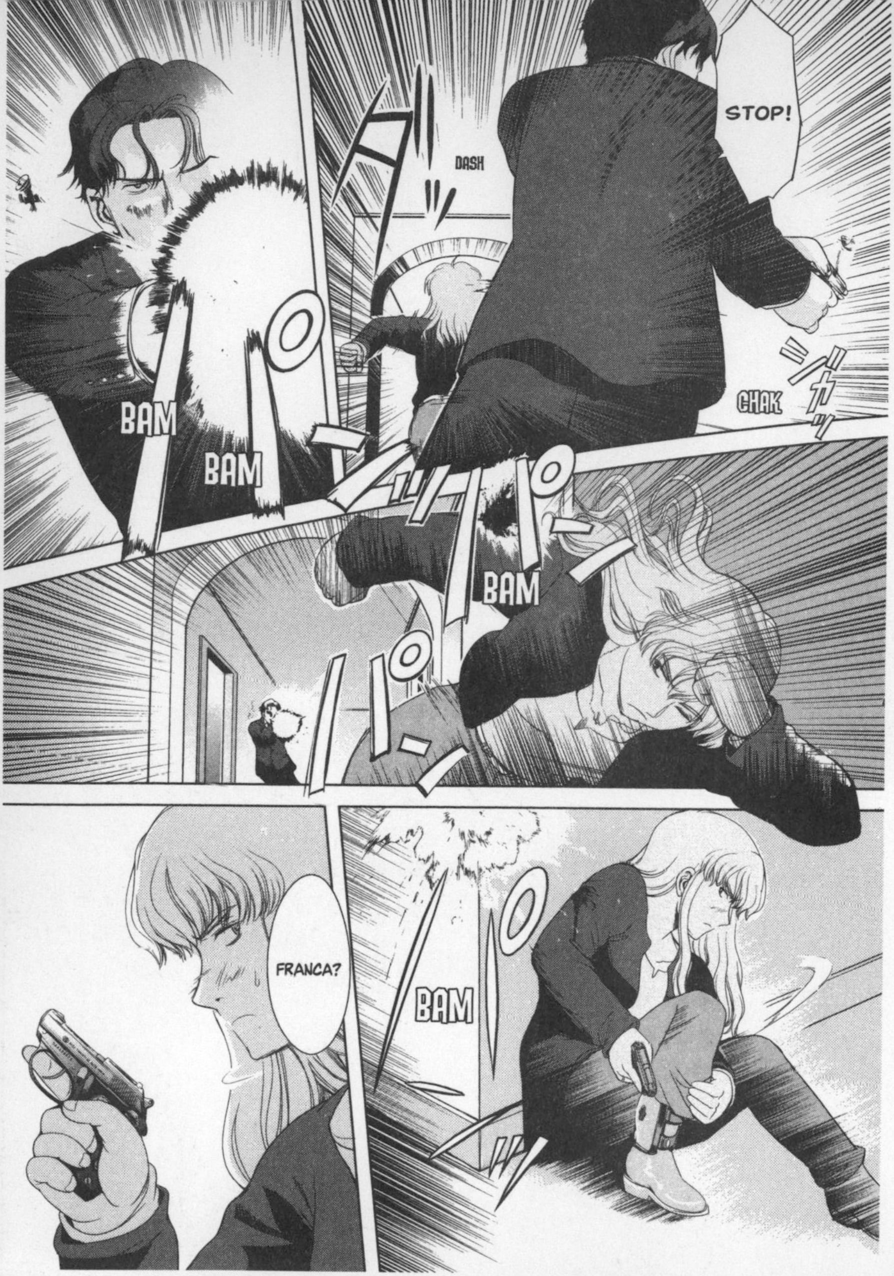
STOP!
DASH
CHAK
BAM
BAM
BAM
BAM
FRANCA?

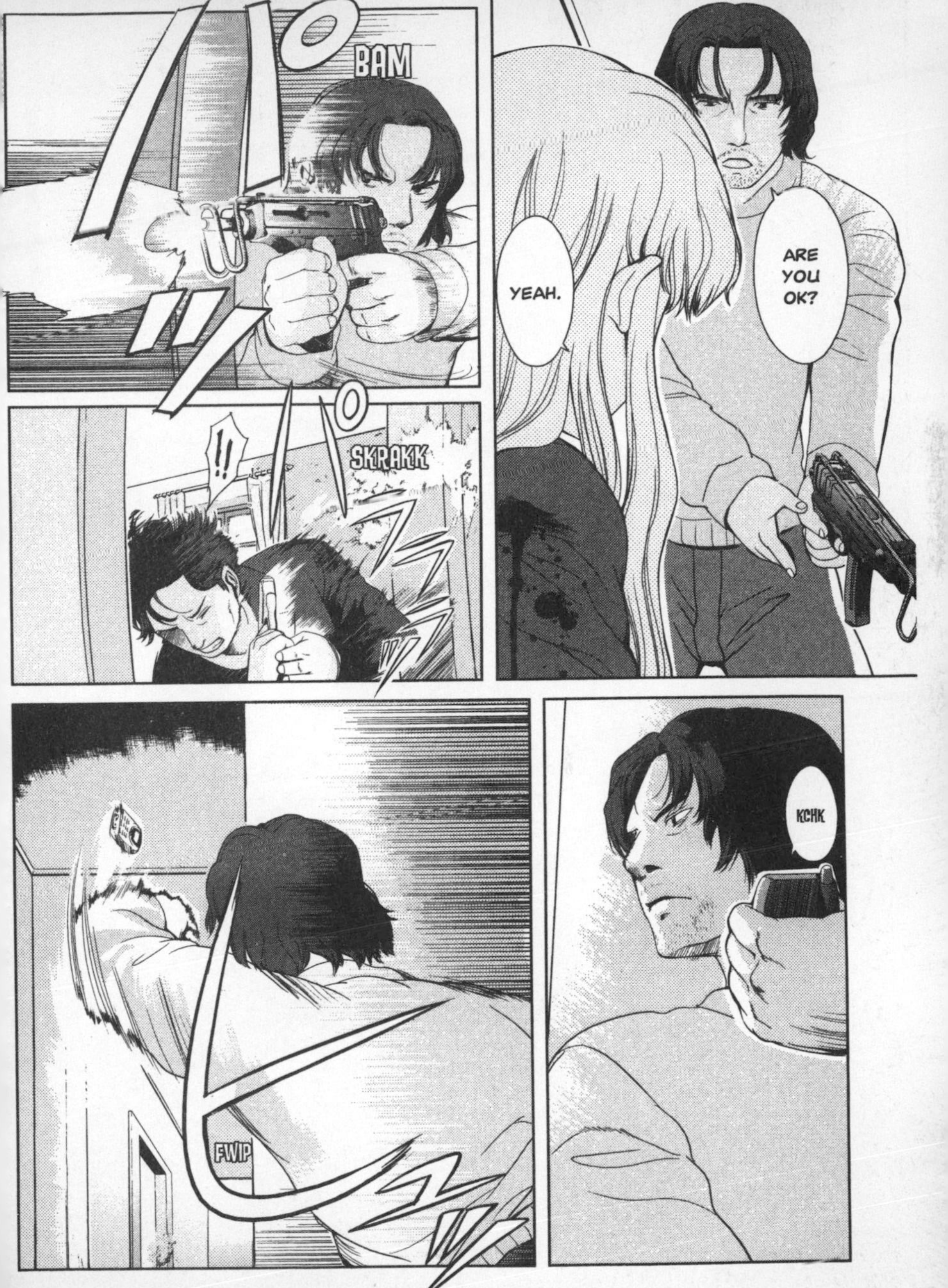
ARE YOU OK?
YEAH.
BAM
SKRAKK
!!
KCHK
FWIP

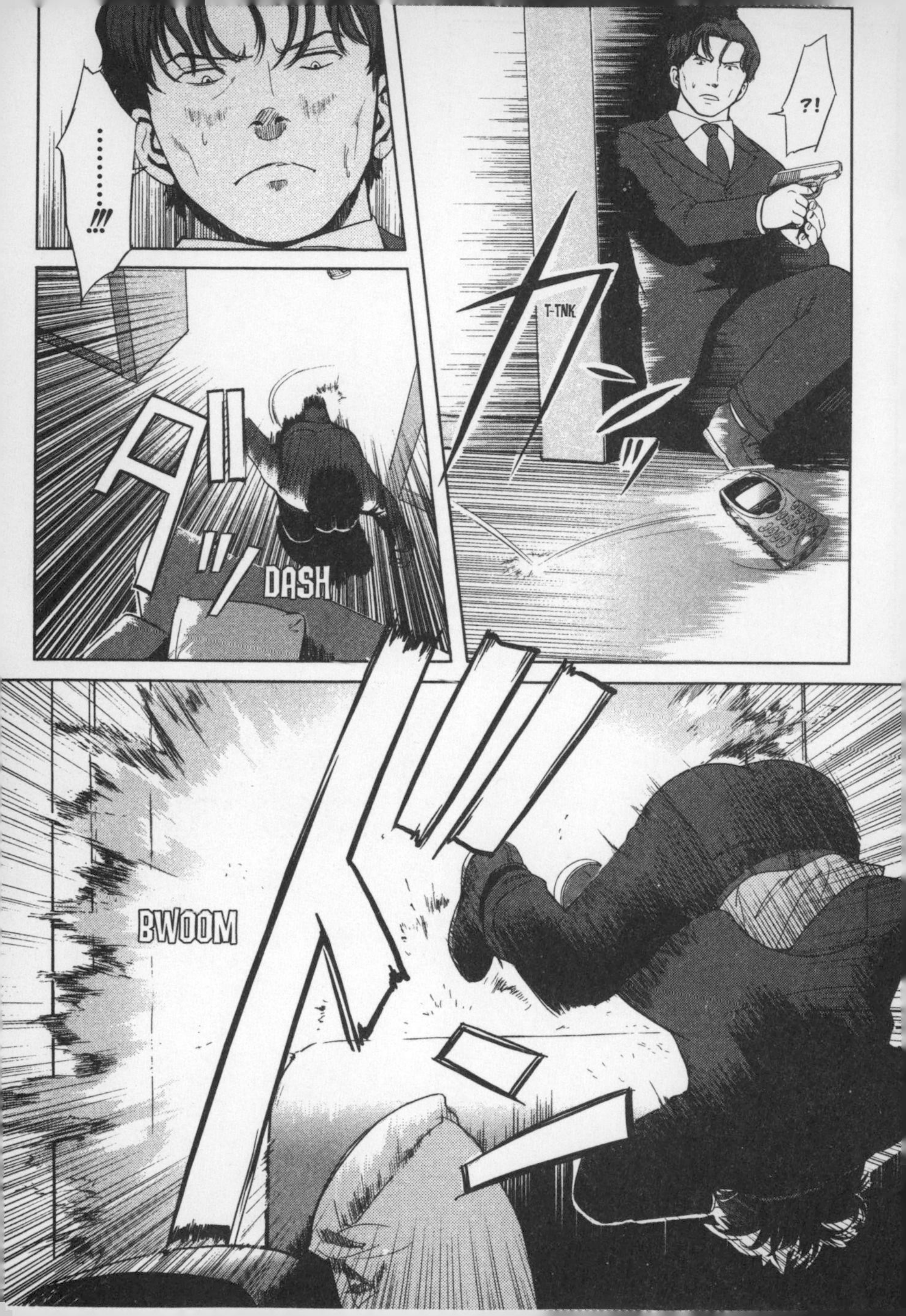
?!
T-TNK
......!!!
DASH
BWOOM

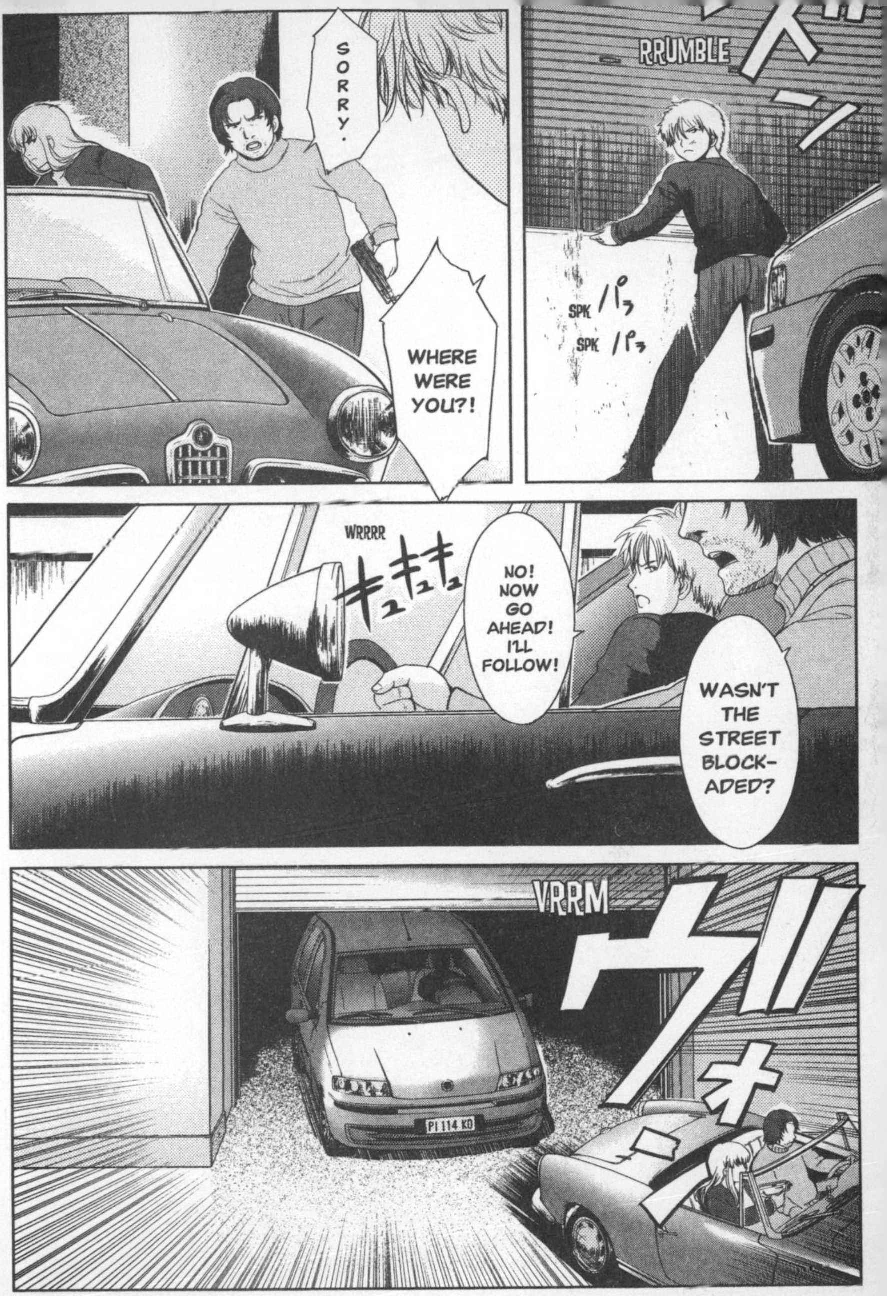
RRUMBLE
SPK
SPK
SORRY.
WHERE WERE YOU?!
WASN'T THE STREET BLOCK-ADED?
NO! NOW GO AHEAD! I'LL FOLLOW!
WRRRR
VRRM
PI 114 KO

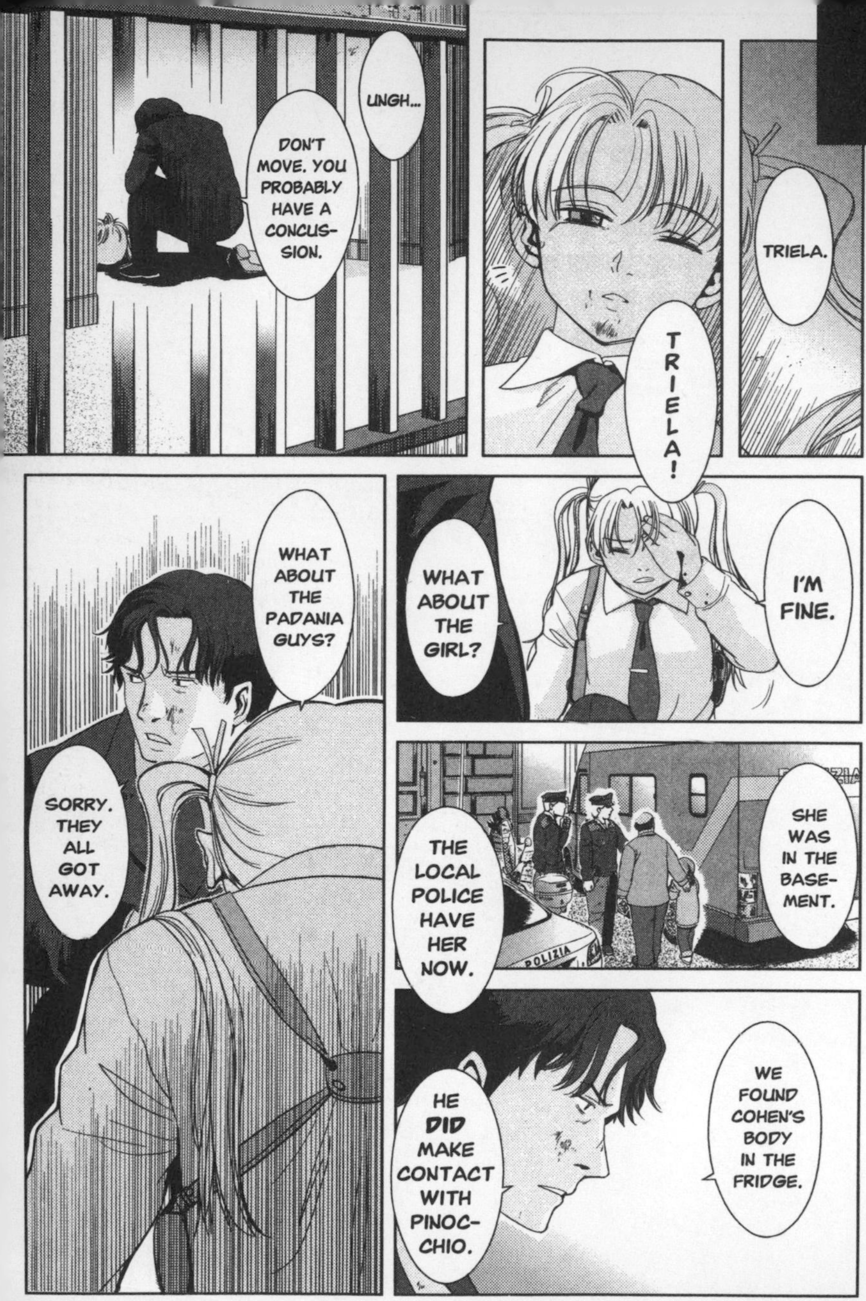
TRIELA.
TRIELA!
UNGH...
DON'T MOVE. YOU PROBABLY HAVE A CONCUSSION.
I'M FINE.
WHAT ABOUT THE GIRL?
SHE WAS IN THE BASEMENT.
THE LOCAL POLICE HAVE HER NOW.
WE FOUND COHEN'S BODY IN THE FRIDGE.
HE **DID** MAKE CONTACT WITH PINOCCHIO.
WHAT ABOUT THE PADANIA GUYS?
SORRY. THEY ALL GOT AWAY.

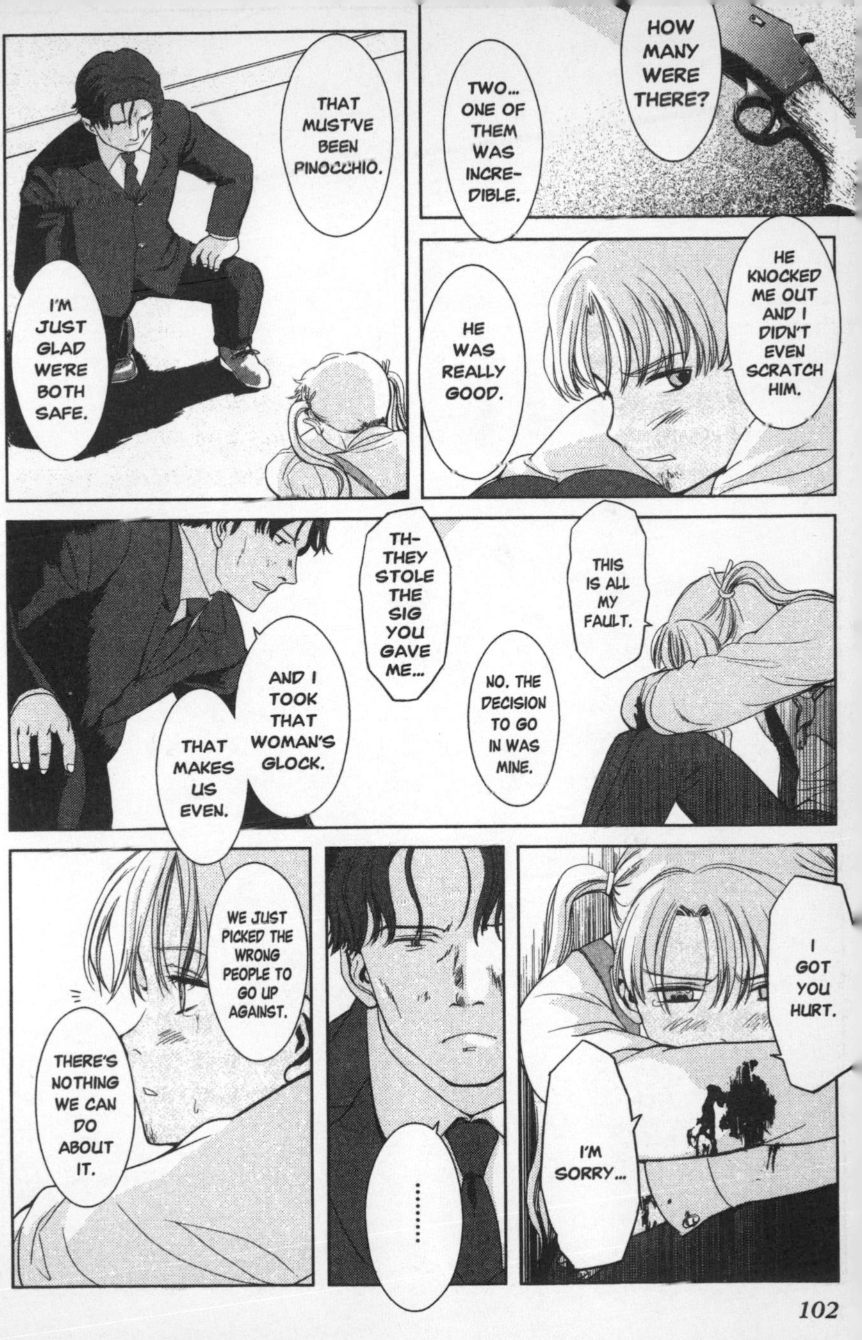
HOW MANY WERE THERE?
TWO... ONE OF THEM WAS INCRE-DIBLE.
HE KNOCKED ME OUT AND I DIDN'T EVEN SCRATCH HIM.
HE WAS REALLY GOOD.
THAT MUST'VE BEEN PINOCCHIO.
I'M JUST GLAD WE'RE BOTH SAFE.
THIS IS ALL MY FAULT.
NO. THE DECISION TO GO IN WAS MINE.
TH-THEY STOLE THE SIG YOU GAVE ME...
AND I TOOK THAT WOMAN'S GLOCK.
THAT MAKES US EVEN.
I GOT YOU HURT.
I'M SORRY...
....
WE JUST PICKED THE WRONG PEOPLE TO GO UP AGAINST.
THERE'S NOTHING WE CAN DO ABOUT IT.

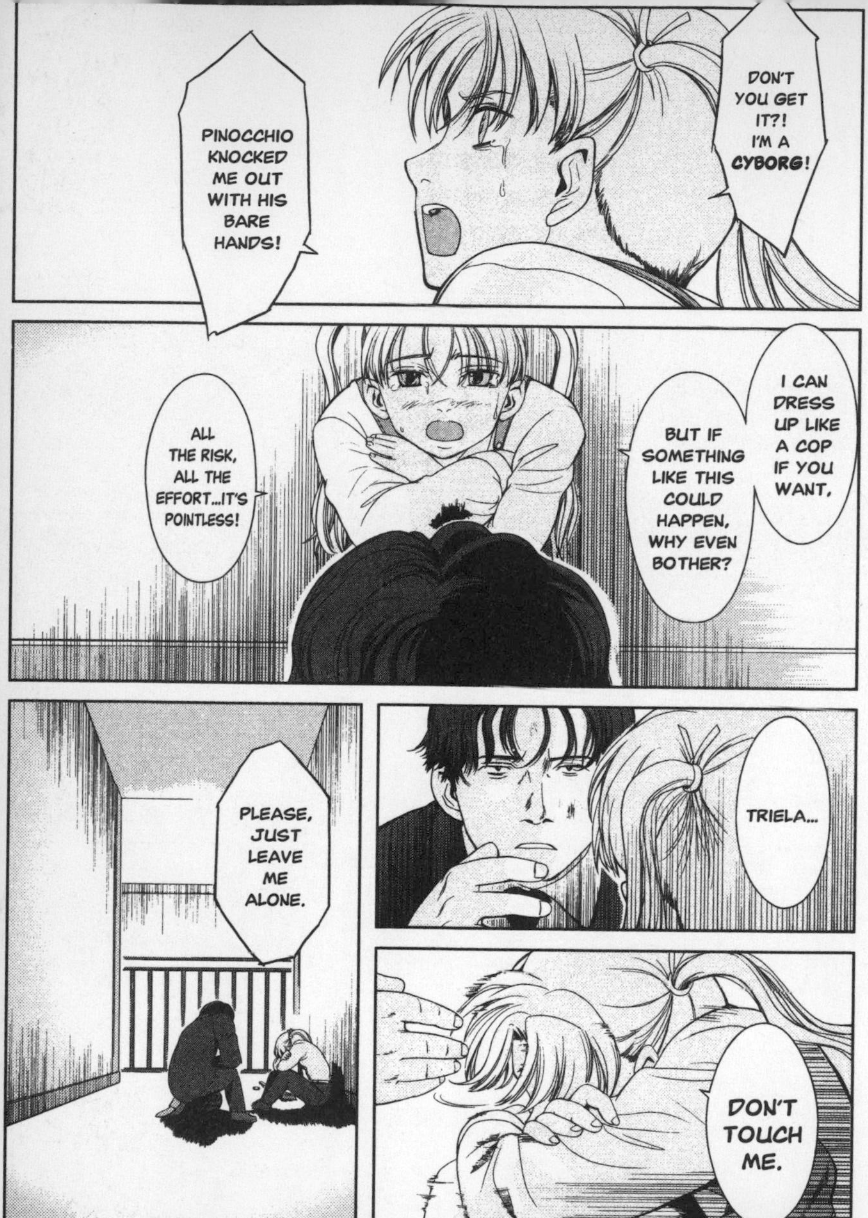
DON'T YOU GET IT?! I'M A **CYBORG**!
PINOCCHIO KNOCKED ME OUT WITH HIS BARE HANDS!
I CAN DRESS UP LIKE A COP IF YOU WANT,
BUT IF SOMETHING LIKE THIS COULD HAPPEN, WHY EVEN BOTHER?
ALL THE RISK, ALL THE EFFORT...IT'S POINTLESS!
TRIELA...
DON'T TOUCH ME.
PLEASE, JUST LEAVE ME ALONE.

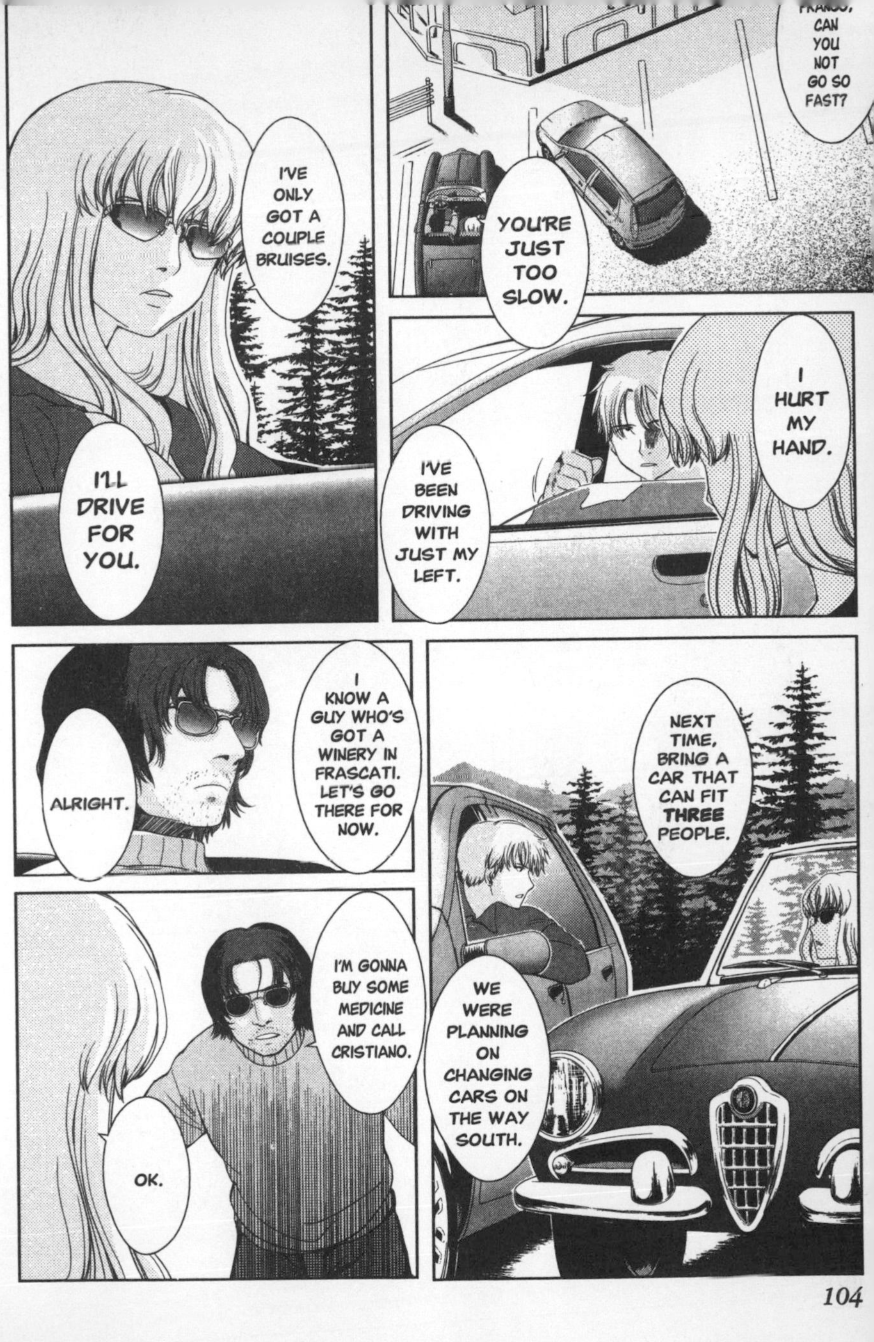
CAN YOU NOT GO SO FAST?
YOU'RE JUST TOO SLOW.
I HURT MY HAND.
I'VE BEEN DRIVING WITH JUST MY LEFT.
I'VE ONLY GOT A COUPLE BRUISES.
I'LL DRIVE FOR YOU.
NEXT TIME, BRING A CAR THAT CAN FIT THREE PEOPLE.
WE WERE PLANNING ON CHANGING CARS ON THE WAY SOUTH.
I KNOW A GUY WHO'S GOT A WINERY IN FRASCATI. LET'S GO THERE FOR NOW.
ALRIGHT.
I'M GONNA BUY SOME MEDICINE AND CALL CRISTIANO.
OK.

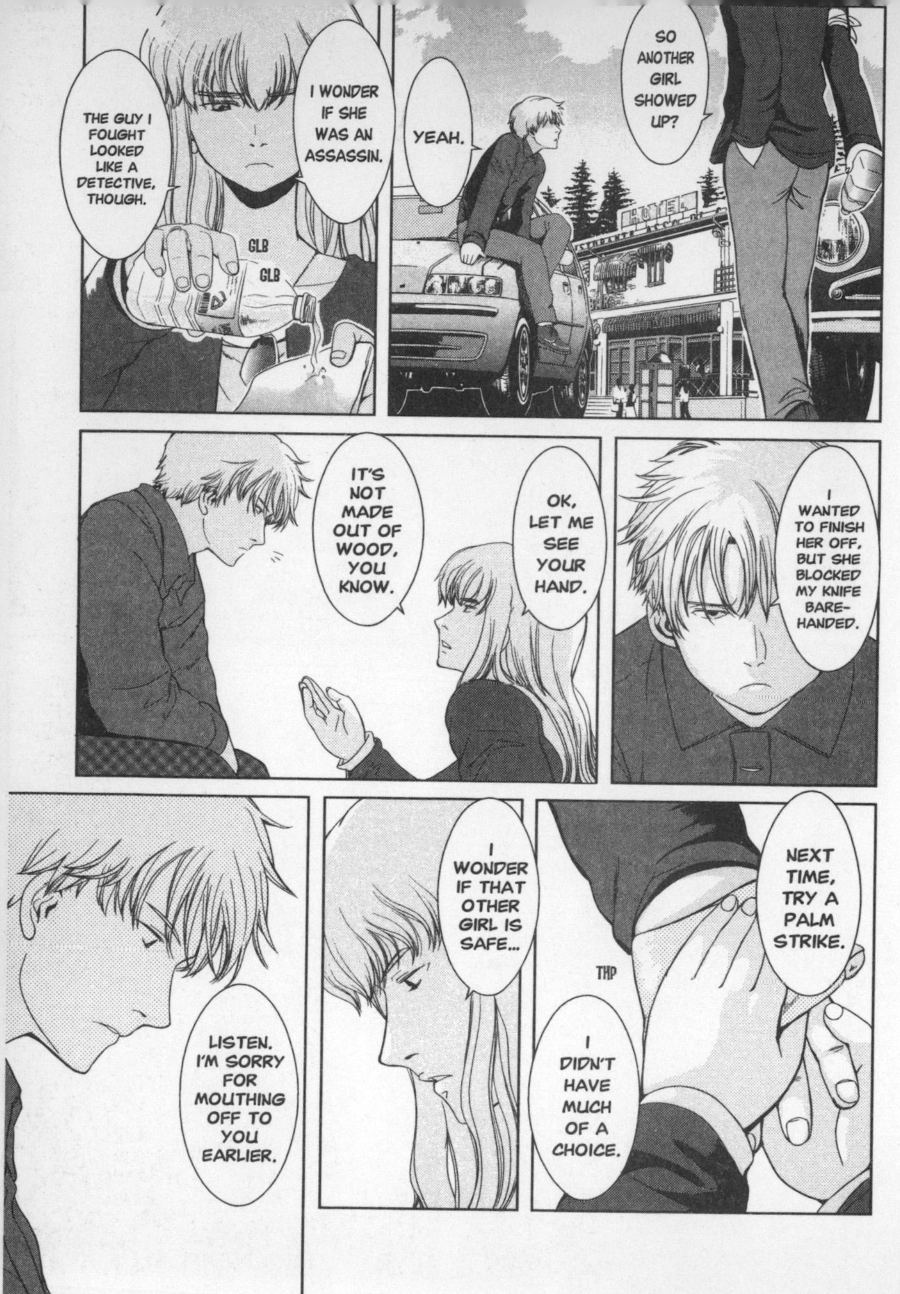
SO ANOTHER GIRL SHOWED UP?
YEAH.
I WONDER IF SHE WAS AN ASSASSIN.
THE GUY I FOUGHT LOOKED LIKE A DETECTIVE, THOUGH.
GLB
GLB
I WANTED TO FINISH HER OFF, BUT SHE BLOCKED MY KNIFE BARE-HANDED.
OK, LET ME SEE YOUR HAND.
IT'S NOT MADE OUT OF WOOD, YOU KNOW.
NEXT TIME, TRY A PALM STRIKE.
THP
I DIDN'T HAVE MUCH OF A CHOICE.
I WONDER IF THAT OTHER GIRL IS SAFE...
LISTEN. I'M SORRY FOR MOUTHING OFF TO YOU EARLIER.

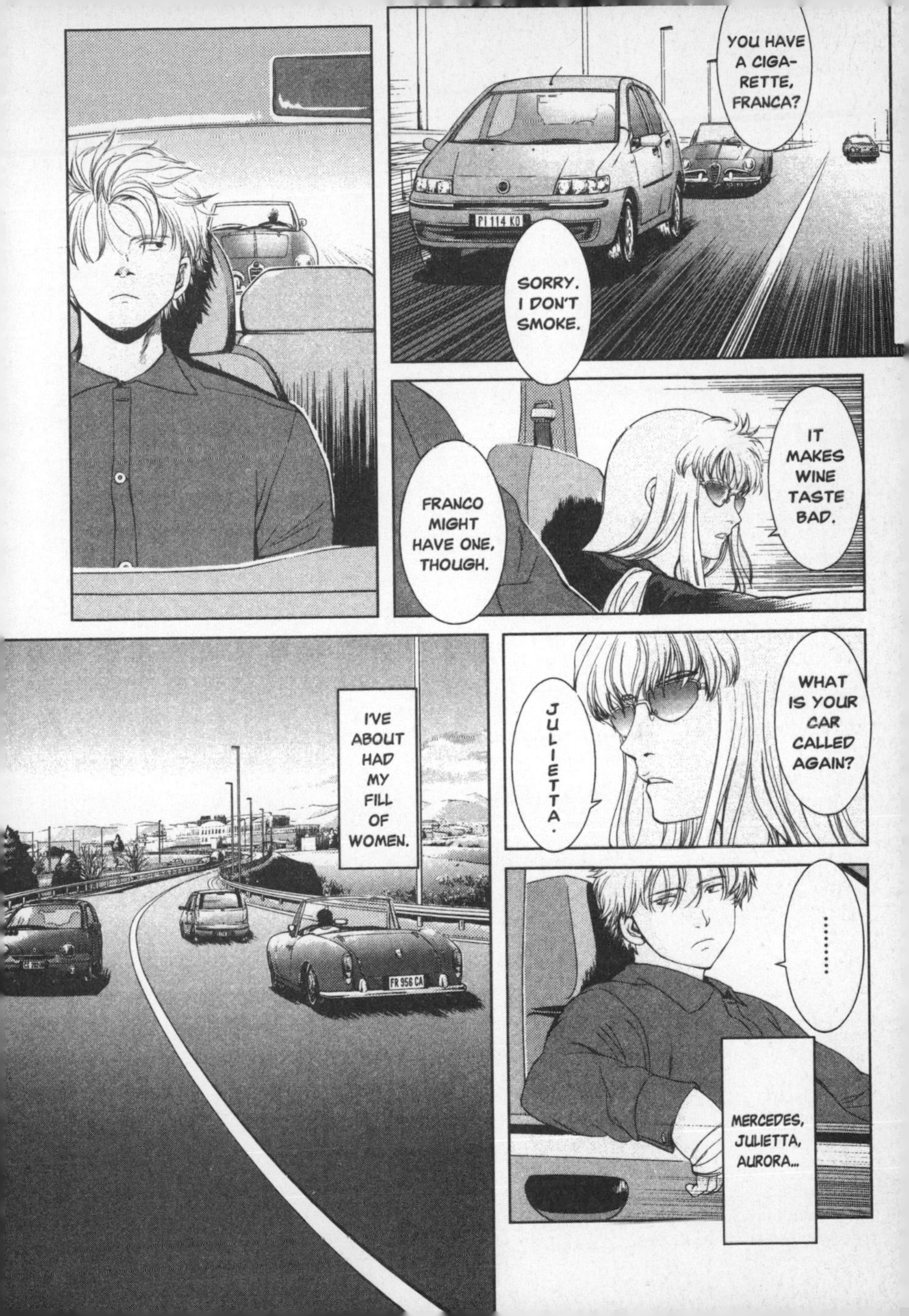
YOU HAVE A CIGARETTE, FRANCA?
SORRY. I DON'T SMOKE.
IT MAKES WINE TASTE BAD.
FRANCO MIGHT HAVE ONE, THOUGH.
WHAT IS YOUR CAR CALLED AGAIN?
JULIETTA.
......
MERCEDES, JULIETTA, AURORA...
I'VE ABOUT HAD MY FILL OF WOMEN.

GUNSLINGERGIRL.

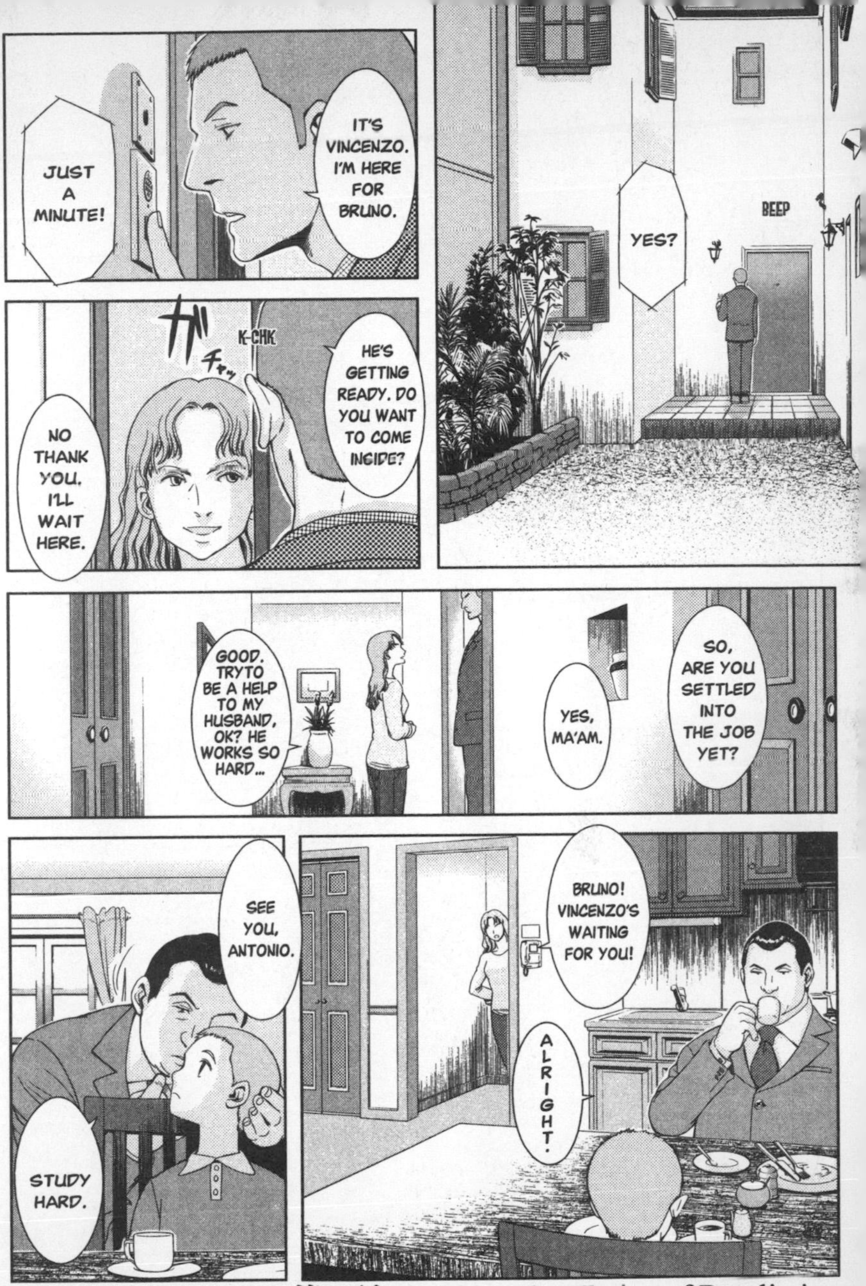
BEEP
YES?
IT'S VINCENZO. I'M HERE FOR BRUNO.
JUST A MINUTE!
ガチャッ
K-CHK
HE'S GETTING READY. DO YOU WANT TO COME INSIDE?
NO THANK YOU. I'LL WAIT HERE.
SO, ARE YOU SETTLED INTO THE JOB YET?
YES, MA'AM.
GOOD. TRYTO BE A HELP TO MY HUSBAND, OK? HE WORKS SO HARD...
BRUNO! VINCENZO'S WAITING FOR YOU!
ALRIGHT.
SEE YOU, ANTONIO.
STUDY HARD.

第16話 Breaking the Chains of Retaliation

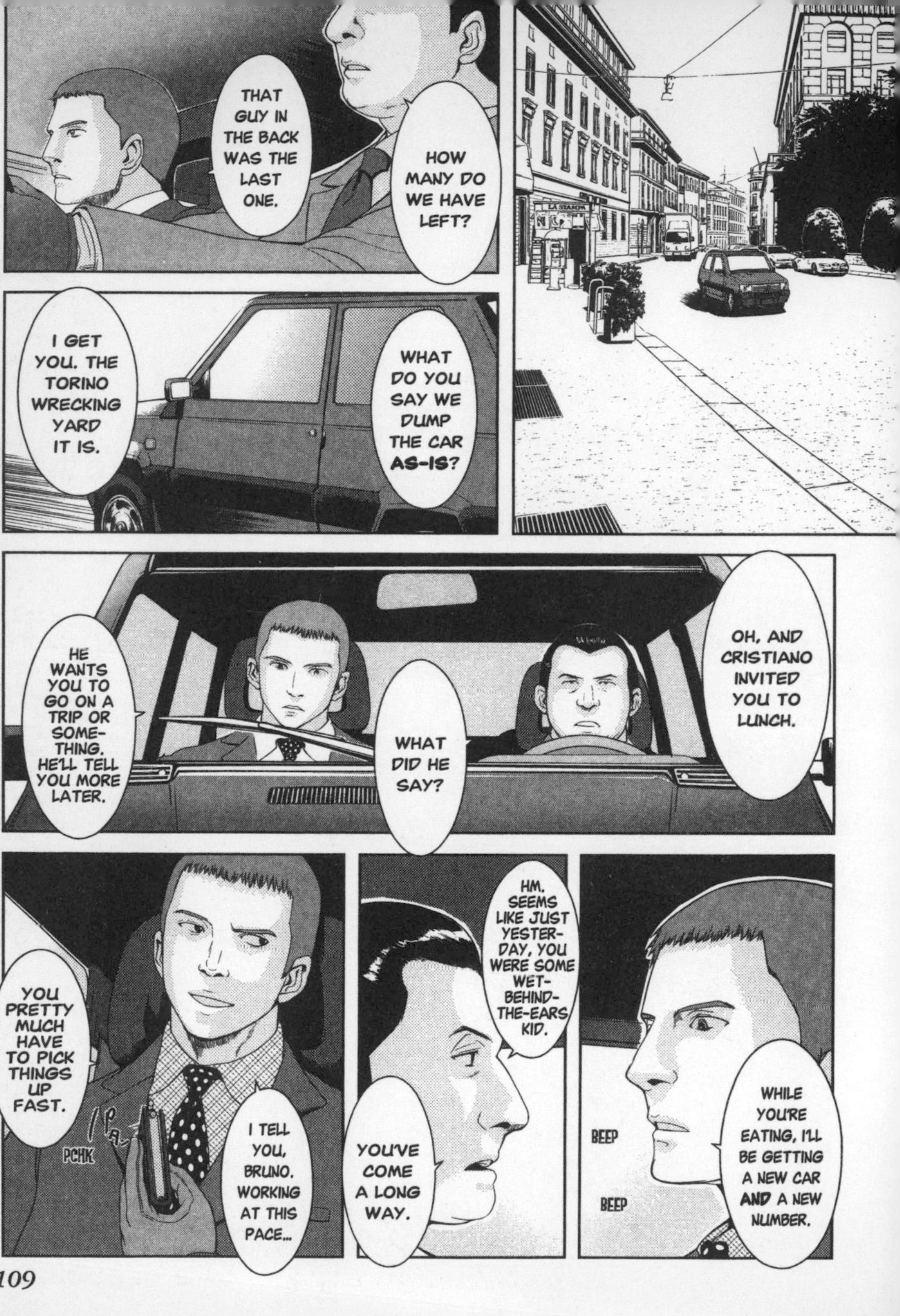
HOW MANY DO WE HAVE LEFT?
THAT GUY IN THE BACK WAS THE LAST ONE.
WHAT DO YOU SAY WE DUMP THE CAR AS-IS?
I GET YOU. THE TORINO WRECKING YARD IT IS.
OH, AND CRISTIANO INVITED YOU TO LUNCH.
WHAT DID HE SAY?
HE WANTS YOU TO GO ON A TRIP OR SOME-THING. HE'LL TELL YOU MORE LATER.
WHILE YOU'RE EATING, I'LL BE GETTING A NEW CAR AND A NEW NUMBER.
BEEP
BEEP
HM. SEEMS LIKE JUST YESTER-DAY, YOU WERE SOME WET-BEHIND-THE-EARS KID.
YOU'VE COME A LONG WAY.
I TELL YOU, BRUNO. WORKING AT THIS PACE...
YOU PRETTY MUCH HAVE TO PICK THINGS UP FAST.
PCHK

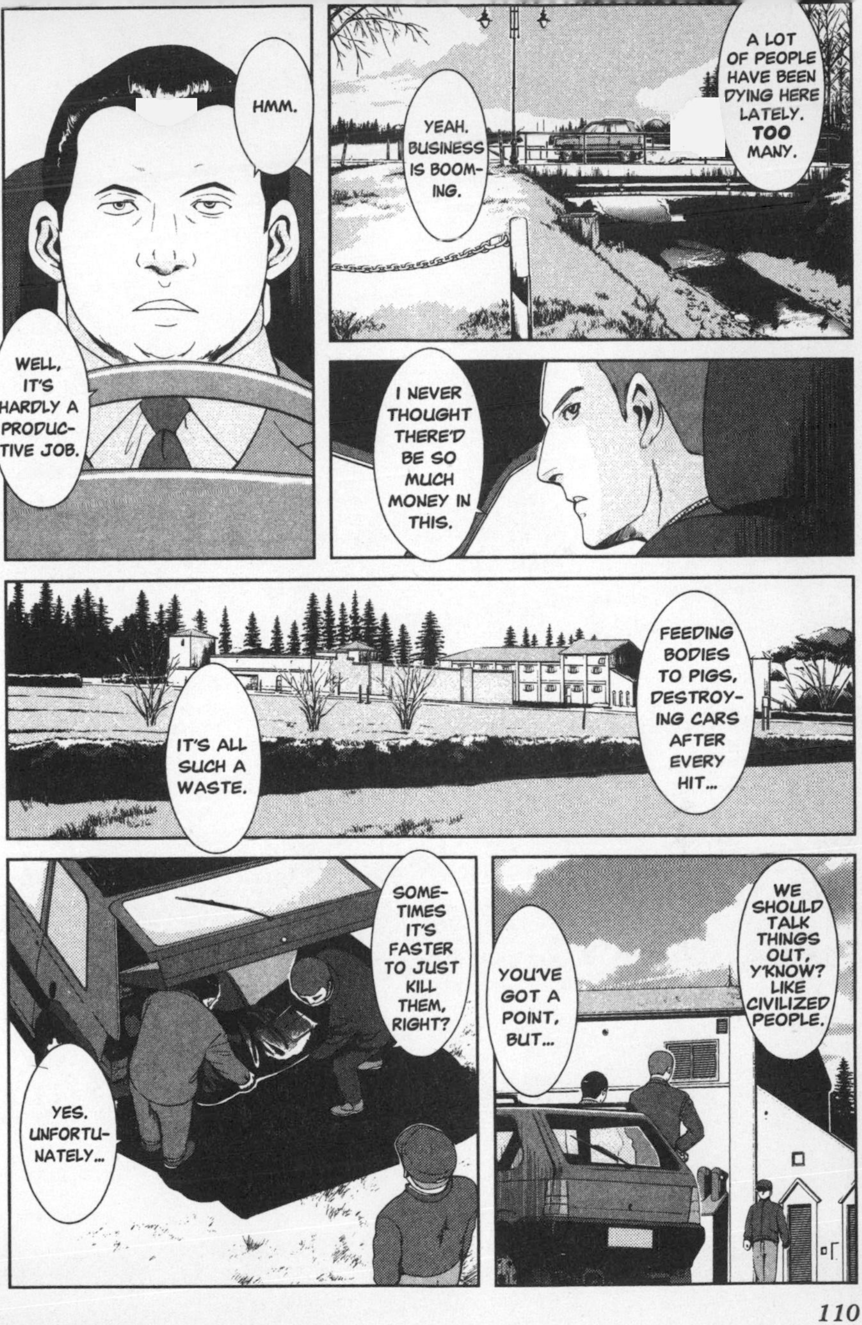
A LOT OF PEOPLE HAVE BEEN DYING HERE LATELY. TOO MANY.
YEAH. BUSINESS IS BOOMING.
I NEVER THOUGHT THERE'D BE SO MUCH MONEY IN THIS.
HMM.
WELL, IT'S HARDLY A PRODUCTIVE JOB.
FEEDING BODIES TO PIGS, DESTROYING CARS AFTER EVERY HIT...
IT'S ALL SUCH A WASTE.
WE SHOULD TALK THINGS OUT, Y'KNOW? LIKE CIVILIZED PEOPLE.
YOU'VE GOT A POINT, BUT...
SOMETIMES IT'S FASTER TO JUST KILL THEM, RIGHT?
YES. UNFORTUNATELY...

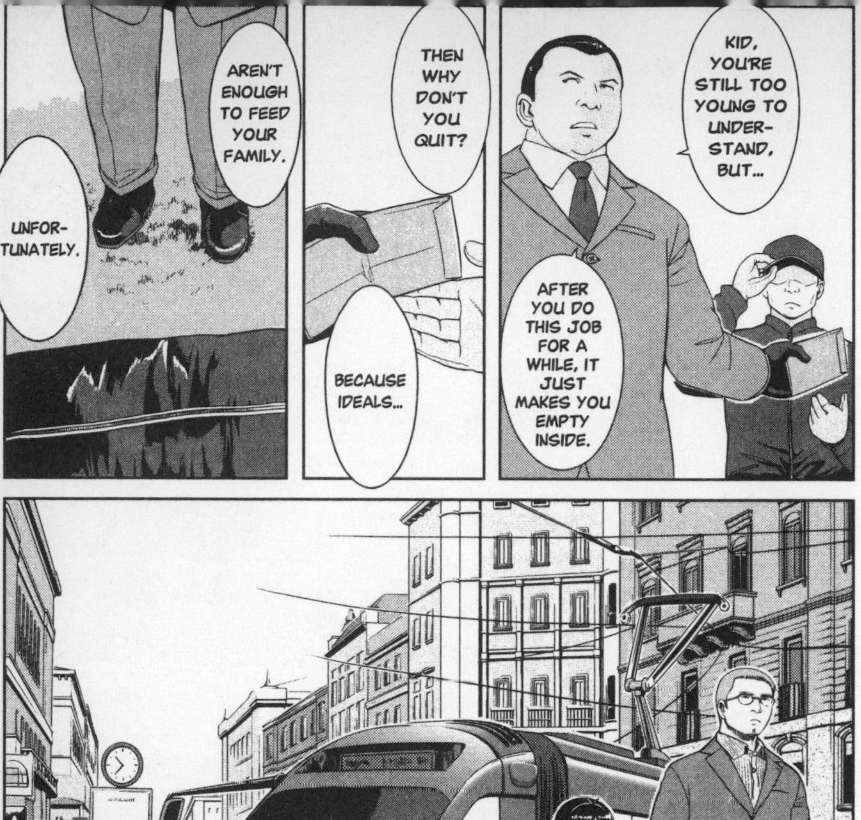
KID, YOU'RE STILL TOO YOUNG TO UNDER-STAND, BUT...
AFTER YOU DO THIS JOB FOR A WHILE, IT JUST MAKES YOU EMPTY INSIDE.
THEN WHY DON'T YOU QUIT?
BECAUSE IDEALS...
AREN'T ENOUGH TO FEED YOUR FAMILY.
UNFOR-TUNATELY.
第16話 Breaking the Chains of Retaliation

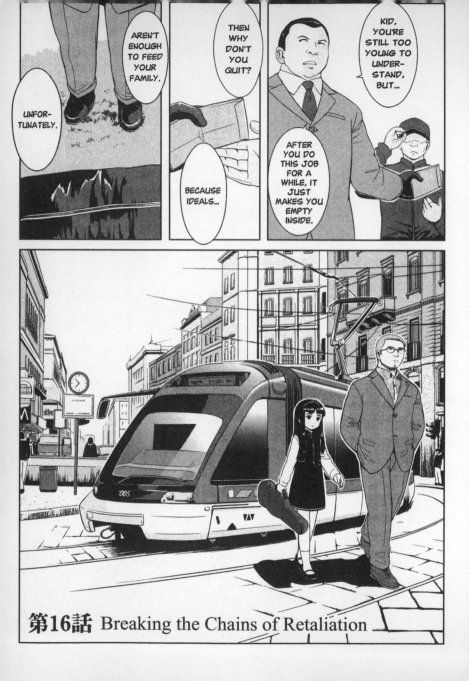

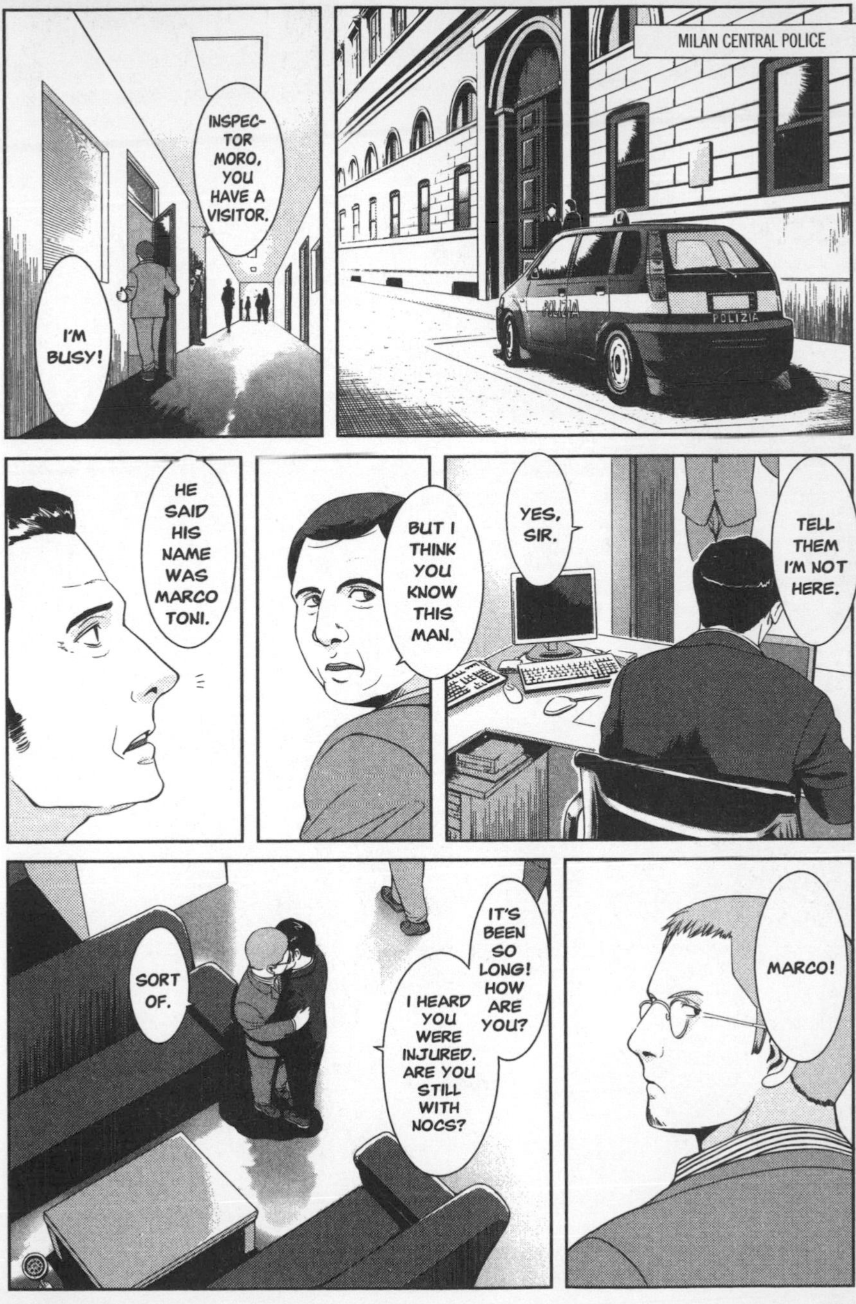
MILAN CENTRAL POLICE
INSPECTOR MORO, YOU HAVE A VISITOR.
I'M BUSY!
TELL THEM I'M NOT HERE.
YES, SIR.
BUT I THINK YOU KNOW THIS MAN.
HE SAID HIS NAME WAS MARCO TONI.
MARCO!
IT'S BEEN SO LONG! HOW ARE YOU?
I HEARD YOU WERE INJURED. ARE YOU STILL WITH NOCS?
SORT OF.

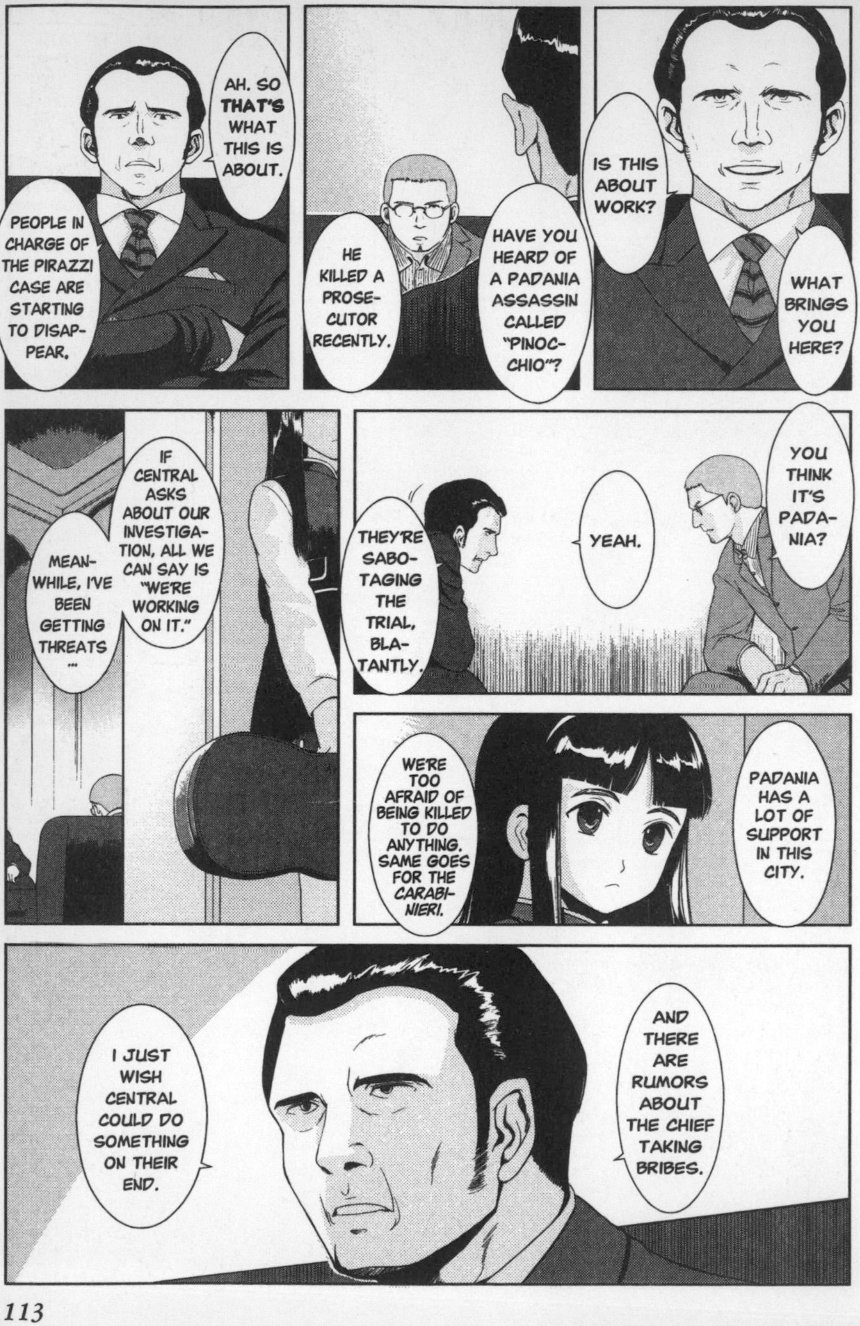
WHAT BRINGS YOU HERE?
IS THIS ABOUT WORK?
HAVE YOU HEARD OF A PADANIA ASSASSIN CALLED "PINOCCHIO"?
HE KILLED A PROSECUTOR RECENTLY.
AH. SO THAT'S WHAT THIS IS ABOUT.
PEOPLE IN CHARGE OF THE PIRAZZI CASE ARE STARTING TO DISAPPEAR.
YOU THINK IT'S PADANIA?
YEAH.
THEY'RE SABOTAGING THE TRIAL, BLATANTLY.
PADANIA HAS A LOT OF SUPPORT IN THIS CITY.
WE'RE TOO AFRAID OF BEING KILLED TO DO ANYTHING. SAME GOES FOR THE CARABINIERI.
IF CENTRAL ASKS ABOUT OUR INVESTIGATION, ALL WE CAN SAY IS "WE'RE WORKING ON IT."
MEANWHILE, I'VE BEEN GETTING THREATS...
AND THERE ARE RUMORS ABOUT THE CHIEF TAKING BRIBES.
I JUST WISH CENTRAL COULD DO SOMETHING ON THEIR END.

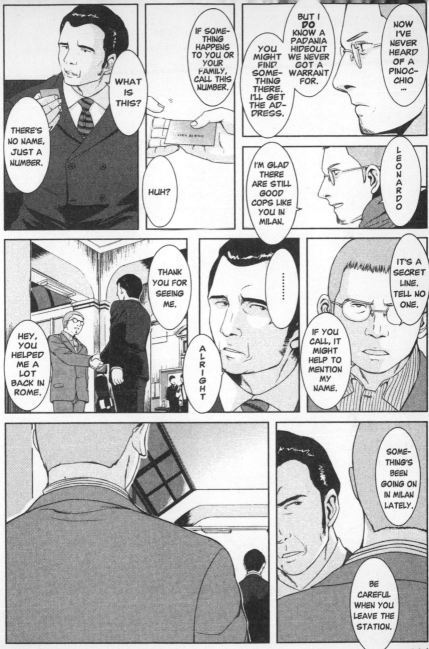

114

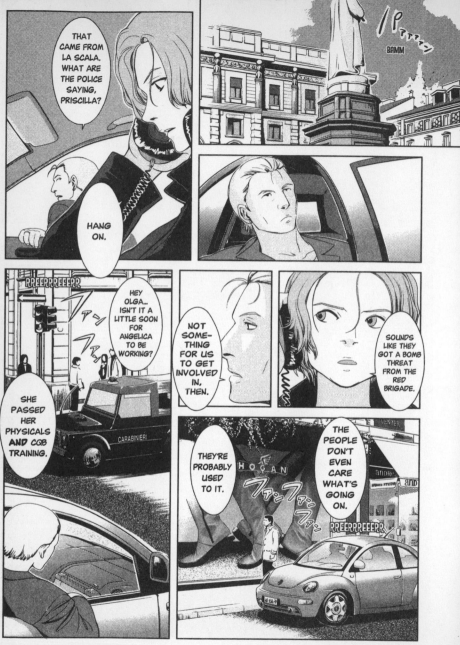

115

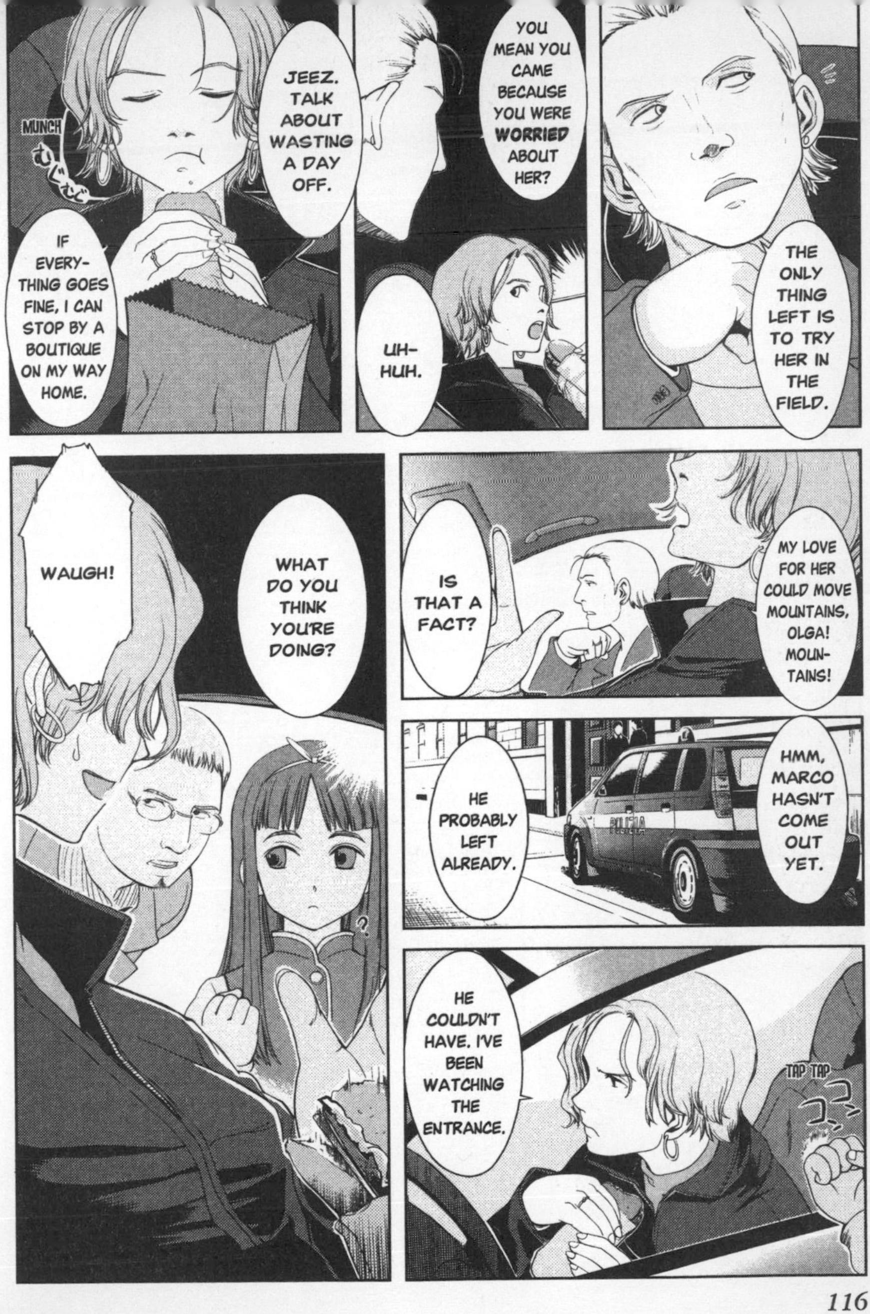
THE ONLY THING LEFT IS TO TRY HER IN THE FIELD.
YOU MEAN YOU CAME BECAUSE YOU WERE WORRIED ABOUT HER?
UH-HUH.
JEEZ. TALK ABOUT WASTING A DAY OFF.
MUNCH
むぐむぐ
IF EVERY-THING GOES FINE, I CAN STOP BY A BOUTIQUE ON MY WAY HOME.
MY LOVE FOR HER COULD MOVE MOUNTAINS, OLGA! MOUN-TAINS!
IS THAT A FACT?
HMM, MARCO HASN'T COME OUT YET.
HE PROBABLY LEFT ALREADY.
TAP TAP
HE COULDN'T HAVE. I'VE BEEN WATCHING THE ENTRANCE.
WHAT DO YOU THINK YOU'RE DOING?
WAUGH!

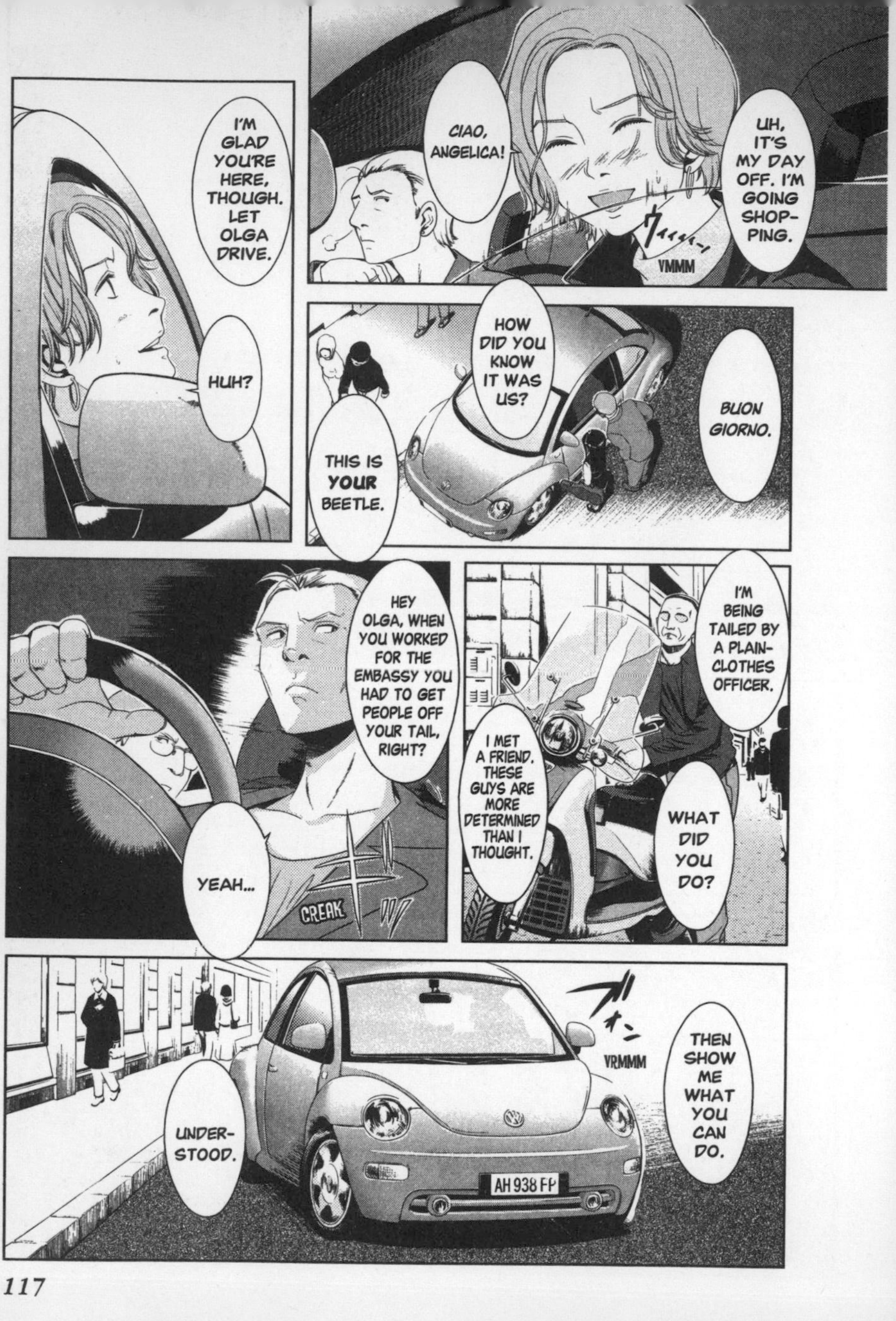
UH, IT'S MY DAY OFF. I'M GOING SHOP-PING.
CIAO, ANGELICA!
VMMM
BUON GIORNO.
HOW DID YOU KNOW IT WAS US?
THIS IS YOUR BEETLE.
I'M GLAD YOU'RE HERE, THOUGH. LET OLGA DRIVE.
HUH?
I'M BEING TAILED BY A PLAIN-CLOTHES OFFICER.
I MET A FRIEND. THESE GUYS ARE MORE DETERMINED THAN I THOUGHT.
WHAT DID YOU DO?
HEY OLGA, WHEN YOU WORKED FOR THE EMBASSY YOU HAD TO GET PEOPLE OFF YOUR TAIL, RIGHT?
YEAH...
CREAK
THEN SHOW ME WHAT YOU CAN DO.
VRMMM
UNDER-STOOD.
AH 938 FP

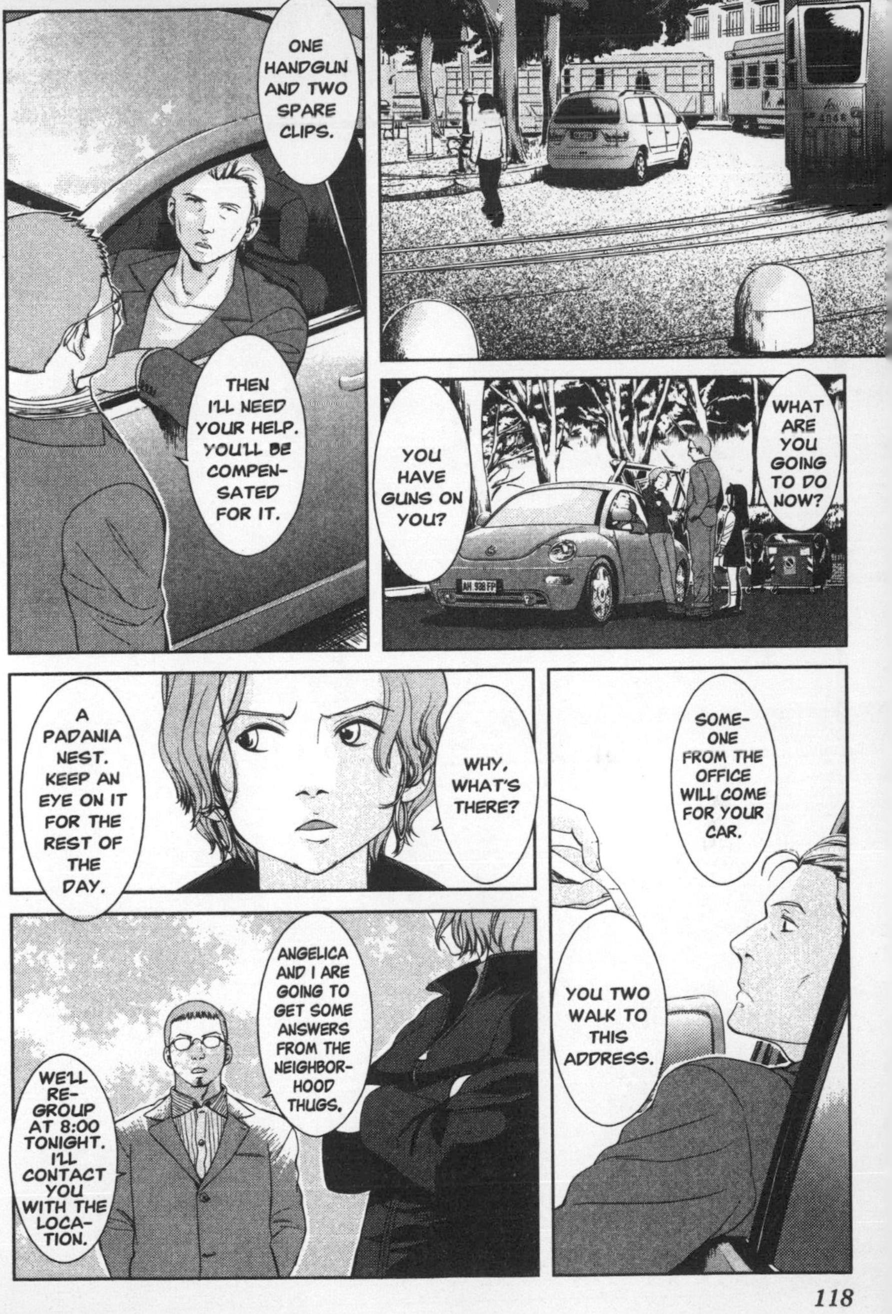
WHAT ARE YOU GOING TO DO NOW?
YOU HAVE GUNS ON YOU?
ONE HANDGUN AND TWO SPARE CLIPS.
THEN I'LL NEED YOUR HELP. YOU'LL BE COMPEN-SATED FOR IT.
SOME-ONE FROM THE OFFICE WILL COME FOR YOUR CAR.
YOU TWO WALK TO THIS ADDRESS.
WHY, WHAT'S THERE?
A PADANIA NEST. KEEP AN EYE ON IT FOR THE REST OF THE DAY.
ANGELICA AND I ARE GOING TO GET SOME ANSWERS FROM THE NEIGHBOR-HOOD THUGS.
WE'LL RE-GROUP AT 8:00 TONIGHT. I'LL CONTACT YOU WITH THE LOCA-TION.

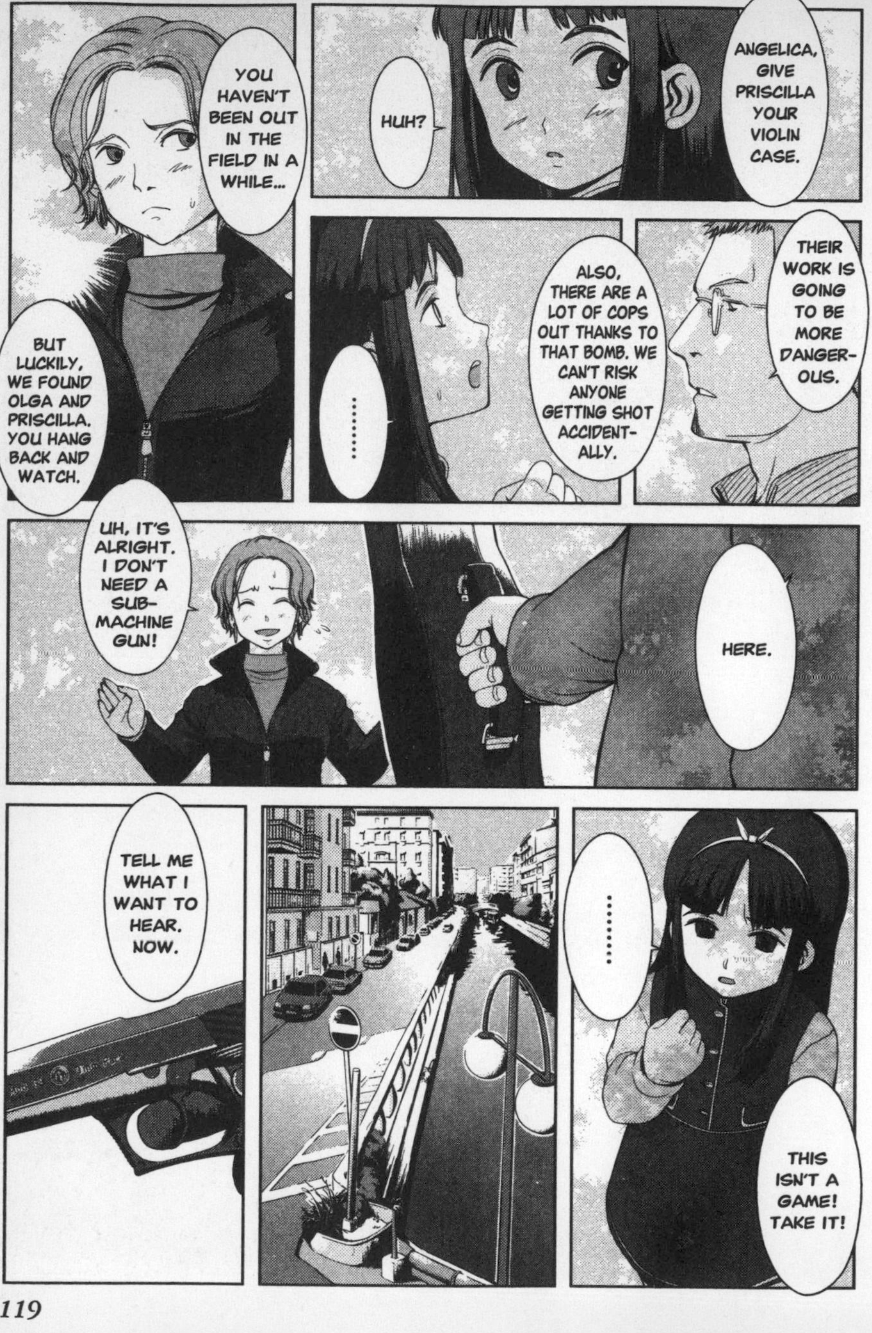
ANGELICA, GIVE PRISCILLA YOUR VIOLIN CASE.
HUH?
THEIR WORK IS GOING TO BE MORE DANGER-OUS.
ALSO, THERE ARE A LOT OF COPS OUT THANKS TO THAT BOMB. WE CAN'T RISK ANYONE GETTING SHOT ACCIDENT-ALLY.
......
YOU HAVEN'T BEEN OUT IN THE FIELD IN A WHILE...
BUT LUCKILY, WE FOUND OLGA AND PRISCILLA. YOU HANG BACK AND WATCH.
HERE.
UH, IT'S ALRIGHT. I DON'T NEED A SUB-MACHINE GUN!
......
THIS ISN'T A GAME! TAKE IT!
TELL ME WHAT I WANT TO HEAR. NOW.

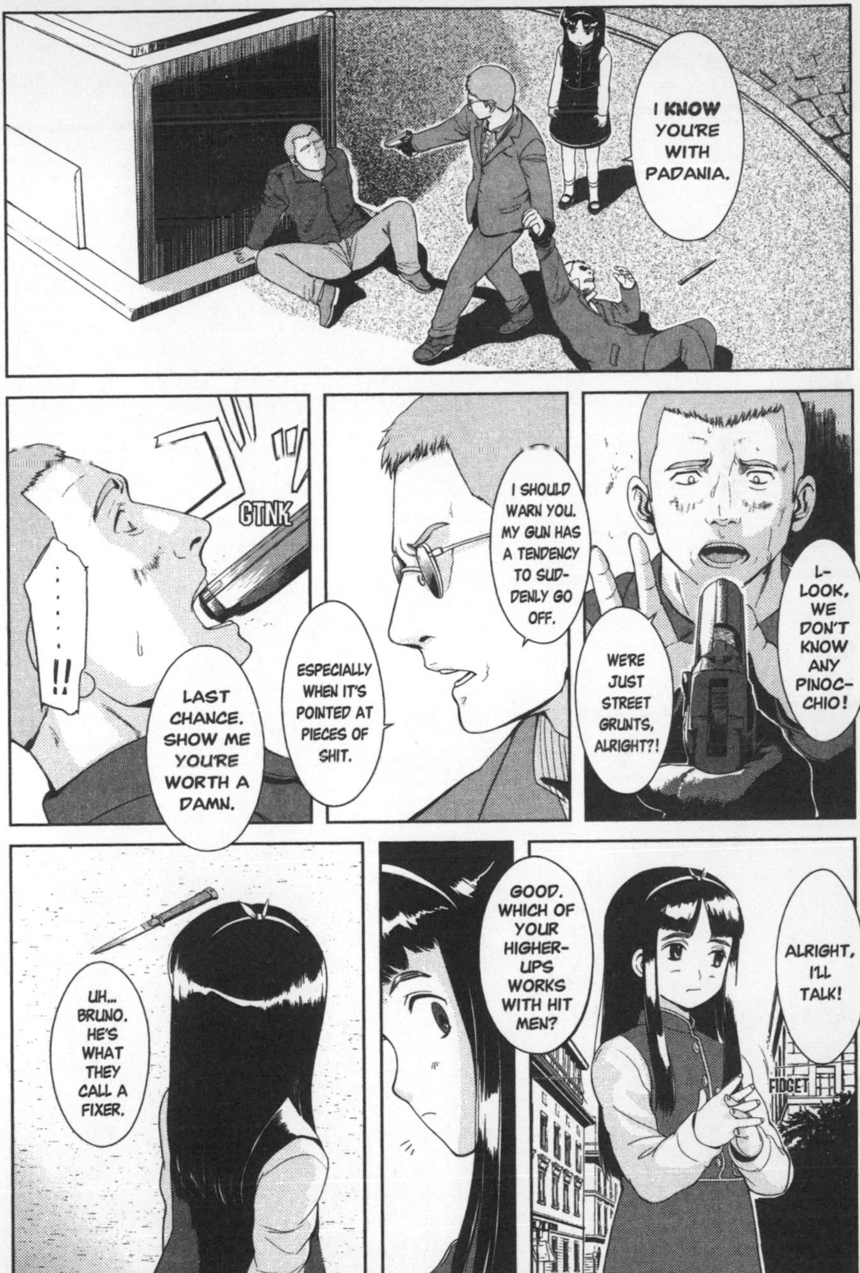
I KNOW YOU'RE WITH PADANIA.
L-LOOK, WE DON'T KNOW ANY PINOCCHIO!
WE'RE JUST STREET GRUNTS, ALRIGHT?!
I SHOULD WARN YOU. MY GUN HAS A TENDENCY TO SUDDENLY GO OFF.
ESPECIALLY WHEN IT'S POINTED AT PIECES OF SHIT.
CTNK
......!!
LAST CHANCE. SHOW ME YOU'RE WORTH A DAMN.
ALRIGHT, I'LL TALK!
FIDGET
GOOD. WHICH OF YOUR HIGHER-UPS WORKS WITH HIT MEN?
UH... BRUNO. HE'S WHAT THEY CALL A FIXER.

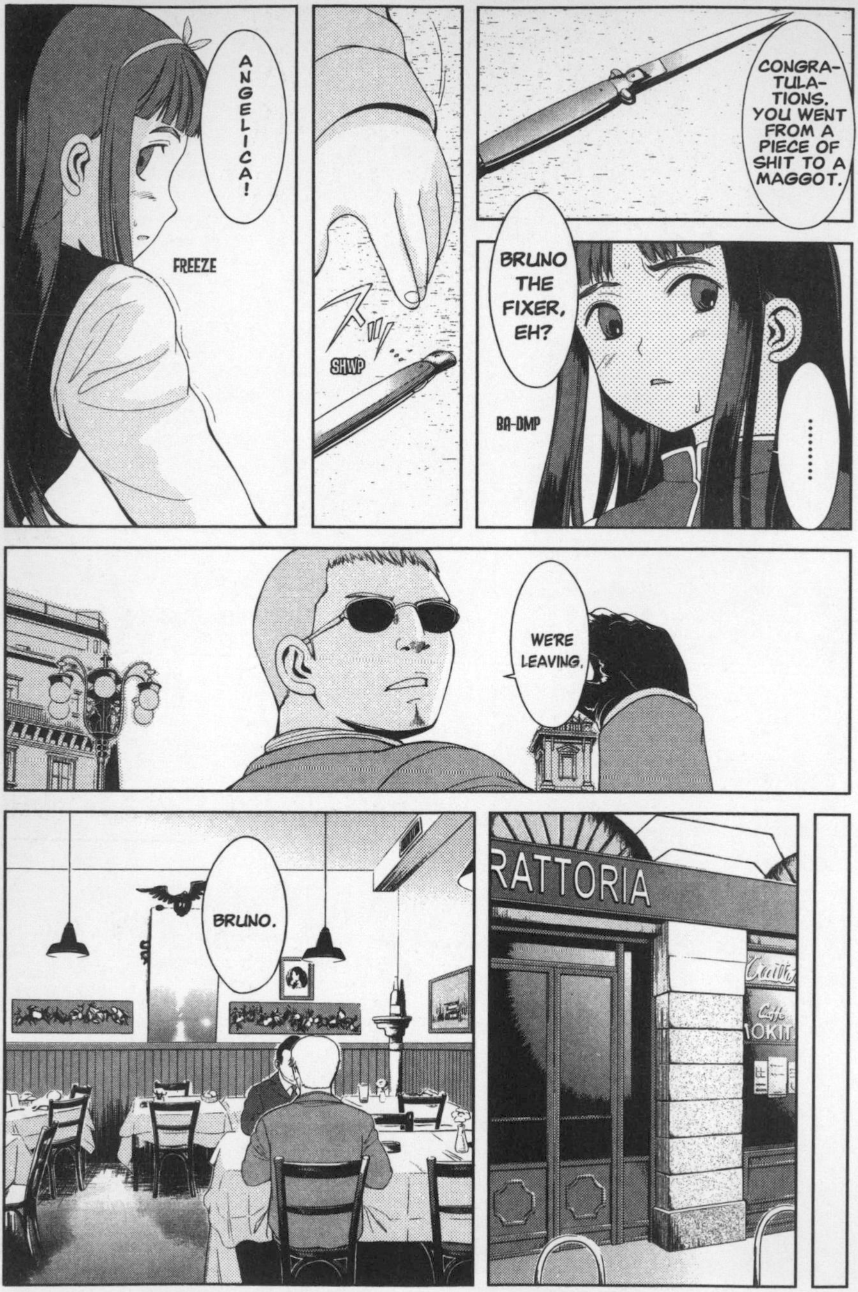

CONGRATULATIONS. YOU WENT FROM A PIECE OF SHIT TO A MAGGOT.
BRUNO THE FIXER, EH?
......
BA-DMP
SHWP
ANGELICA!
FREEZE
WE'RE LEAVING.
RATTORIA
BRUNO.

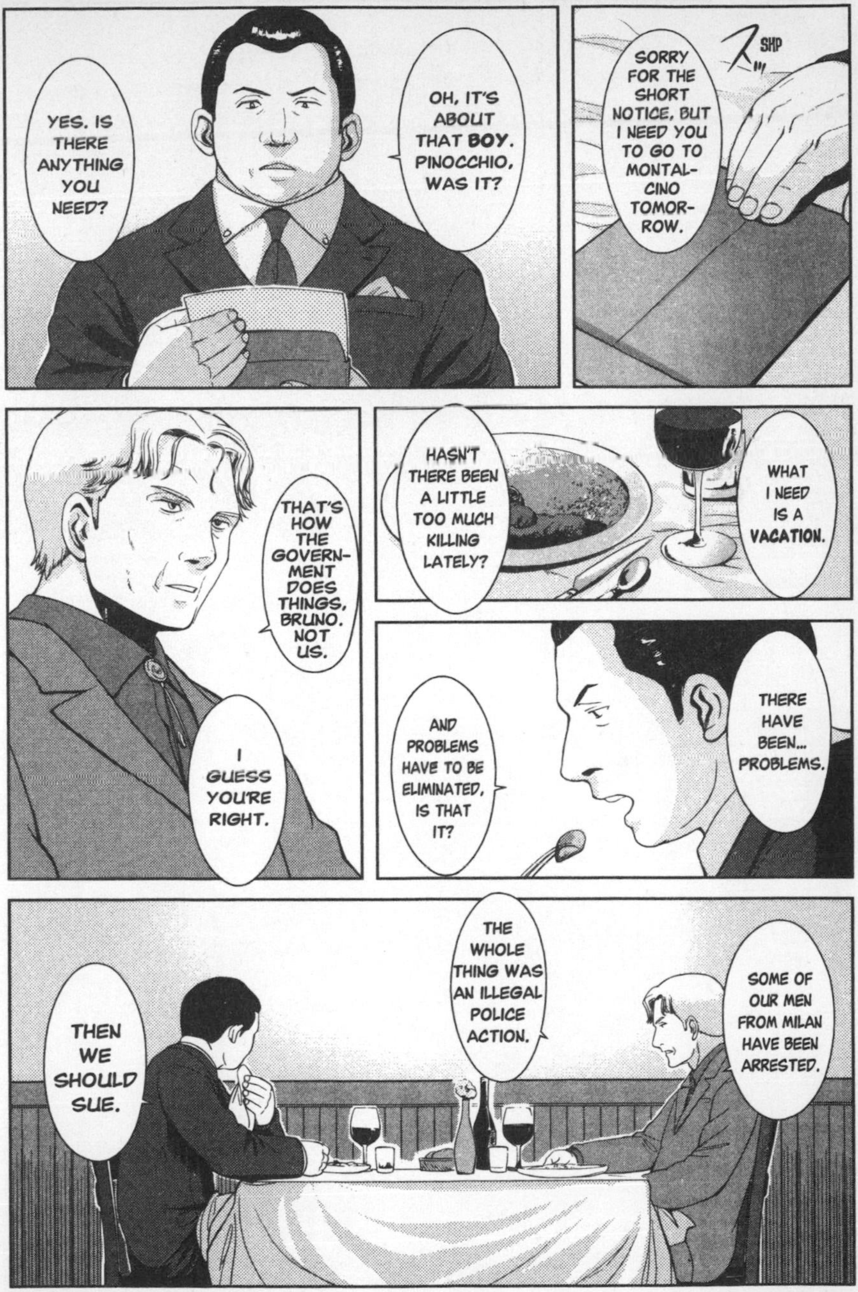
ス SHP
SORRY FOR THE SHORT NOTICE, BUT I NEED YOU TO GO TO MONTAL-CINO TOMOR-ROW.
OH, IT'S ABOUT THAT BOY. PINOCCHIO, WAS IT?
YES. IS THERE ANYTHING YOU NEED?
WHAT I NEED IS A VACATION.
HASN'T THERE BEEN A LITTLE TOO MUCH KILLING LATELY?
THERE HAVE BEEN... PROBLEMS.
AND PROBLEMS HAVE TO BE ELIMINATED, IS THAT IT?
THAT'S HOW THE GOVERN-MENT DOES THINGS, BRUNO. NOT US.
I GUESS YOU'RE RIGHT.
SOME OF OUR MEN FROM MILAN HAVE BEEN ARRESTED.
THE WHOLE THING WAS AN ILLEGAL POLICE ACTION.
THEN WE SHOULD SUE.

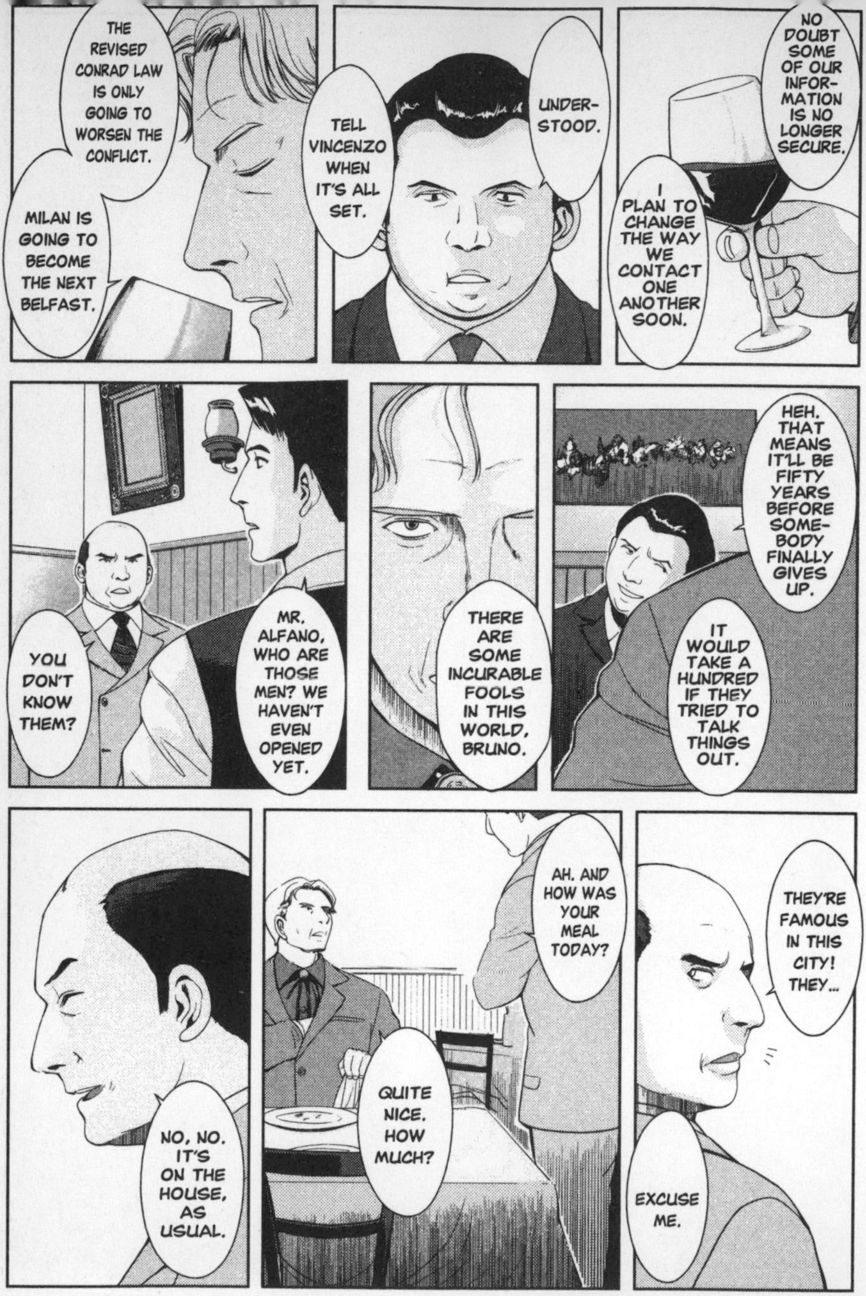
NO DOUBT SOME OF OUR INFORMATION IS NO LONGER SECURE.
I PLAN TO CHANGE THE WAY WE CONTACT ONE ANOTHER SOON.
UNDERSTOOD.
TELL VINCENZO WHEN IT'S ALL SET.
THE REVISED CONRAD LAW IS ONLY GOING TO WORSEN THE CONFLICT.
MILAN IS GOING TO BECOME THE NEXT BELFAST.
HEH. THAT MEANS IT'LL BE FIFTY YEARS BEFORE SOMEBODY FINALLY GIVES UP.
IT WOULD TAKE A HUNDRED IF THEY TRIED TO TALK THINGS OUT.
THERE ARE SOME INCURABLE FOOLS IN THIS WORLD, BRUNO.
MR. ALFANO, WHO ARE THOSE MEN? WE HAVEN'T EVEN OPENED YET.
YOU DON'T KNOW THEM?
THEY'RE FAMOUS IN THIS CITY! THEY...
EXCUSE ME.
AH. AND HOW WAS YOUR MEAL TODAY?
QUITE NICE. HOW MUCH?
NO, NO. IT'S ON THE HOUSE, AS USUAL.

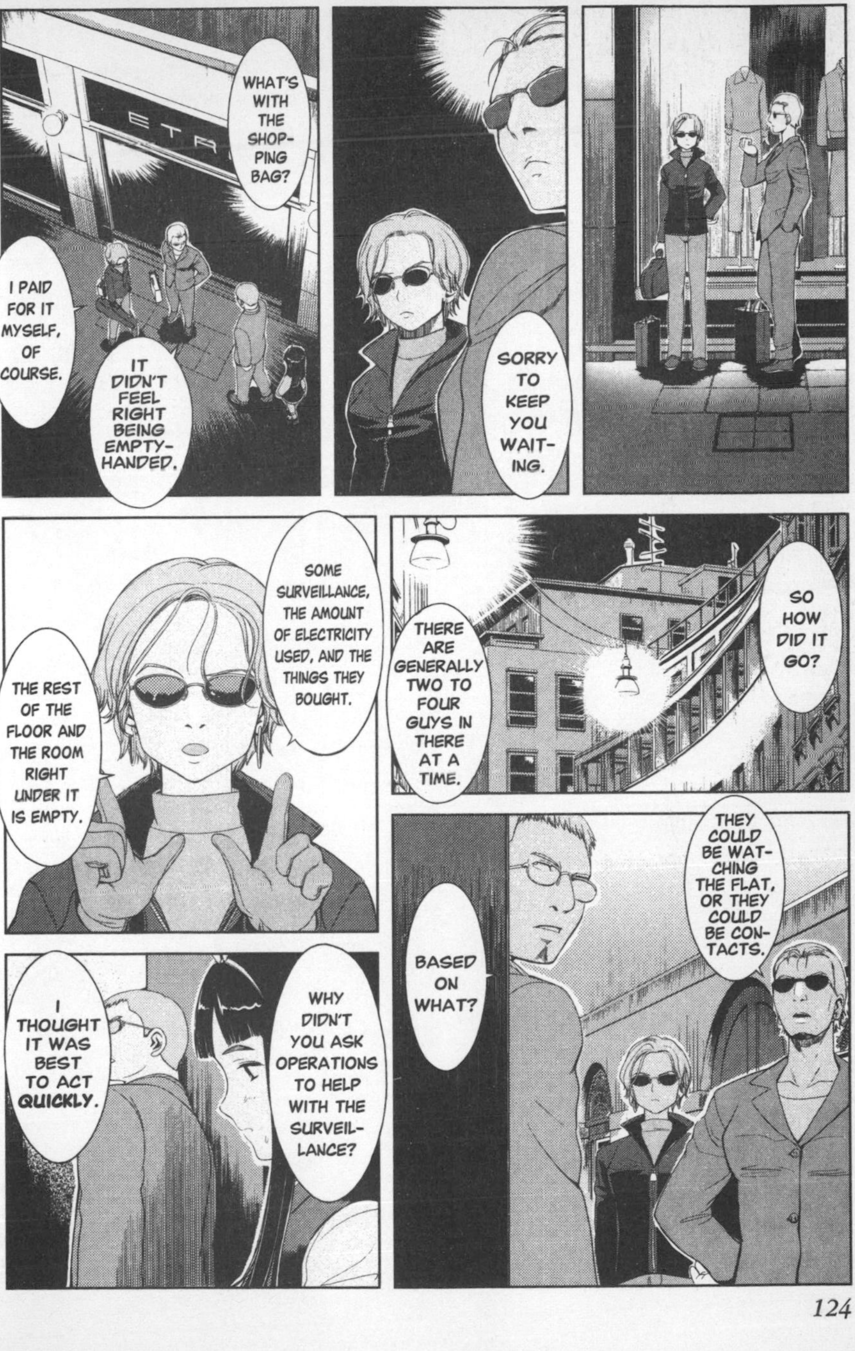
SORRY TO KEEP YOU WAIT-ING.
WHAT'S WITH THE SHOP-PING BAG?
I PAID FOR IT MYSELF, OF COURSE.
IT DIDN'T FEEL RIGHT BEING EMPTY-HANDED.
SO HOW DID IT GO?
THERE ARE GENERALLY TWO TO FOUR GUYS IN THERE AT A TIME.
SOME SURVEILLANCE, THE AMOUNT OF ELECTRICITY USED, AND THE THINGS THEY BOUGHT.
THE REST OF THE FLOOR AND THE ROOM RIGHT UNDER IT IS EMPTY.
THEY COULD BE WAT-CHING THE FLAT, OR THEY COULD BE CON-TACTS.
BASED ON WHAT?
WHY DIDN'T YOU ASK OPERATIONS TO HELP WITH THE SURVEIL-LANCE?
I THOUGHT IT WAS BEST TO ACT QUICKLY.

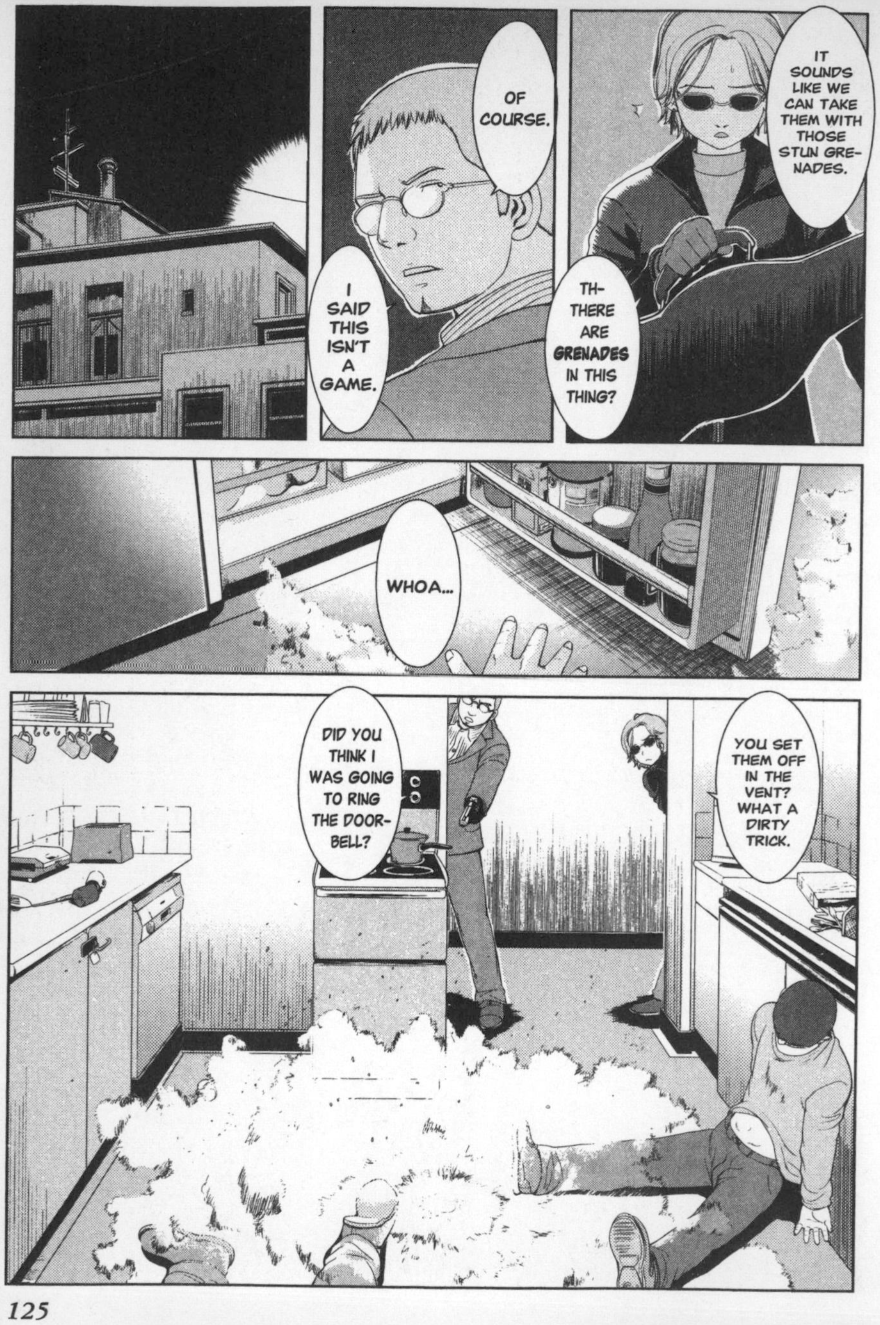
IT SOUNDS LIKE WE CAN TAKE THEM WITH THOSE STUN GRE-NADES.
TH-THERE ARE GRENADES IN THIS THING?
OF COURSE.
I SAID THIS ISN'T A GAME.
WHOA...
YOU SET THEM OFF IN THE VENT? WHAT A DIRTY TRICK.
DID YOU THINK I WAS GOING TO RING THE DOOR-BELL?

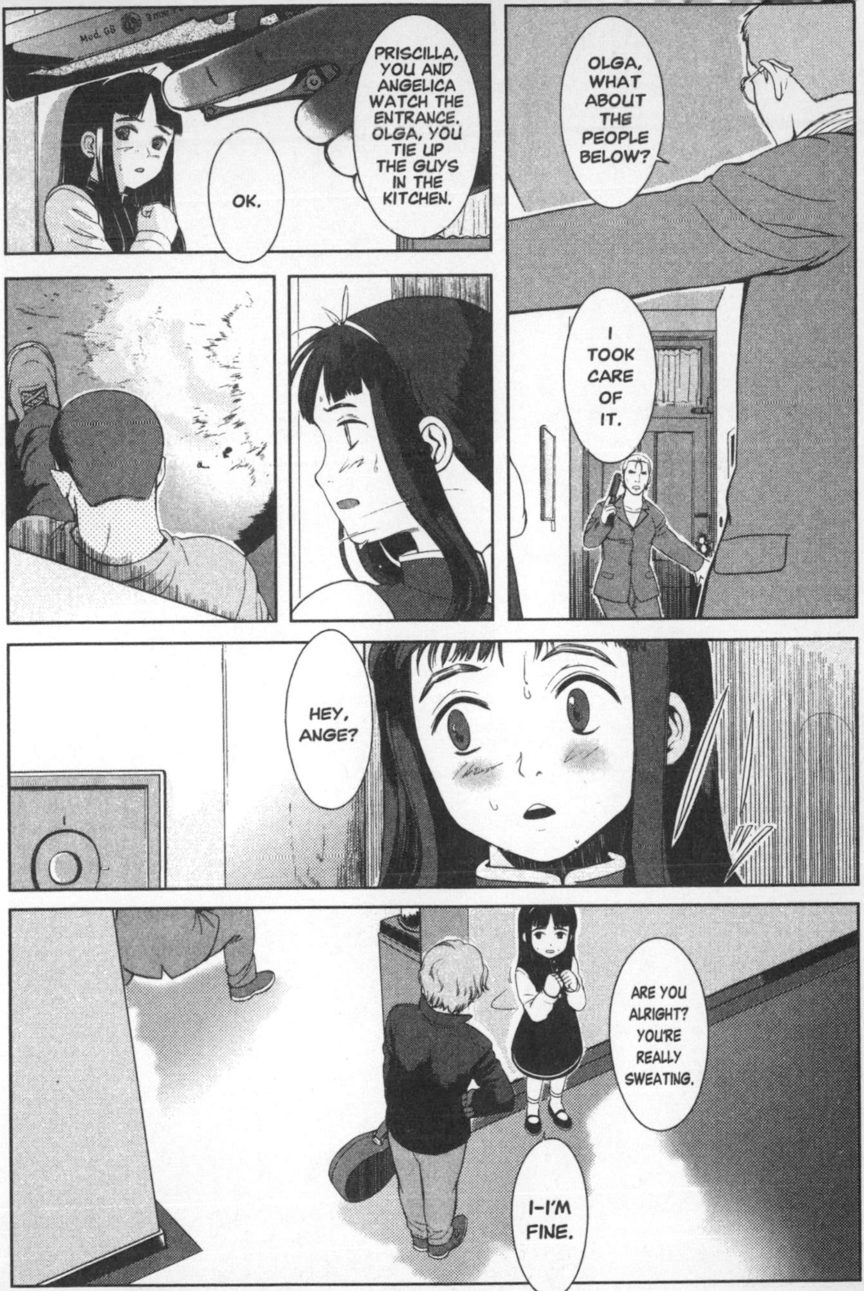
OLGA, WHAT ABOUT THE PEOPLE BELOW?
I TOOK CARE OF IT.
PRISCILLA, YOU AND ANGELICA WATCH THE ENTRANCE. OLGA, YOU TIE UP THE GUYS IN THE KITCHEN.
OK.
HEY, ANGE?
ARE YOU ALRIGHT? YOU'RE REALLY SWEATING.
I-I'M FINE.

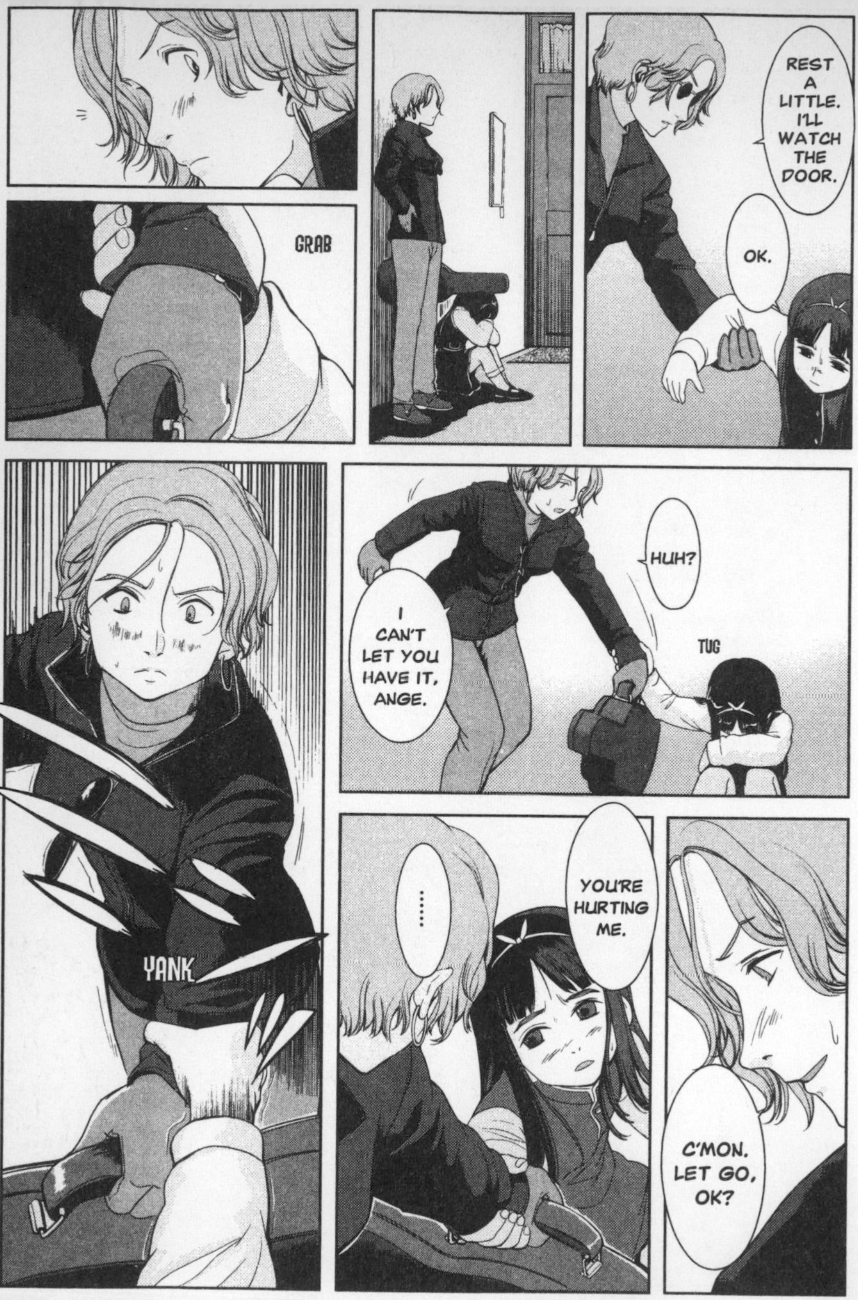
REST A LITTLE. I'LL WATCH THE DOOR.
OK.
GRAB
HUH?
TUG
I CAN'T LET YOU HAVE IT, ANGE.
C'MON. LET GO, OK?
YOU'RE HURTING ME.
......
YANK

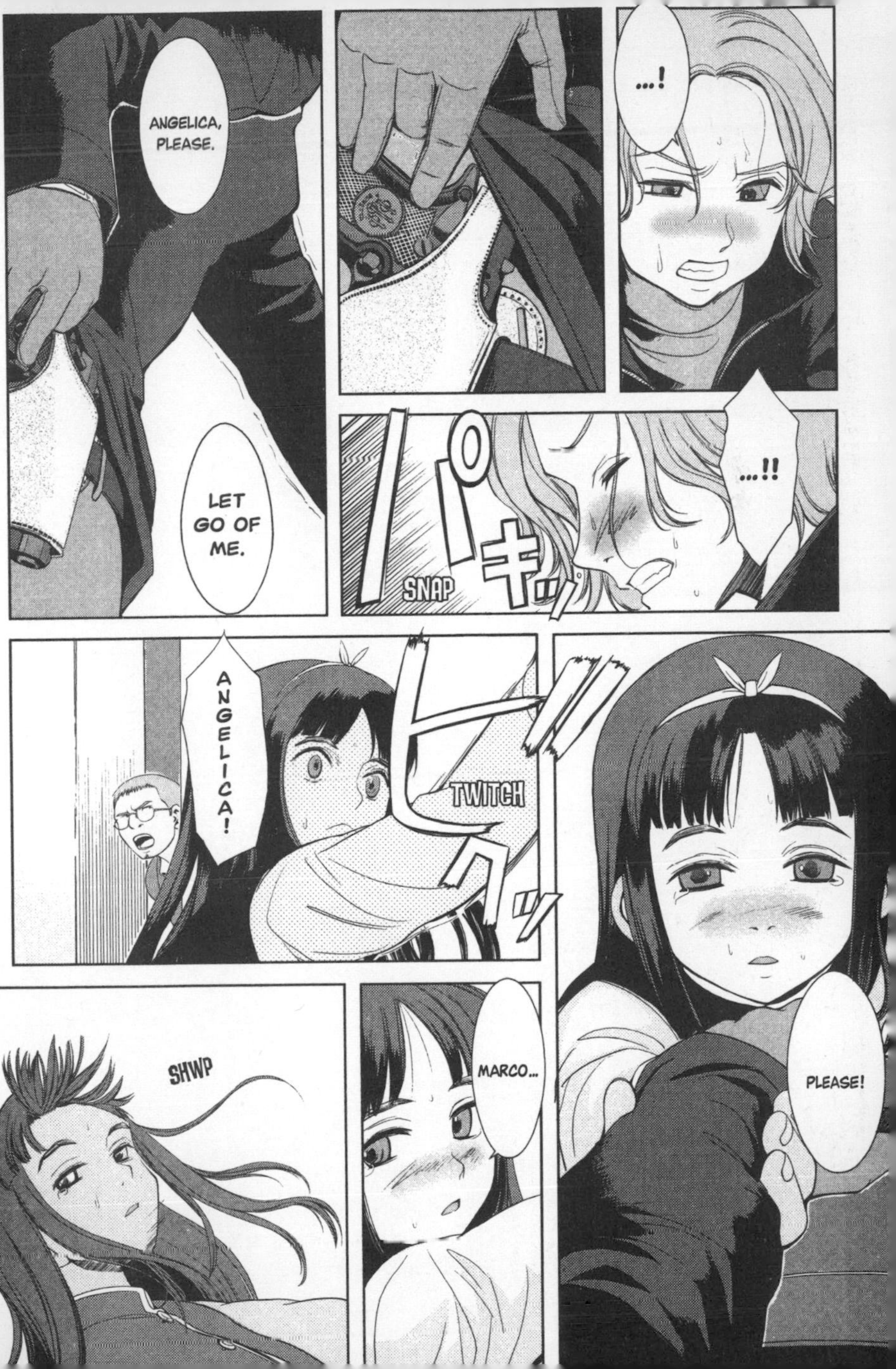
...!
...!!
SNAP
パキッ
ANGELICA, PLEASE.
LET GO OF ME.
PLEASE!
ANGELICA!
ピクッ
TWITCH
MARCO...
SHWP

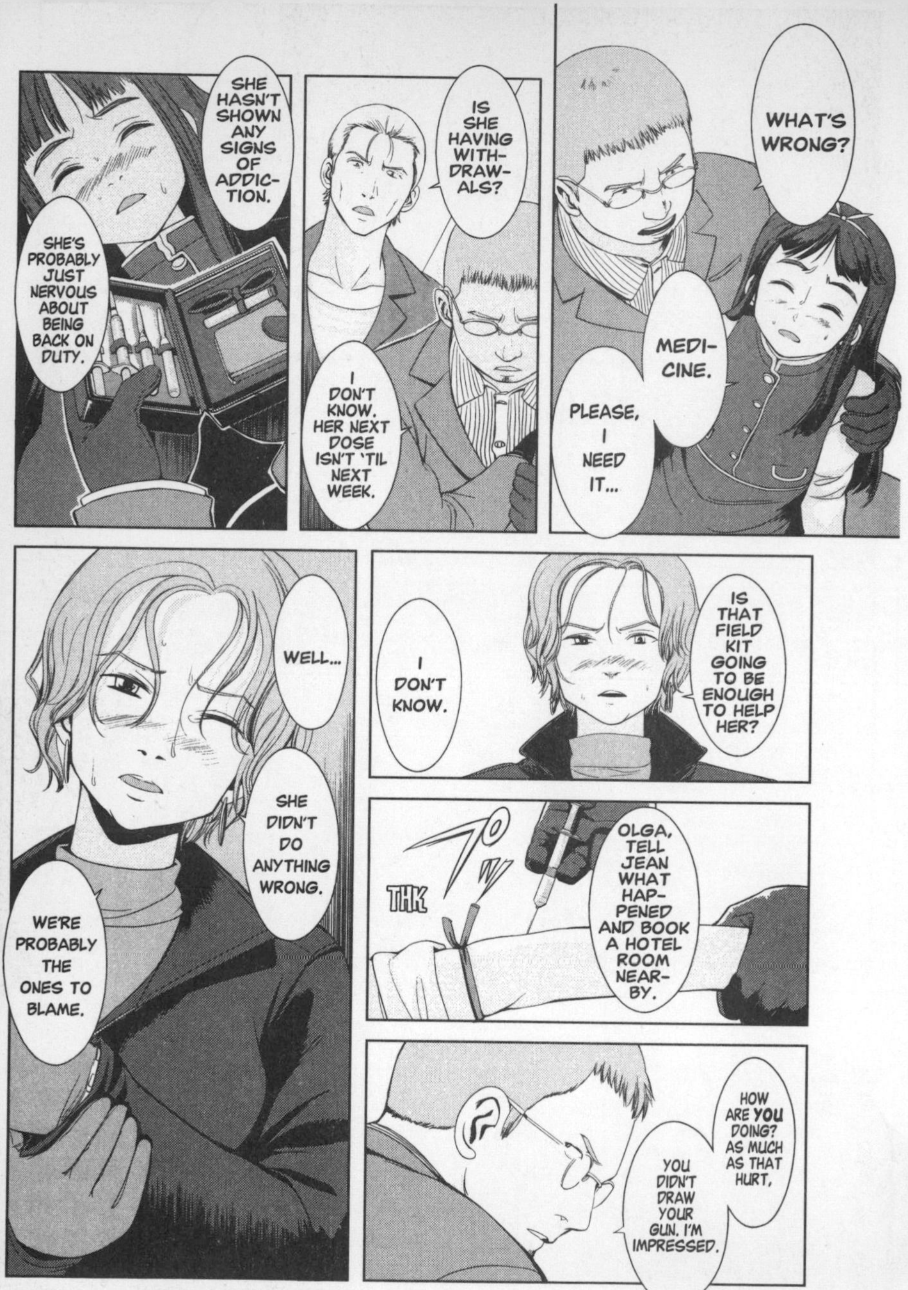
WHAT'S WRONG?
MEDICINE.
PLEASE, I NEED IT...
IS SHE HAVING WITHDRAWALS?
I DON'T KNOW. HER NEXT DOSE ISN'T 'TIL NEXT WEEK.
SHE HASN'T SHOWN ANY SIGNS OF ADDICTION.
SHE'S PROBABLY JUST NERVOUS ABOUT BEING BACK ON DUTY.
IS THAT FIELD KIT GOING TO BE ENOUGH TO HELP HER?
I DON'T KNOW.
OLGA, TELL JEAN WHAT HAPPENED AND BOOK A HOTEL ROOM NEARBY.
THK
HOW ARE YOU DOING? AS MUCH AS THAT HURT,
YOU DIDN'T DRAW YOUR GUN. I'M IMPRESSED.
WELL...
SHE DIDN'T DO ANYTHING WRONG.
WE'RE PROBABLY THE ONES TO BLAME.

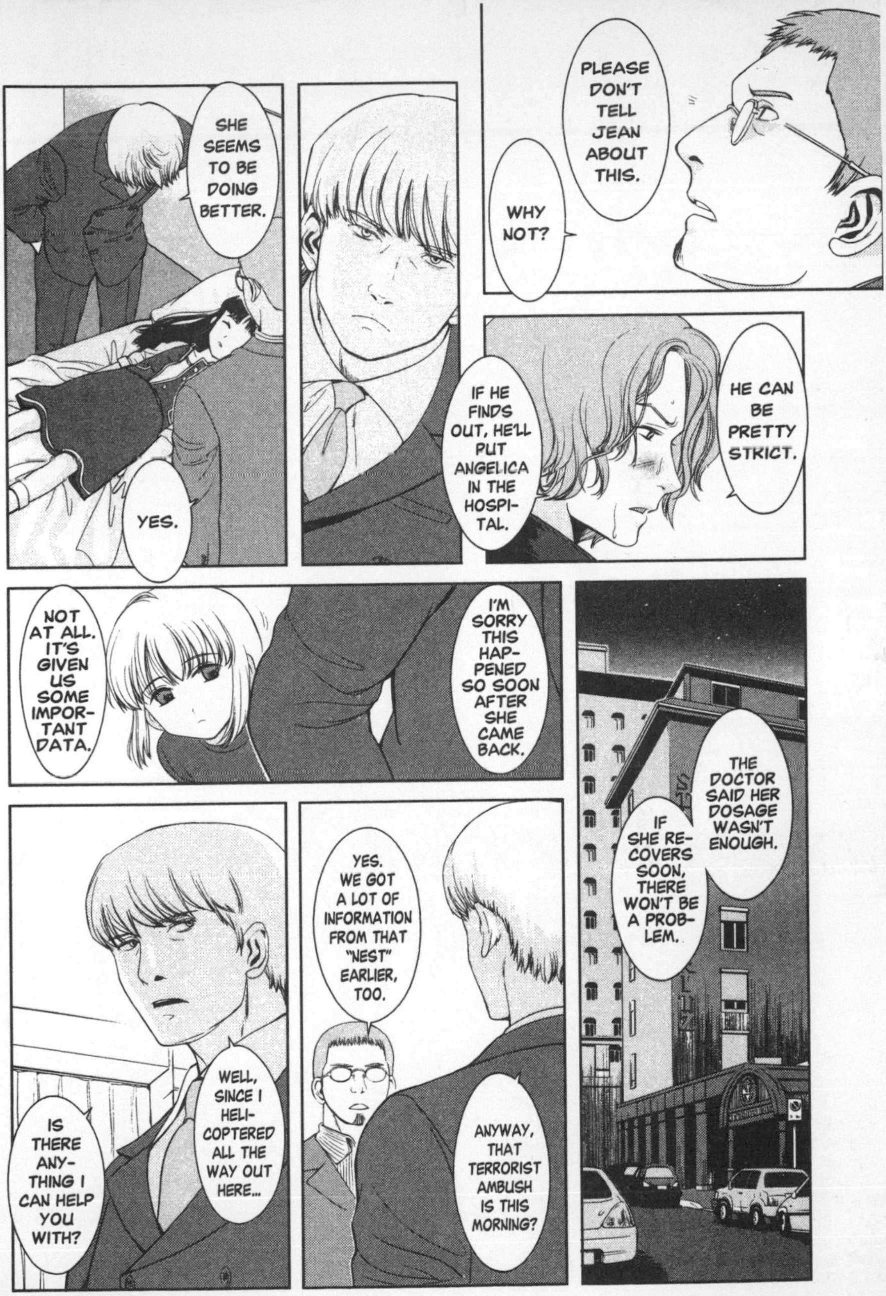
PLEASE DON'T TELL JEAN ABOUT THIS.
WHY NOT?
HE CAN BE PRETTY STRICT.
IF HE FINDS OUT, HE'LL PUT ANGELICA IN THE HOSPI-TAL.
SHE SEEMS TO BE DOING BETTER.
YES.
THE DOCTOR SAID HER DOSAGE WASN'T ENOUGH.
IF SHE RE-COVERS SOON, THERE WON'T BE A PROB-LEM.
I'M SORRY THIS HAP-PENED SO SOON AFTER SHE CAME BACK.
NOT AT ALL. IT'S GIVEN US SOME IMPOR-TANT DATA.
YES. WE GOT A LOT OF INFORMATION FROM THAT "NEST" EARLIER, TOO.
ANYWAY, THAT TERRORIST AMBUSH IS THIS MORNING?
WELL, SINCE I HELI-COPTERED ALL THE WAY OUT HERE...
IS THERE ANY-THING I CAN HELP YOU WITH?

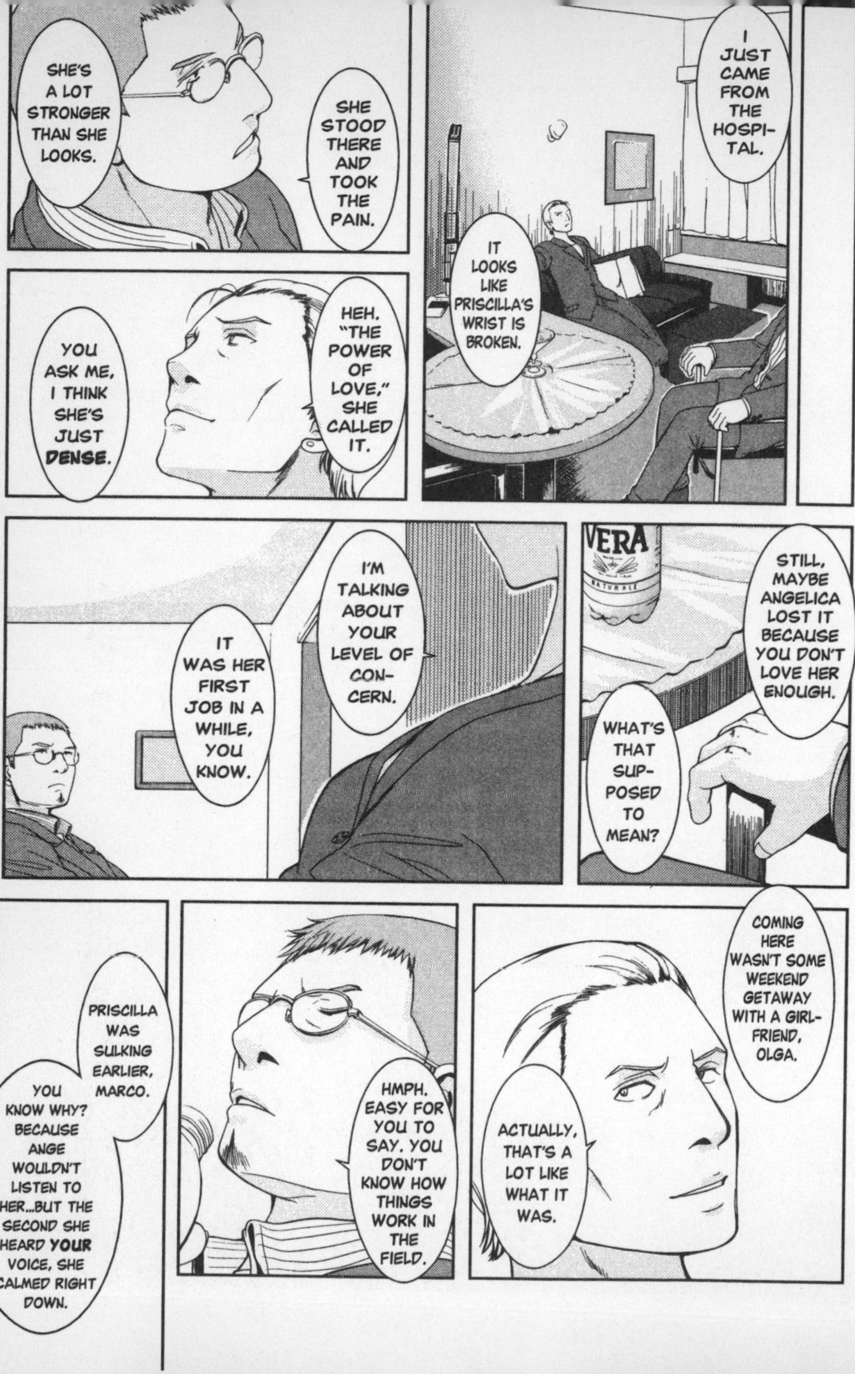
I JUST CAME FROM THE HOSPITAL.
IT LOOKS LIKE PRISCILLA'S WRIST IS BROKEN.
SHE STOOD THERE AND TOOK THE PAIN.
SHE'S A LOT STRONGER THAN SHE LOOKS.
HEH. "THE POWER OF LOVE," SHE CALLED IT.
YOU ASK ME, I THINK SHE'S JUST **DENSE**.
STILL, MAYBE ANGELICA LOST IT BECAUSE YOU DON'T LOVE HER ENOUGH.
WHAT'S THAT SUPPOSED TO MEAN?
I'M TALKING ABOUT YOUR LEVEL OF CONCERN.
IT WAS HER FIRST JOB IN A WHILE, YOU KNOW.
COMING HERE WASN'T SOME WEEKEND GETAWAY WITH A GIRLFRIEND, OLGA.
ACTUALLY, THAT'S A LOT LIKE WHAT IT WAS.
HMPH. EASY FOR YOU TO SAY. YOU DON'T KNOW HOW THINGS WORK IN THE FIELD.
PRISCILLA WAS SULKING EARLIER, MARCO.
YOU KNOW WHY? BECAUSE ANGE WOULDN'T LISTEN TO HER...BUT THE SECOND SHE HEARD **YOUR** VOICE, SHE CALMED RIGHT DOWN.

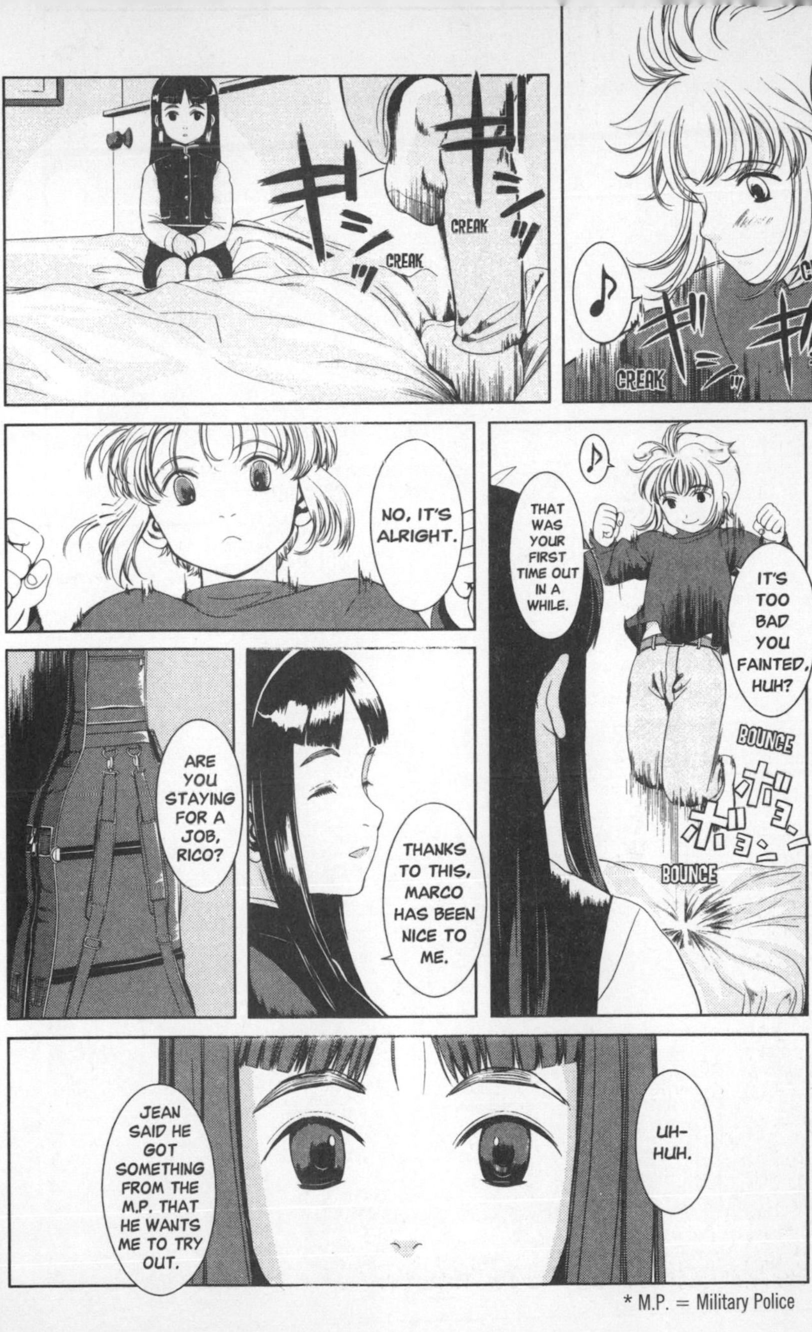
♪
CREAK
♪
CREAK
CREAK
CREAK
♪
THAT WAS YOUR FIRST TIME OUT IN A WHILE.
IT'S TOO BAD YOU FAINTED, HUH?
BOUNCE
BOUNCE
NO, IT'S ALRIGHT.
THANKS TO THIS, MARCO HAS BEEN NICE TO ME.
ARE YOU STAYING FOR A JOB, RICO?
UH-HUH.
JEAN SAID HE GOT SOMETHING FROM THE M.P. THAT HE WANTS ME TO TRY OUT.

* M.P. = Military Police

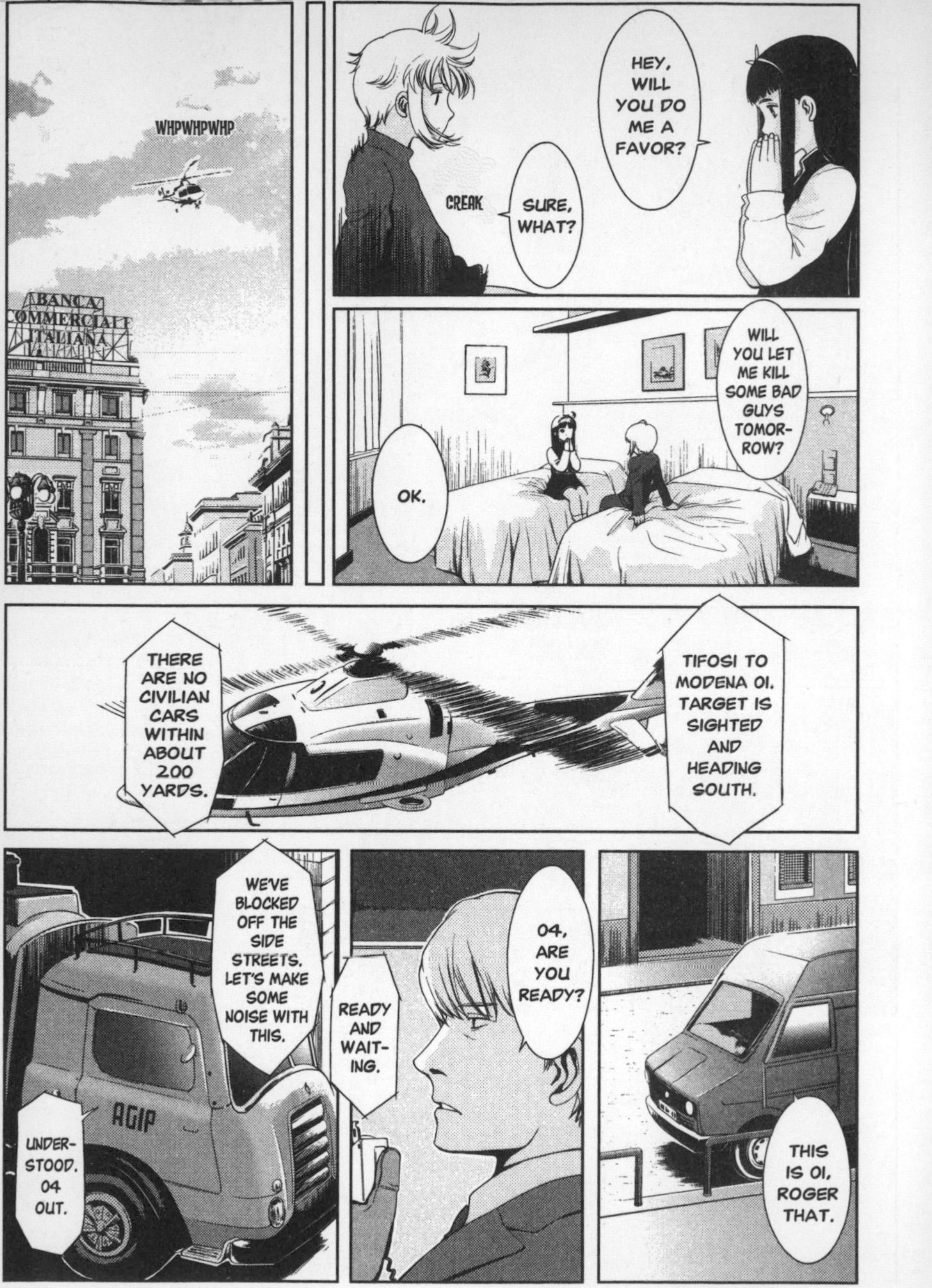
HEY, WILL YOU DO ME A FAVOR?
CREAK
SURE, WHAT?
WILL YOU LET ME KILL SOME BAD GUYS TOMORROW?
OK.
WHPWHPWHP
BANCA COMMERCIALE ITALIANA
TIFOSI TO MODENA 01. TARGET IS SIGHTED AND HEADING SOUTH.
THERE ARE NO CIVILIAN CARS WITHIN ABOUT 200 YARDS.
THIS IS 01, ROGER THAT.
04, ARE YOU READY?
READY AND WAITING.
WE'VE BLOCKED OFF THE SIDE STREETS. LET'S MAKE SOME NOISE WITH THIS.
AGIP
UNDER-STOOD. 04 OUT.

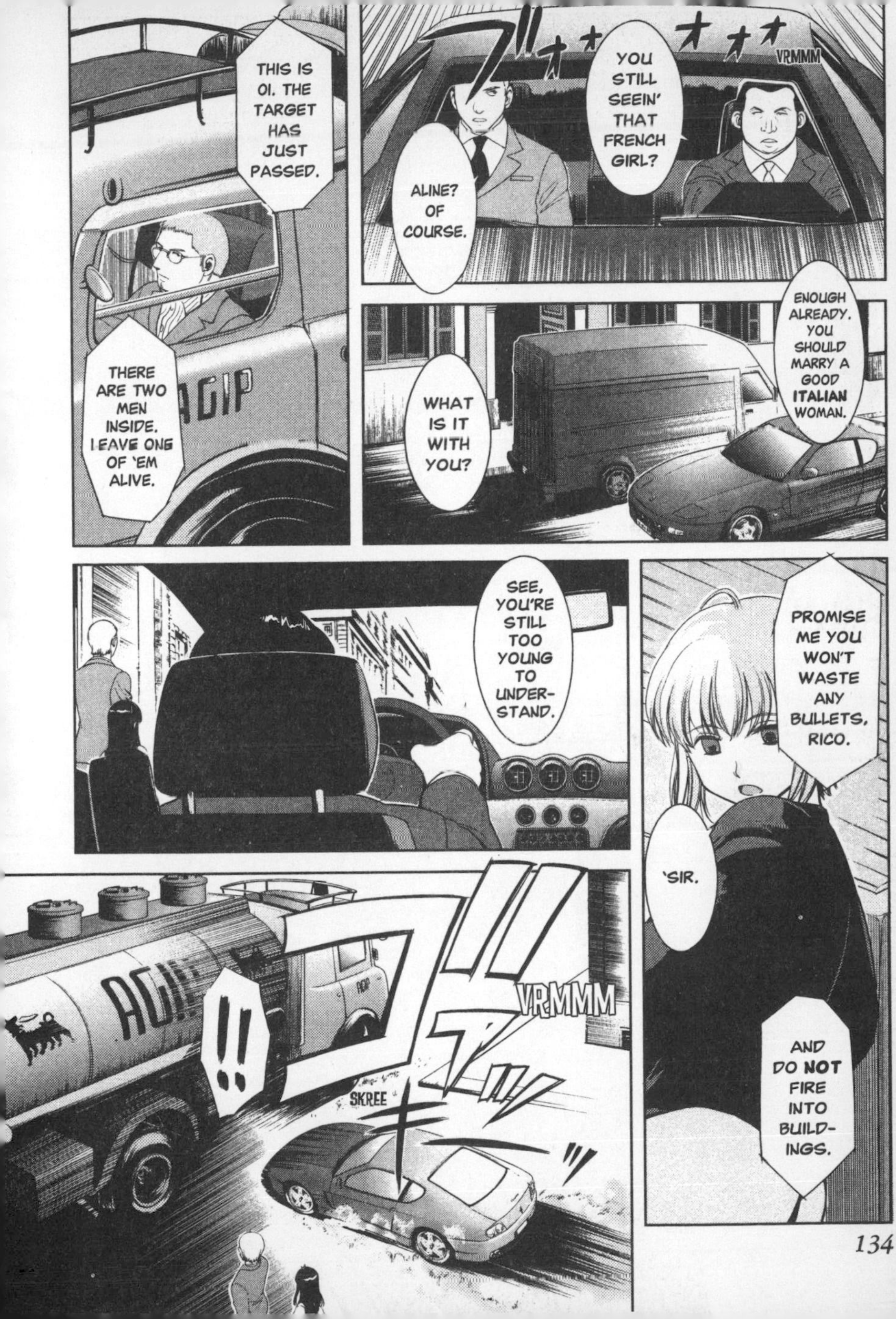
VRMMM
YOU STILL SEEIN' THAT FRENCH GIRL?
ALINE? OF COURSE.
ENOUGH ALREADY. YOU SHOULD MARRY A GOOD ITALIAN WOMAN.
WHAT IS IT WITH YOU?
THIS IS 01. THE TARGET HAS JUST PASSED.
THERE ARE TWO MEN INSIDE. LEAVE ONE OF 'EM ALIVE.
PROMISE ME YOU WON'T WASTE ANY BULLETS, RICO.
'SIR.
AND DO NOT FIRE INTO BUILDINGS.
SEE, YOU'RE STILL TOO YOUNG TO UNDER-STAND.
VRMMM
!!
SKREE

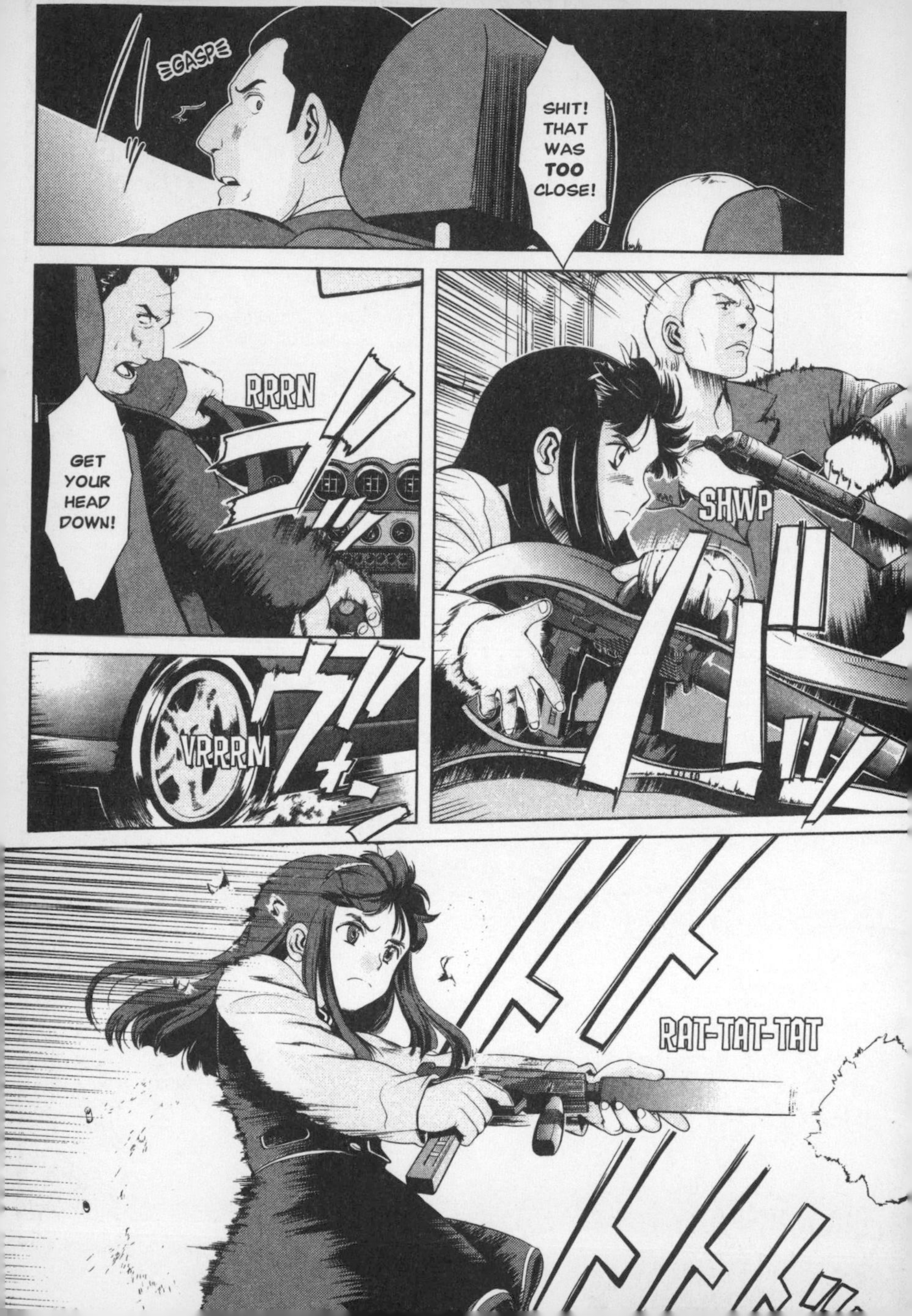
SHIT! THAT WAS TOO CLOSE!
GASP
SHWP
RRRN
GET YOUR HEAD DOWN!
VRRRM
RAT-TAT-TAT

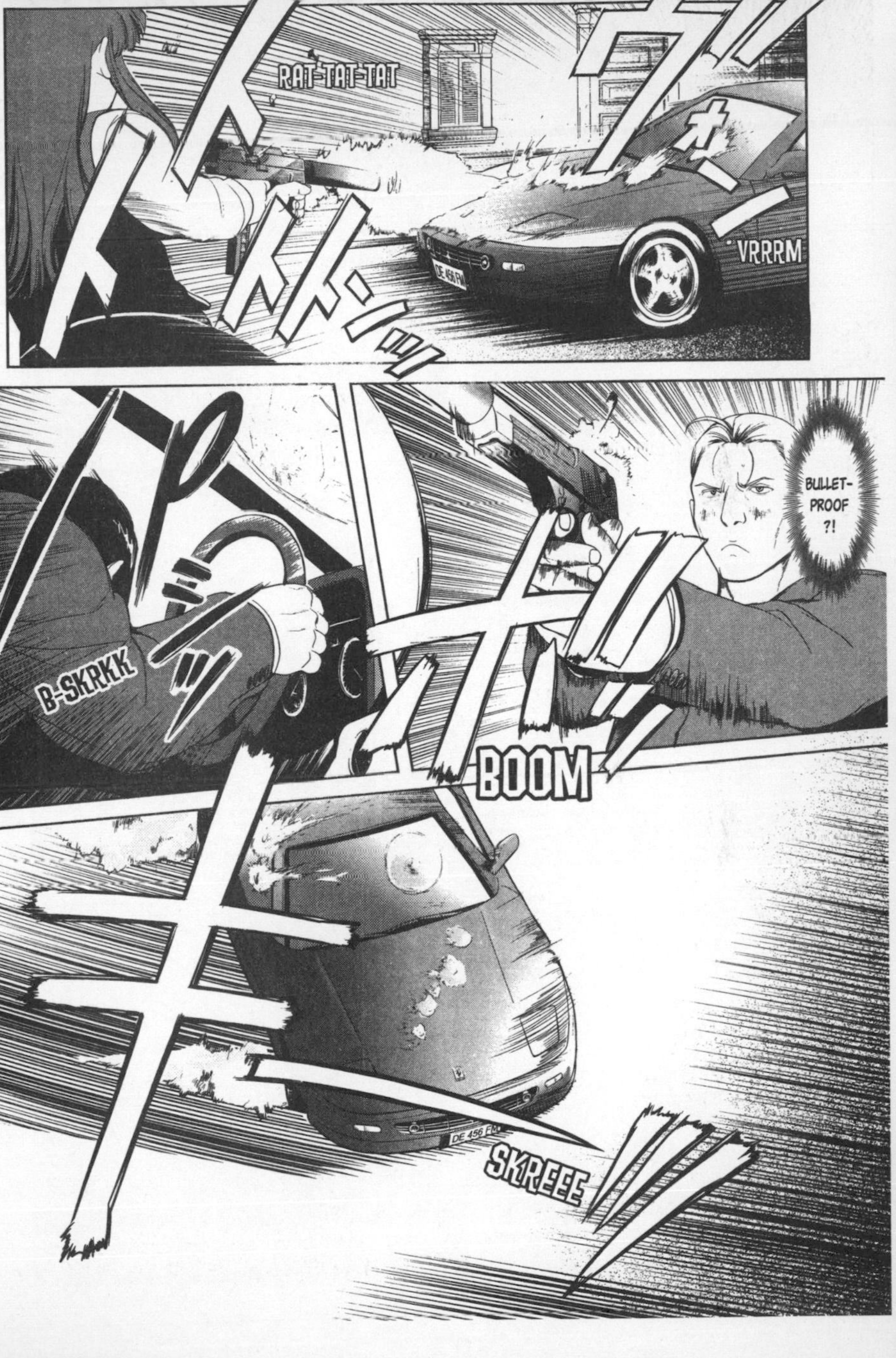
RAT-TAT-TAT
VRRRM
BULLET-PROOF ?!
B-SKRKK
BOOM
SKREEE

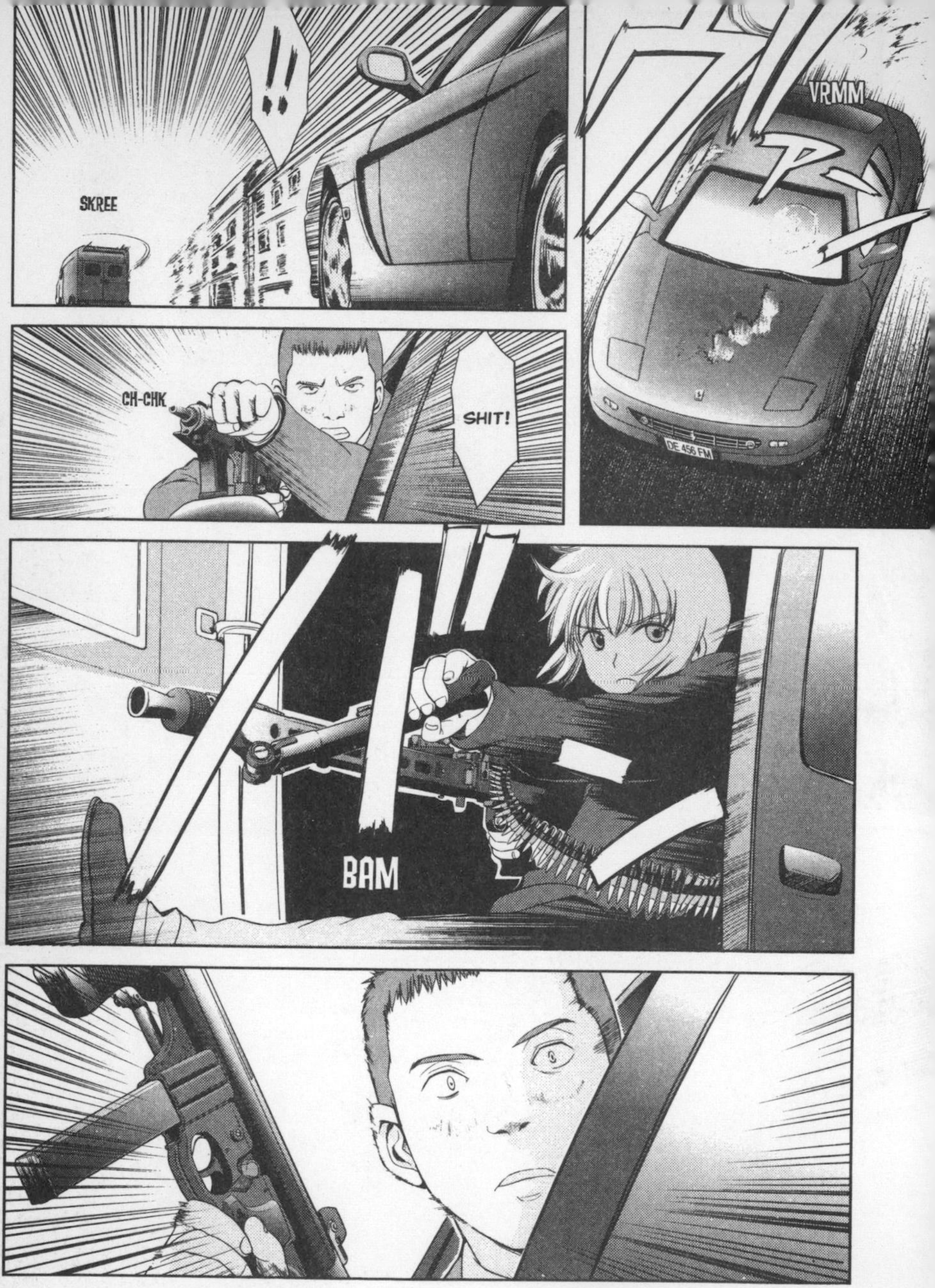
VRMM
!!
SKREE
SHIT!
CH-CHK
BAM

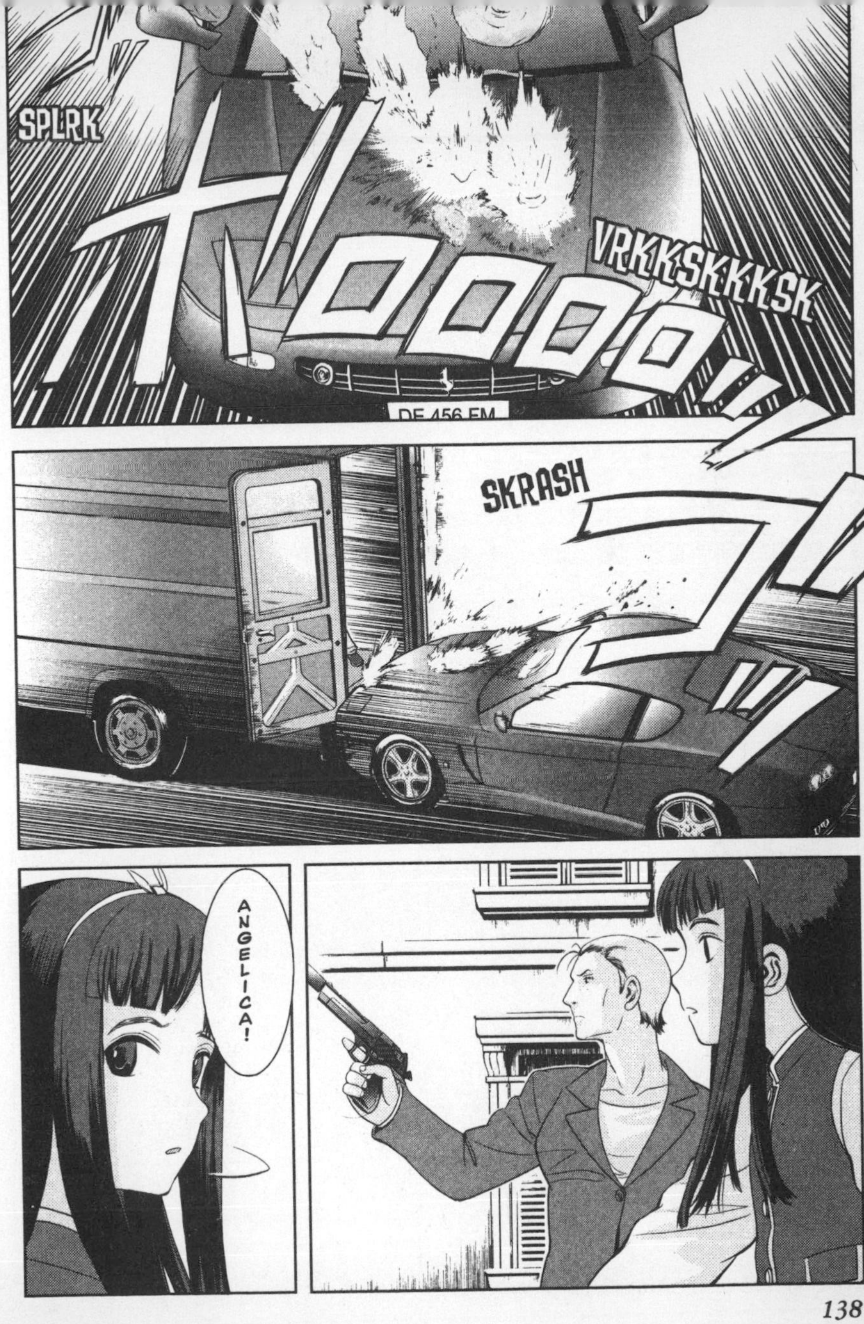
SPLRK
VRKKSKKKSK
SKRASH
ANGELICA!

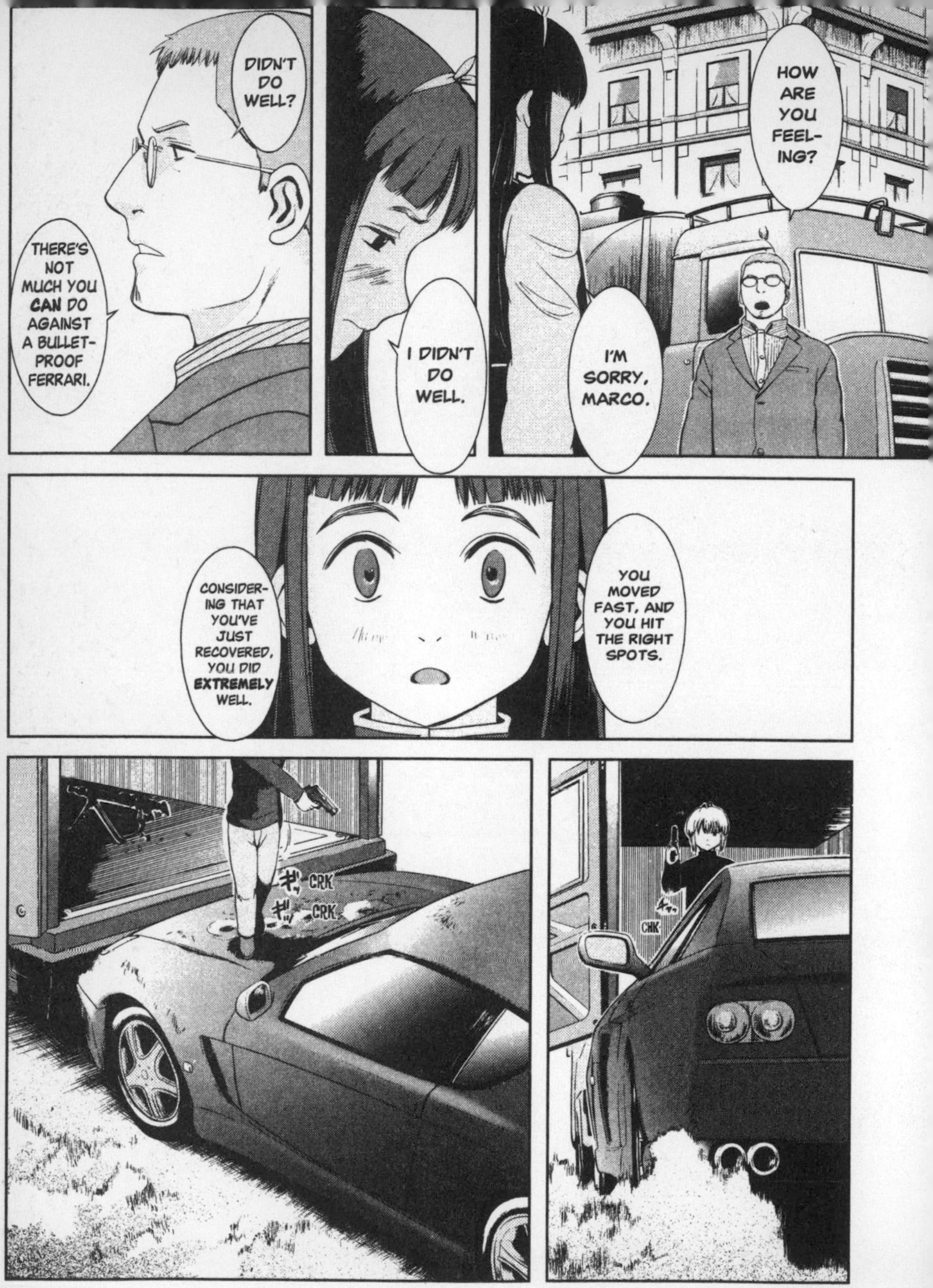
HOW ARE YOU FEEL-ING?
I'M SORRY, MARCO.
I DIDN'T DO WELL.
DIDN'T DO WELL?
THERE'S NOT MUCH YOU **CAN** DO AGAINST A BULLET-PROOF FERRARI.
YOU MOVED FAST, AND YOU HIT THE RIGHT SPOTS.
CONSIDER-ING THAT YOU'VE JUST RECOVERED, YOU DID **EXTREMELY** WELL.
CHK
CRK
CRK

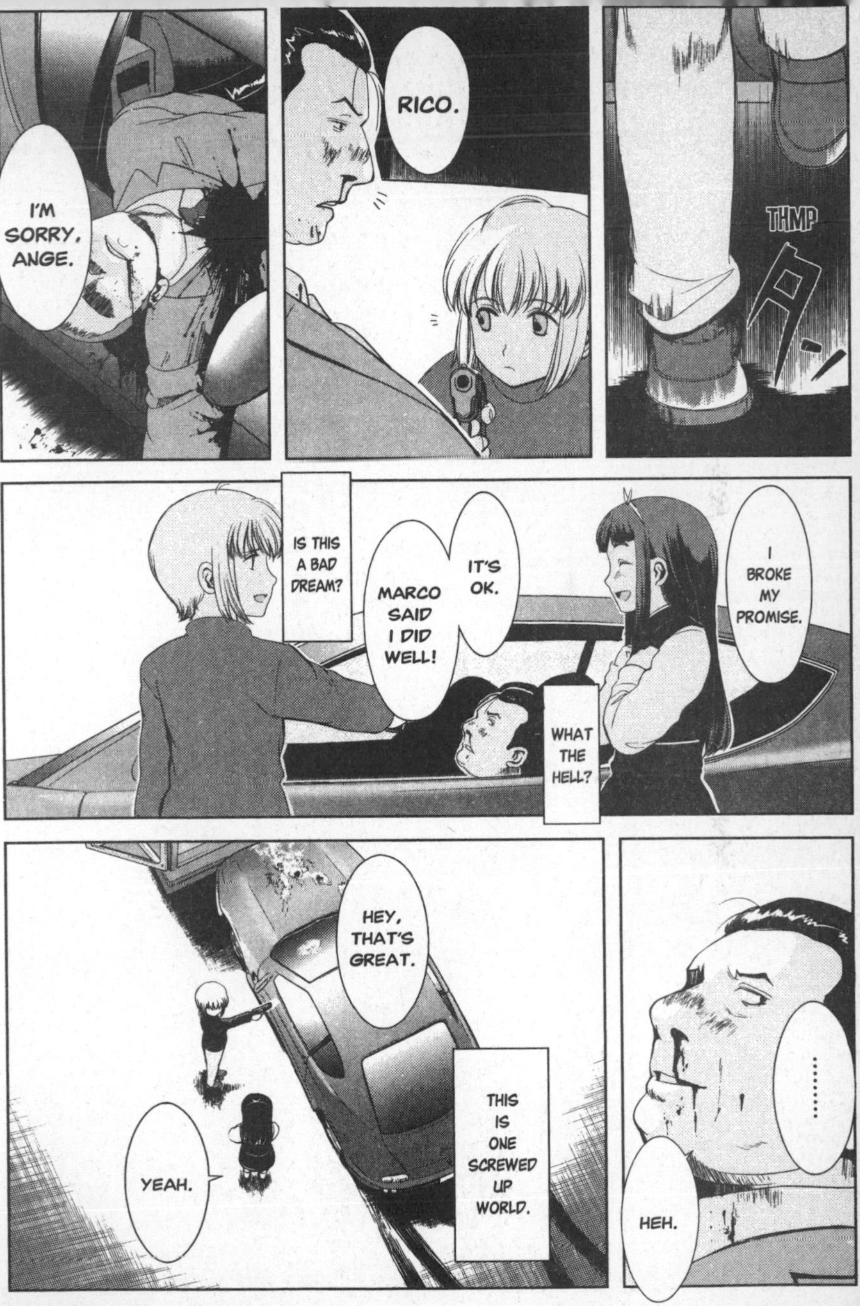
THMP
RICO.
I'M SORRY, ANGE.
I BROKE MY PROMISE.
IT'S OK.
MARCO SAID I DID WELL!
IS THIS A BAD DREAM?
WHAT THE HELL?
....
HEH.
HEY, THAT'S GREAT.
THIS IS ONE SCREWED UP WORLD.
YEAH.

GUNSLINGERGIRL.

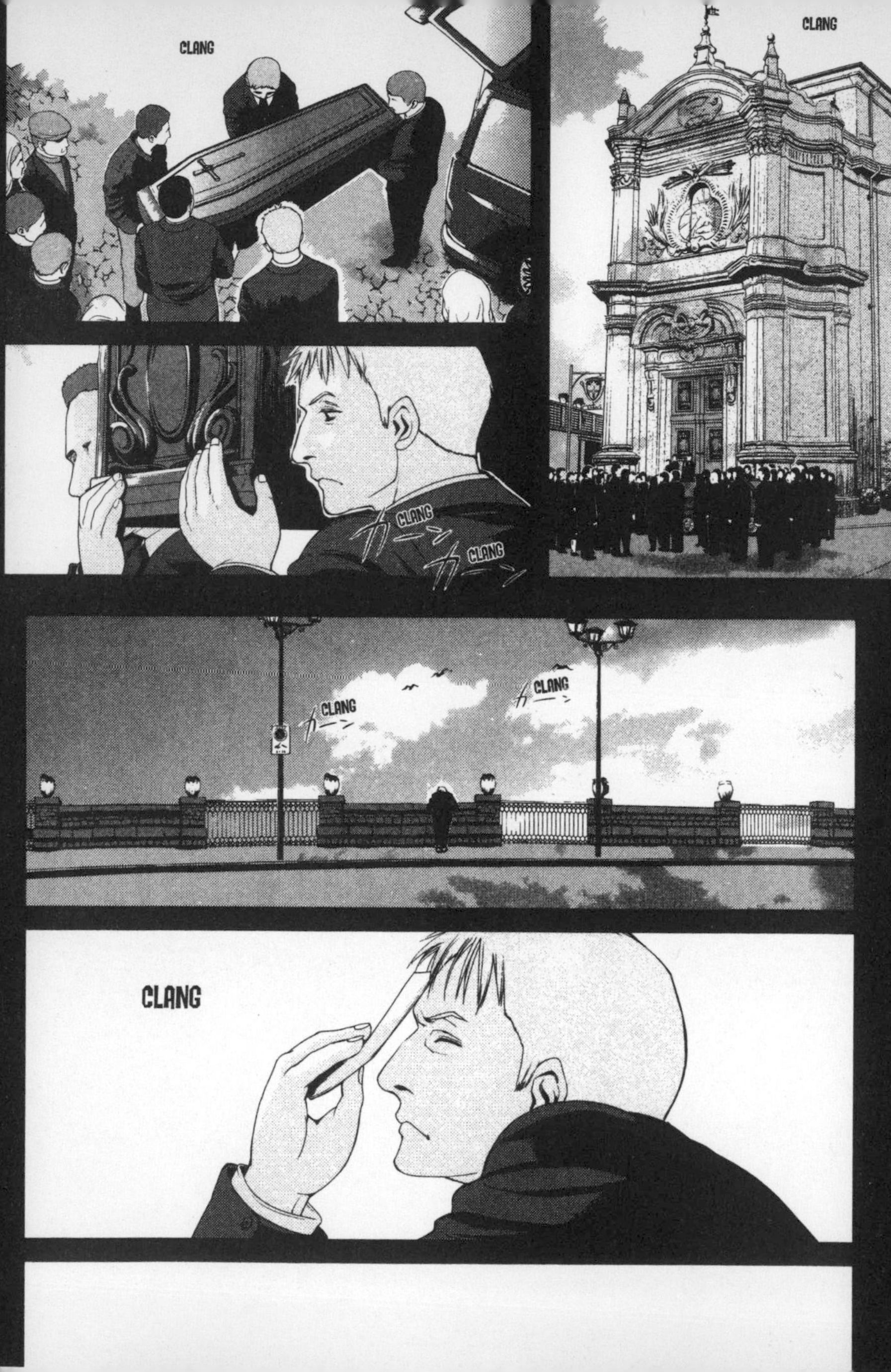
CLANG
CLANG
CLANG
カーン
CLANG
カーン
CLANG
カーン
CLANG
カーン
CLANG

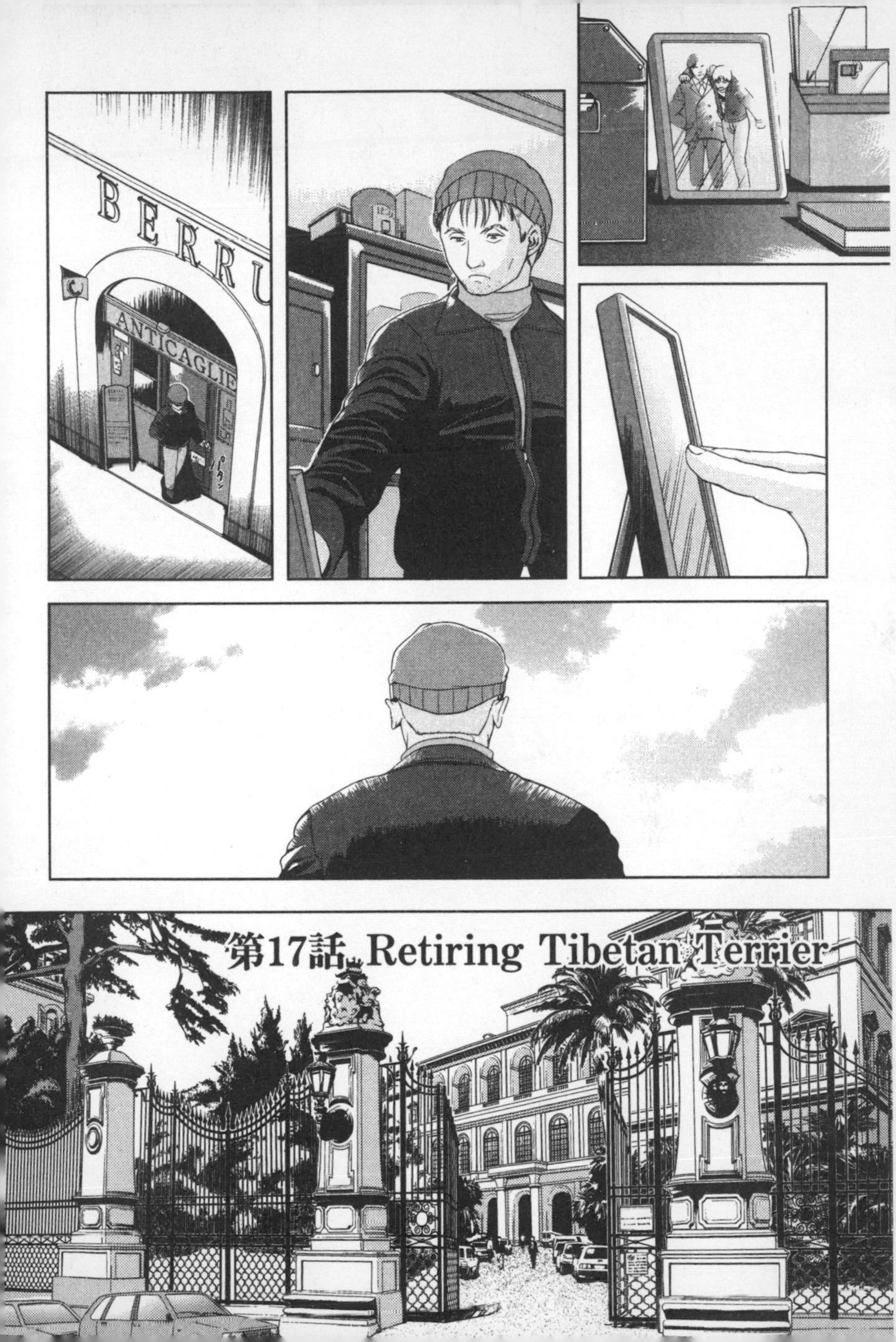
BERRU
ANTICAGLIE
第17話 Retiring Tibetan Terrier

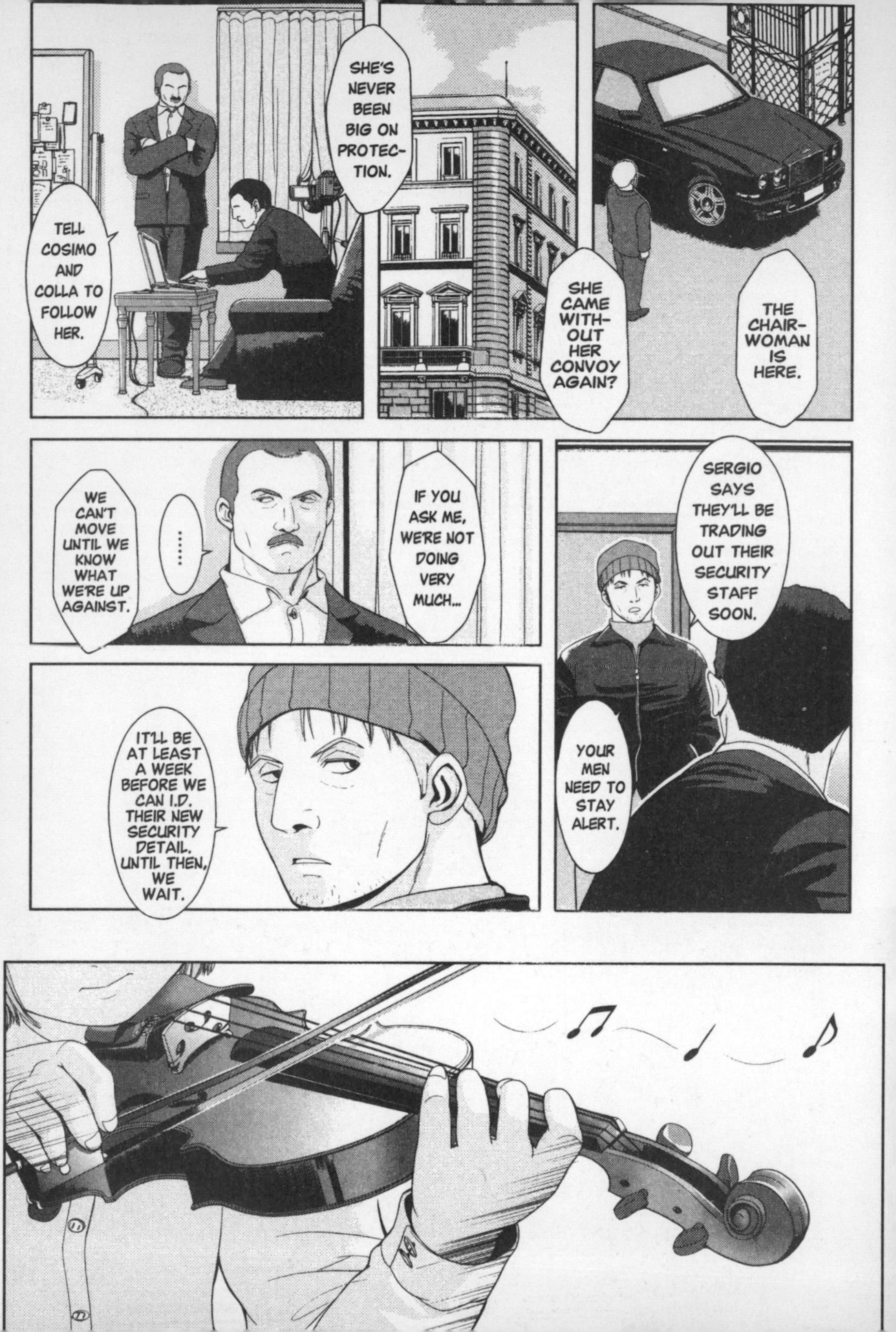
THE CHAIR-WOMAN IS HERE.
SHE CAME WITH-OUT HER CONVOY AGAIN?
SHE'S NEVER BEEN BIG ON PROTEC-TION.
TELL COSIMO AND COLLA TO FOLLOW HER.
SERGIO SAYS THEY'LL BE TRADING OUT THEIR SECURITY STAFF SOON.
YOUR MEN NEED TO STAY ALERT.
IF YOU ASK ME, WE'RE NOT DOING VERY MUCH...
......
WE CAN'T MOVE UNTIL WE KNOW WHAT WE'RE UP AGAINST.
IT'LL BE AT LEAST A WEEK BEFORE WE CAN I.D. THEIR NEW SECURITY DETAIL. UNTIL THEN, WE WAIT.

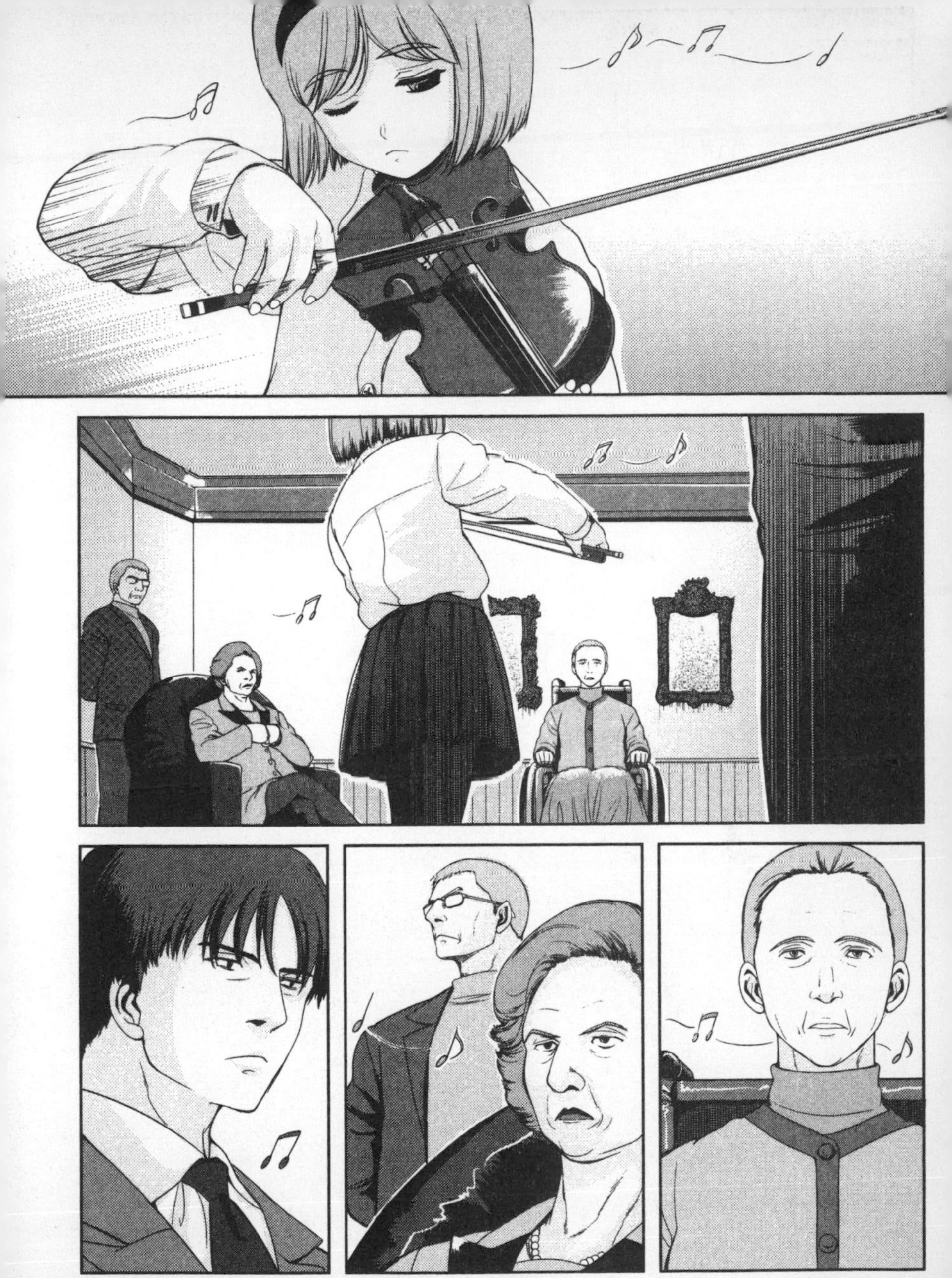

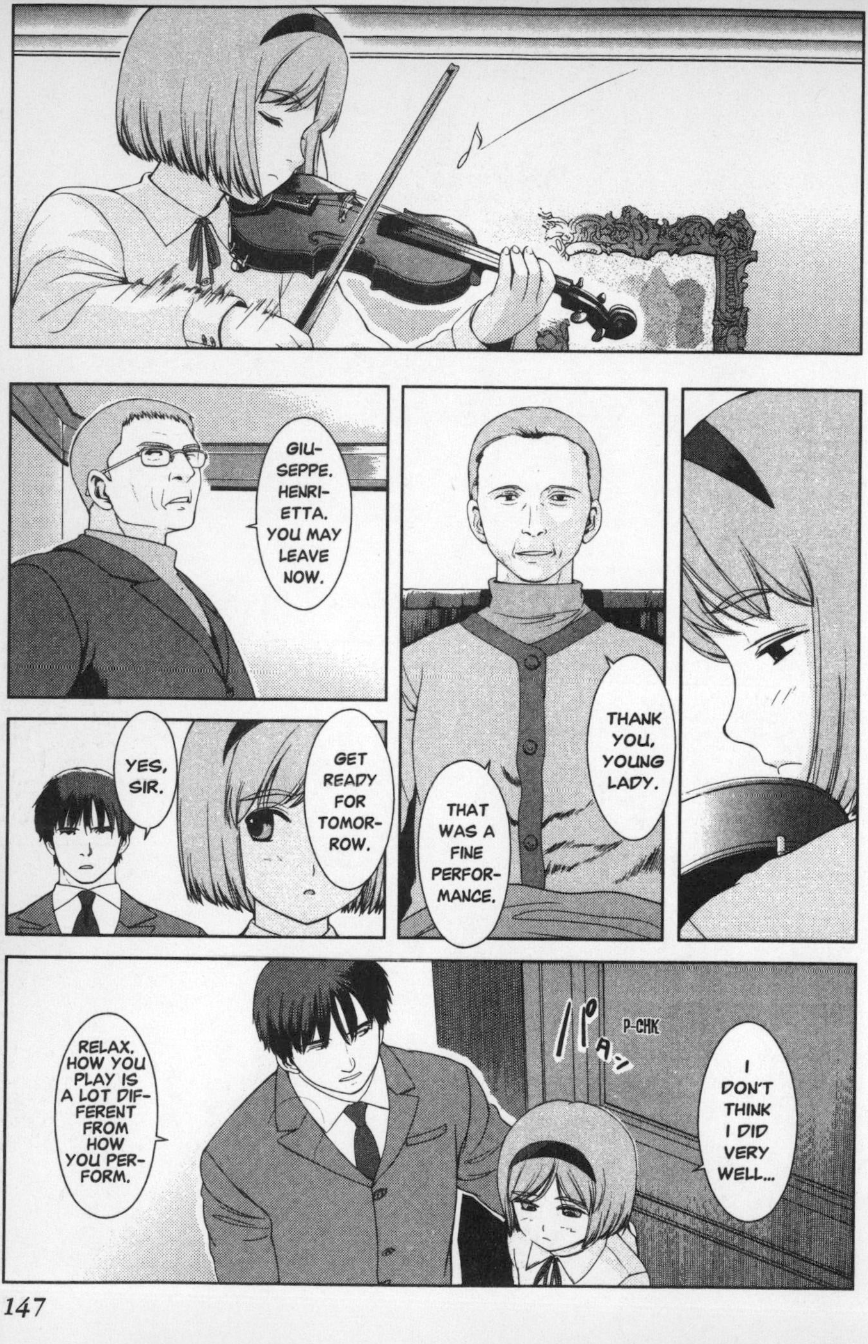
THANK YOU, YOUNG LADY.
THAT WAS A FINE PERFORMANCE.
GIUSEPPE. HENRIETTA. YOU MAY LEAVE NOW.
GET READY FOR TOMORROW.
YES, SIR.
P-CHK
I DON'T THINK I DID VERY WELL...
RELAX. HOW YOU PLAY IS A LOT DIFFERENT FROM HOW YOU PERFORM.

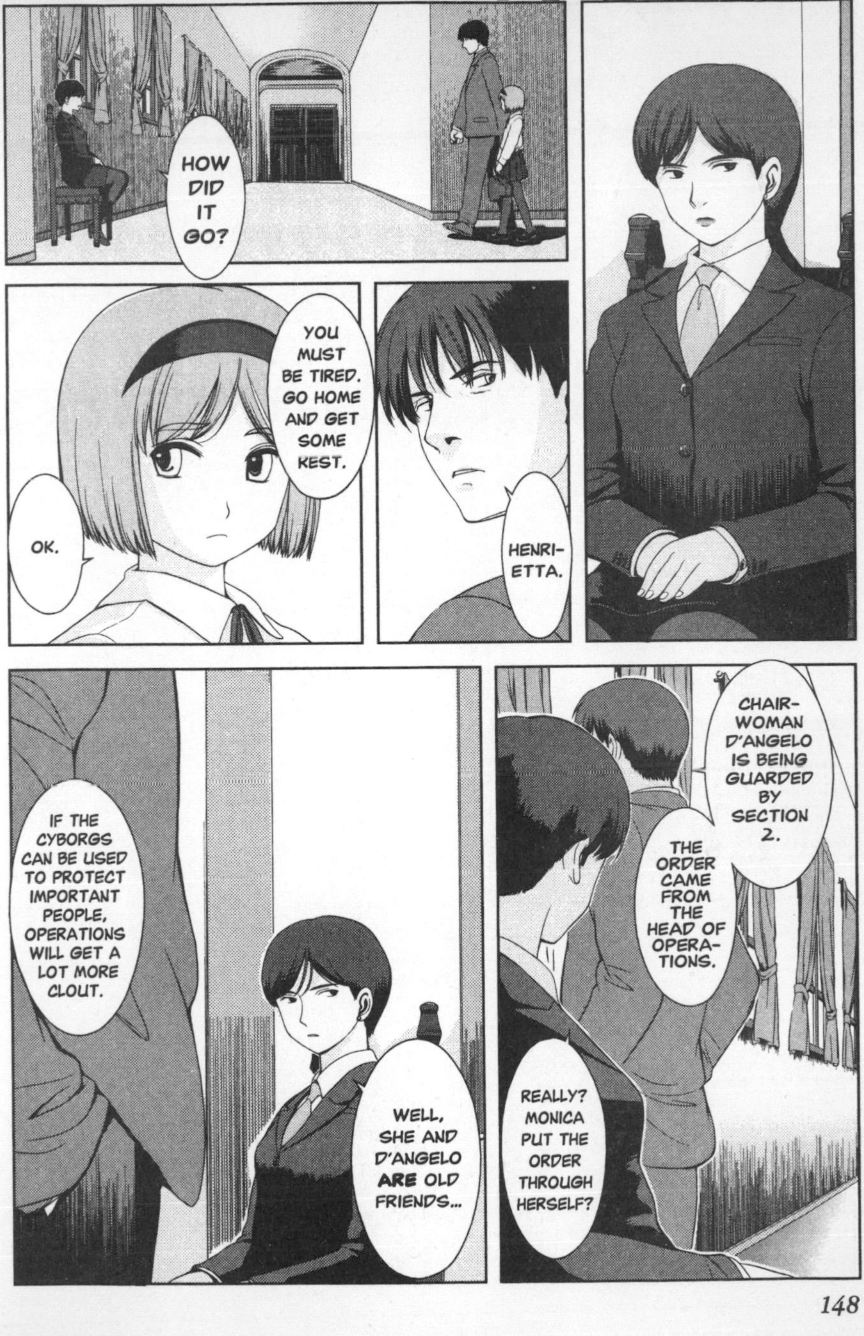
HOW DID IT GO?
HENRI-ETTA.
YOU MUST BE TIRED. GO HOME AND GET SOME KEST.
OK.
CHAIR-WOMAN D'ANGELO IS BEING GUARDED BY SECTION 2.
THE ORDER CAME FROM THE HEAD OF OPERA-TIONS.
REALLY? MONICA PUT THE ORDER THROUGH HERSELF?
WELL, SHE AND D'ANGELO **ARE** OLD FRIENDS...
IF THE CYBORGS CAN BE USED TO PROTECT IMPORTANT PEOPLE, OPERATIONS WILL GET A LOT MORE CLOUT.

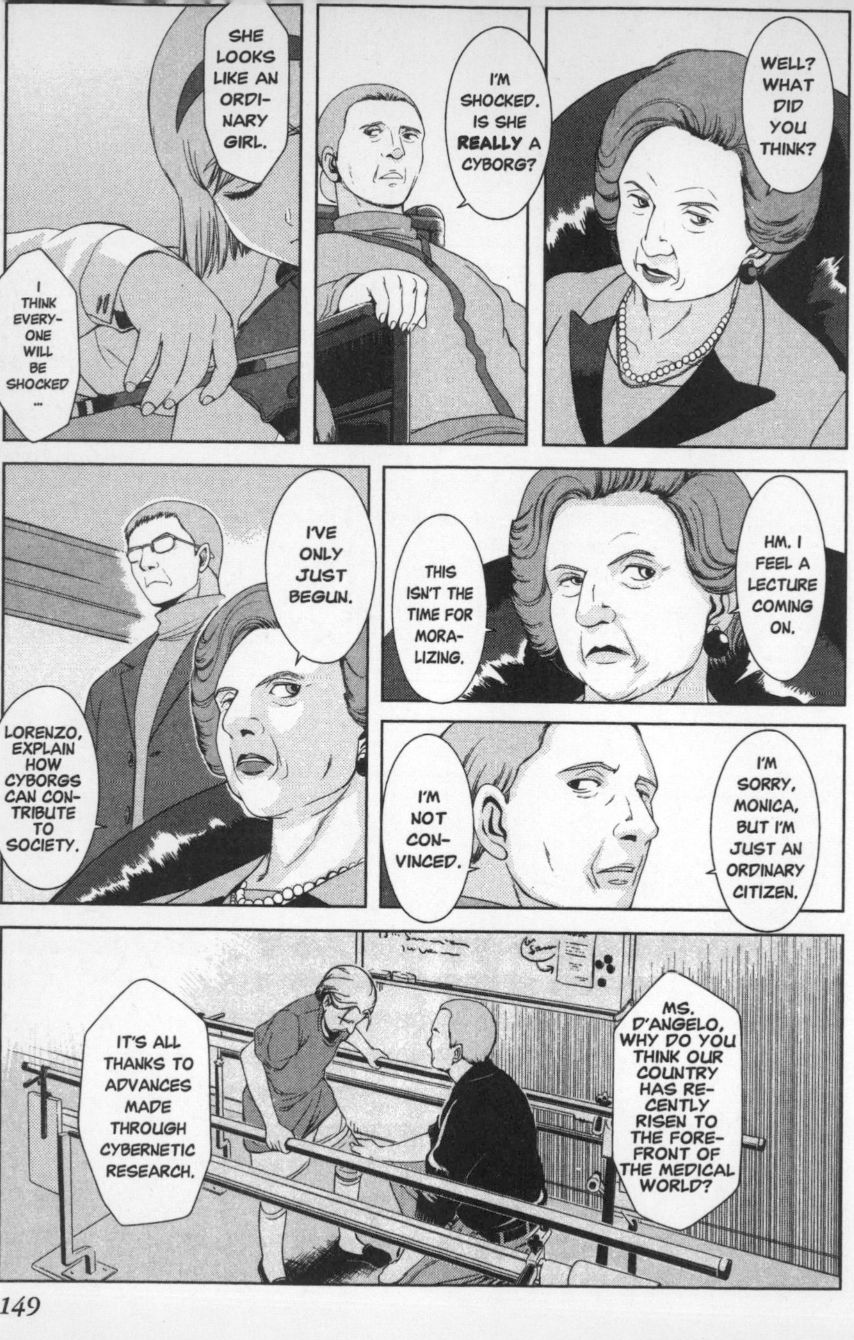
WELL? WHAT DID YOU THINK?
I'M SHOCKED. IS SHE **REALLY** A CYBORG?
SHE LOOKS LIKE AN ORDINARY GIRL.
I THINK EVERYONE WILL BE SHOCKED ...
HM. I FEEL A LECTURE COMING ON.
THIS ISN'T THE TIME FOR MORALIZING.
I'M SORRY, MONICA, BUT I'M JUST AN ORDINARY CITIZEN.
I'M NOT CONVINCED.
I'VE ONLY JUST BEGUN.
LORENZO, EXPLAIN HOW CYBORGS CAN CONTRIBUTE TO SOCIETY.
MS. D'ANGELO, WHY DO YOU THINK OUR COUNTRY HAS RECENTLY RISEN TO THE FOREFRONT OF THE MEDICAL WORLD?
IT'S ALL THANKS TO ADVANCES MADE THROUGH CYBERNETIC RESEARCH.

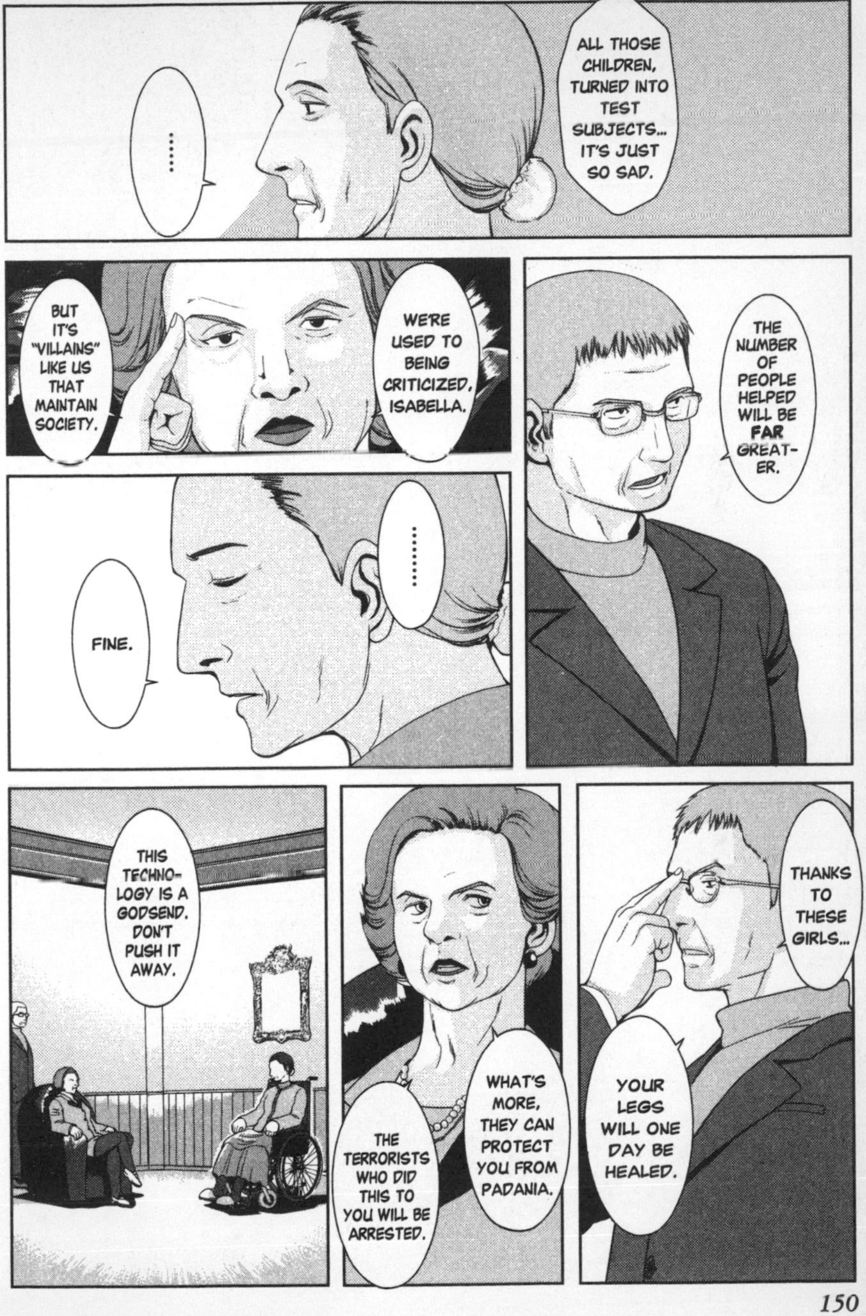
ALL THOSE CHILDREN, TURNED INTO TEST SUBJECTS... IT'S JUST SO SAD.
......
THE NUMBER OF PEOPLE HELPED WILL BE FAR GREATER.
WE'RE USED TO BEING CRITICIZED, ISABELLA.
BUT IT'S "VILLAINS" LIKE US THAT MAINTAIN SOCIETY.
....
FINE.
THANKS TO THESE GIRLS...
YOUR LEGS WILL ONE DAY BE HEALED.
WHAT'S MORE, THEY CAN PROTECT YOU FROM PADANIA.
THE TERRORISTS WHO DID THIS TO YOU WILL BE ARRESTED.
THIS TECHNOLOGY IS A GODSEND. DON'T PUSH IT AWAY.

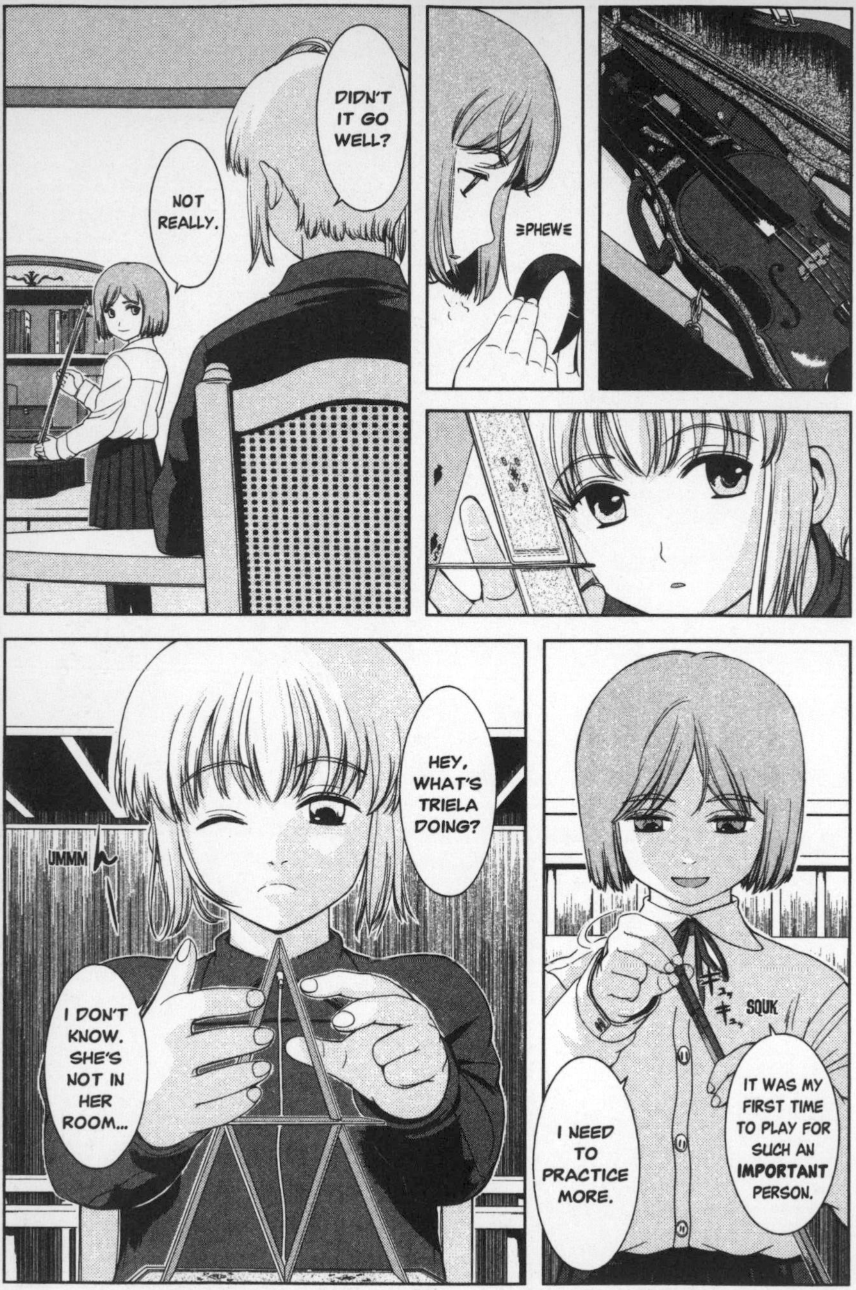

≡PHEW≡
DIDN'T IT GO WELL?
NOT REALLY.
SQUK
IT WAS MY FIRST TIME TO PLAY FOR SUCH AN IMPORTANT PERSON.
I NEED TO PRACTICE MORE.
HEY, WHAT'S TRIELA DOING?
UMMM
I DON'T KNOW. SHE'S NOT IN HER ROOM...

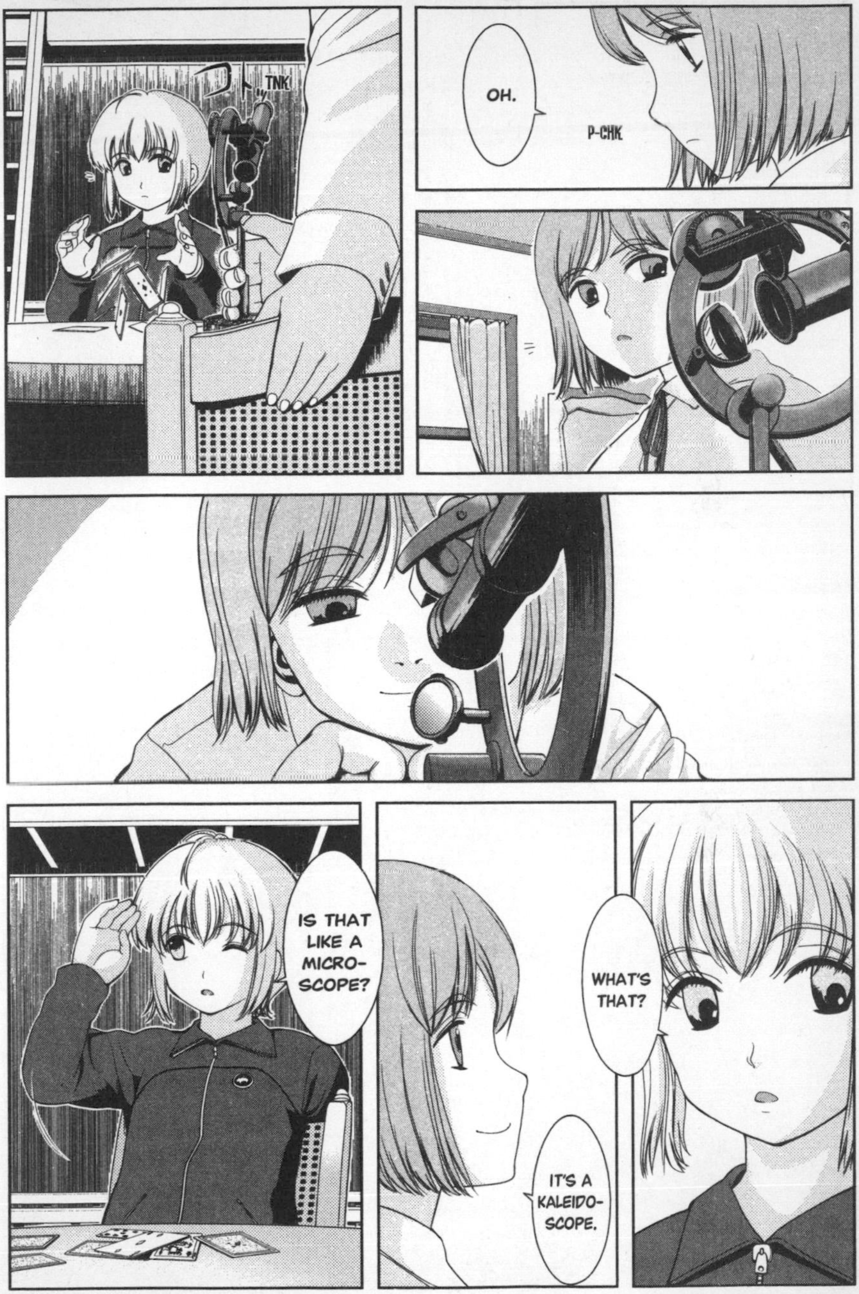
OH.
P-CHK
コトッ
TNK
WHAT'S THAT?
IT'S A KALEIDO-SCOPE.
IS THAT LIKE A MICRO-SCOPE?

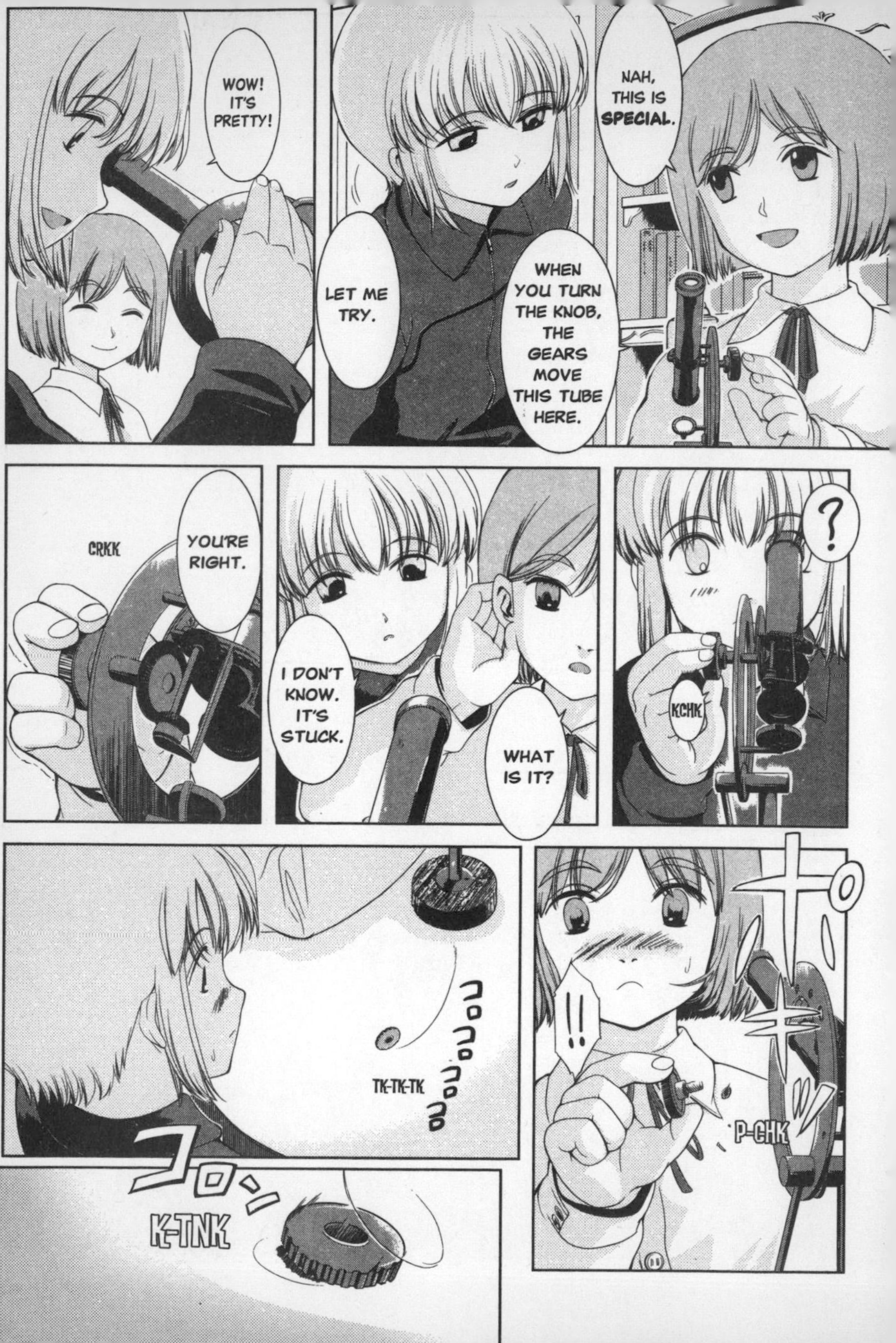

NAH, THIS IS **SPECIAL.**
WHEN YOU TURN THE KNOB, THE GEARS MOVE THIS TUBE HERE.
LET ME TRY.
WOW! IT'S PRETTY!
?
KCHK
WHAT IS IT?
I DON'T KNOW. IT'S STUCK.
YOU'RE RIGHT.
CRKK
!!
P-CHK
TK-TK-TK
K-TNK

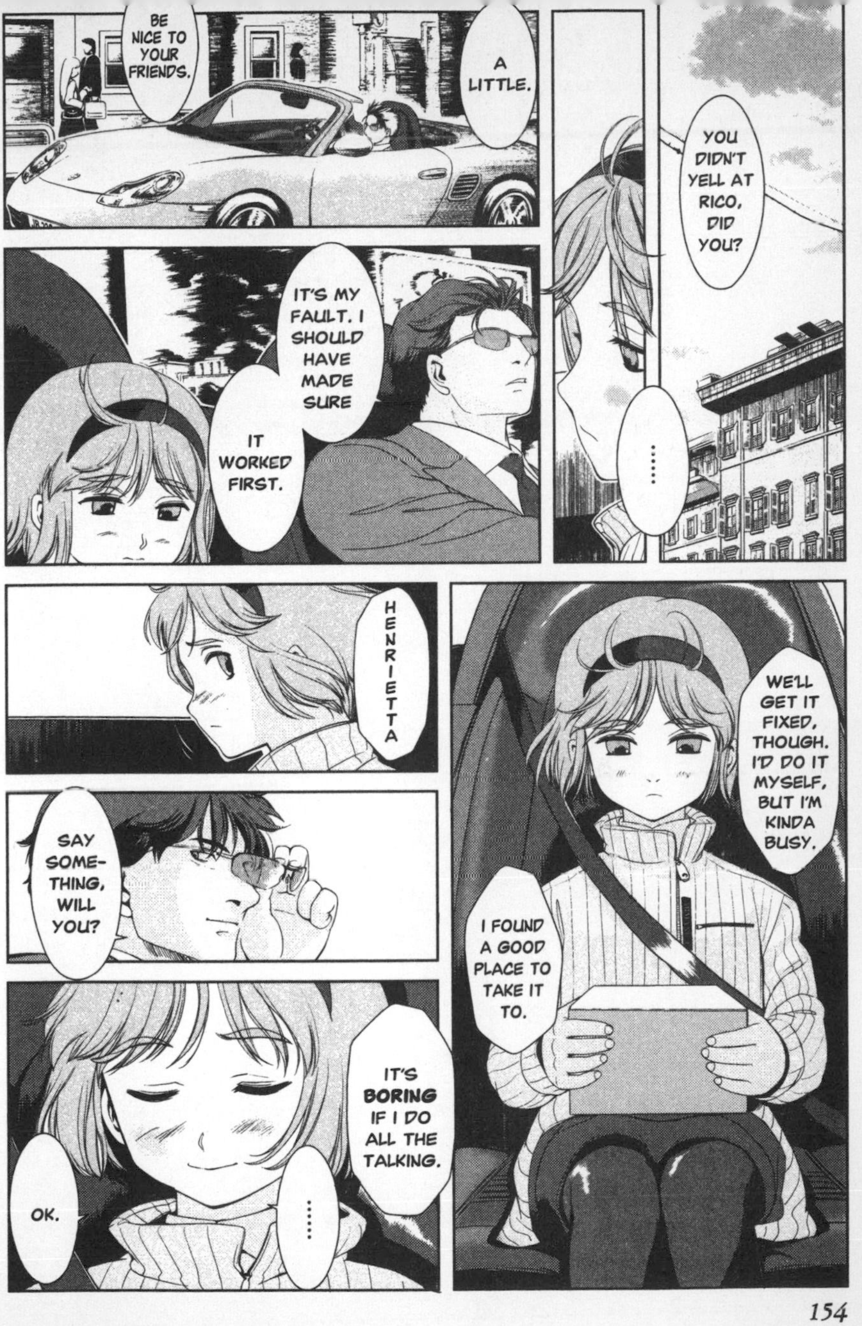
YOU DIDN'T YELL AT RICO, DID YOU?
……
A LITTLE.
BE NICE TO YOUR FRIENDS.
IT'S MY FAULT. I SHOULD HAVE MADE SURE
IT WORKED FIRST.
WE'LL GET IT FIXED, THOUGH. I'D DO IT MYSELF, BUT I'M KINDA BUSY.
I FOUND A GOOD PLACE TO TAKE IT TO.
HENRIETTA
SAY SOME-THING, WILL YOU?
IT'S BORING IF I DO ALL THE TALKING.
……
OK.

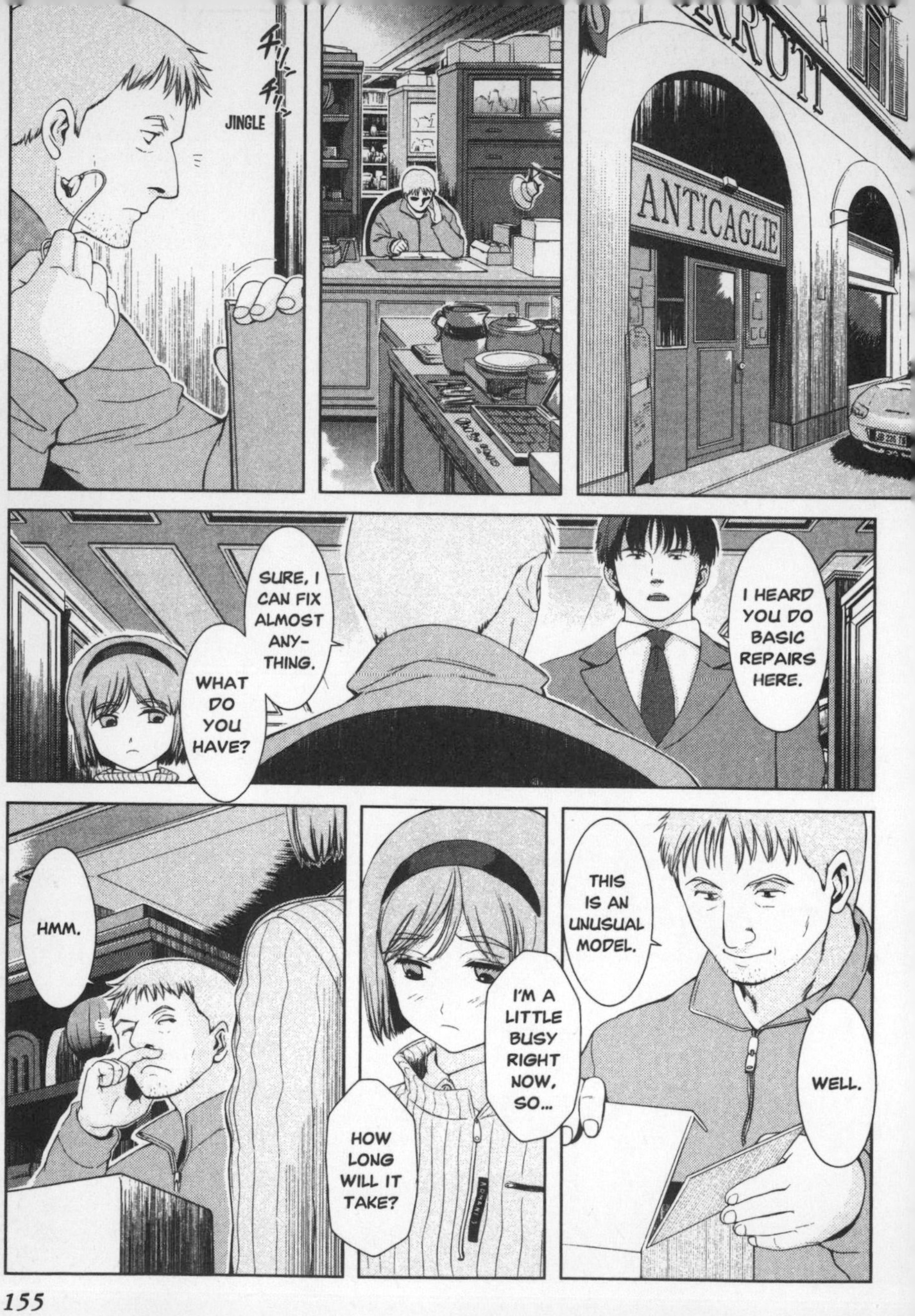
ANTICAGLIE
チリン チリン
JINGLE
I HEARD YOU DO BASIC REPAIRS HERE.
SURE, I CAN FIX ALMOST ANY-THING.
WHAT DO YOU HAVE?
THIS IS AN UNUSUAL MODEL.
WELL.
I'M A LITTLE BUSY RIGHT NOW, SO...
HOW LONG WILL IT TAKE?
HMM.

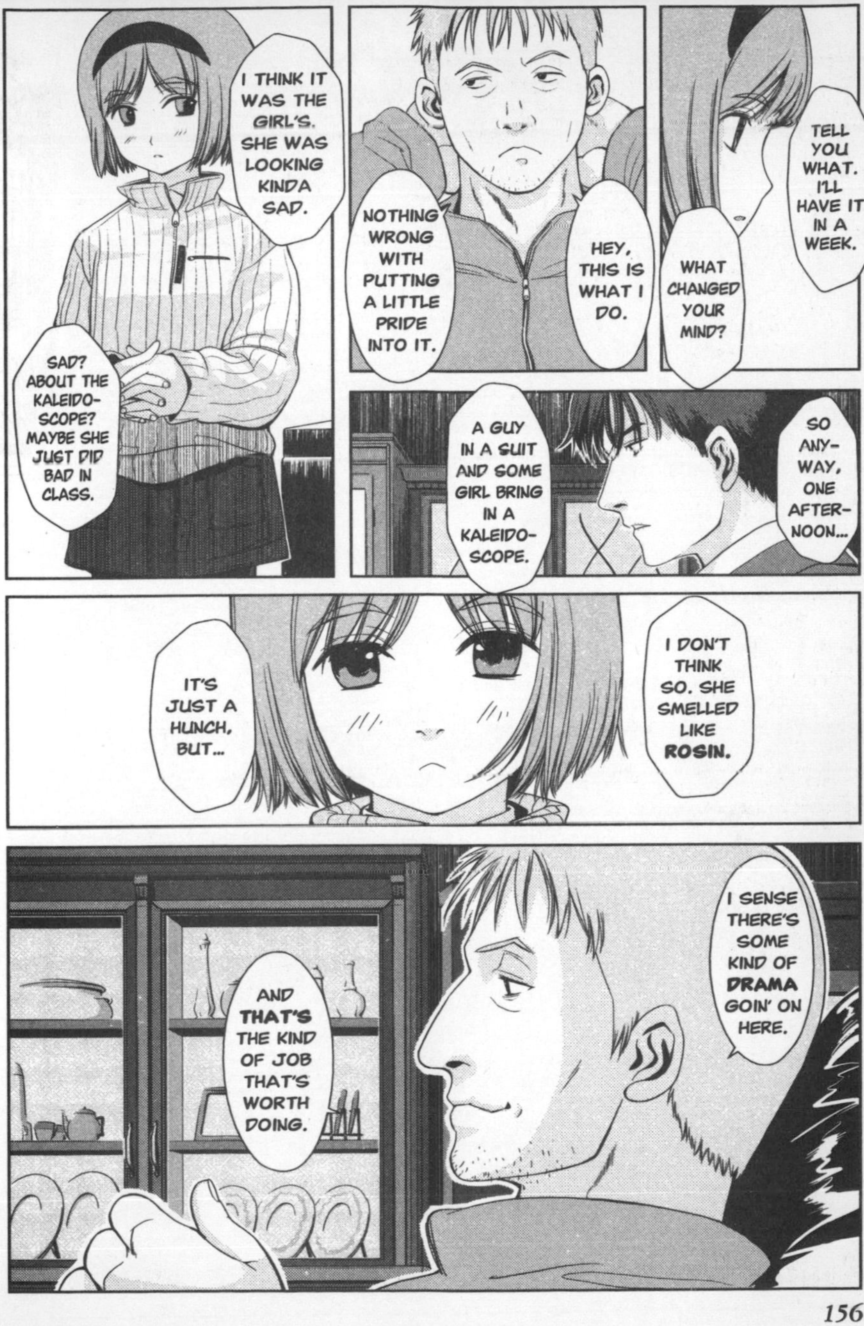
TELL YOU WHAT. I'LL HAVE IT IN A WEEK.
WHAT CHANGED YOUR MIND?
HEY, THIS IS WHAT I DO.
NOTHING WRONG WITH PUTTING A LITTLE PRIDE INTO IT.
SO ANYWAY, ONE AFTERNOON...
A GUY IN A SUIT AND SOME GIRL BRING IN A KALEIDOSCOPE.
I THINK IT WAS THE GIRL'S. SHE WAS LOOKING KINDA SAD.
SAD? ABOUT THE KALEIDOSCOPE? MAYBE SHE JUST DID BAD IN CLASS.
I DON'T THINK SO. SHE SMELLED LIKE **ROSIN.**
IT'S JUST A HUNCH, BUT...
I SENSE THERE'S SOME KIND OF **DRAMA** GOIN' ON HERE.
AND **THAT'S** THE KIND OF JOB THAT'S WORTH DOING.

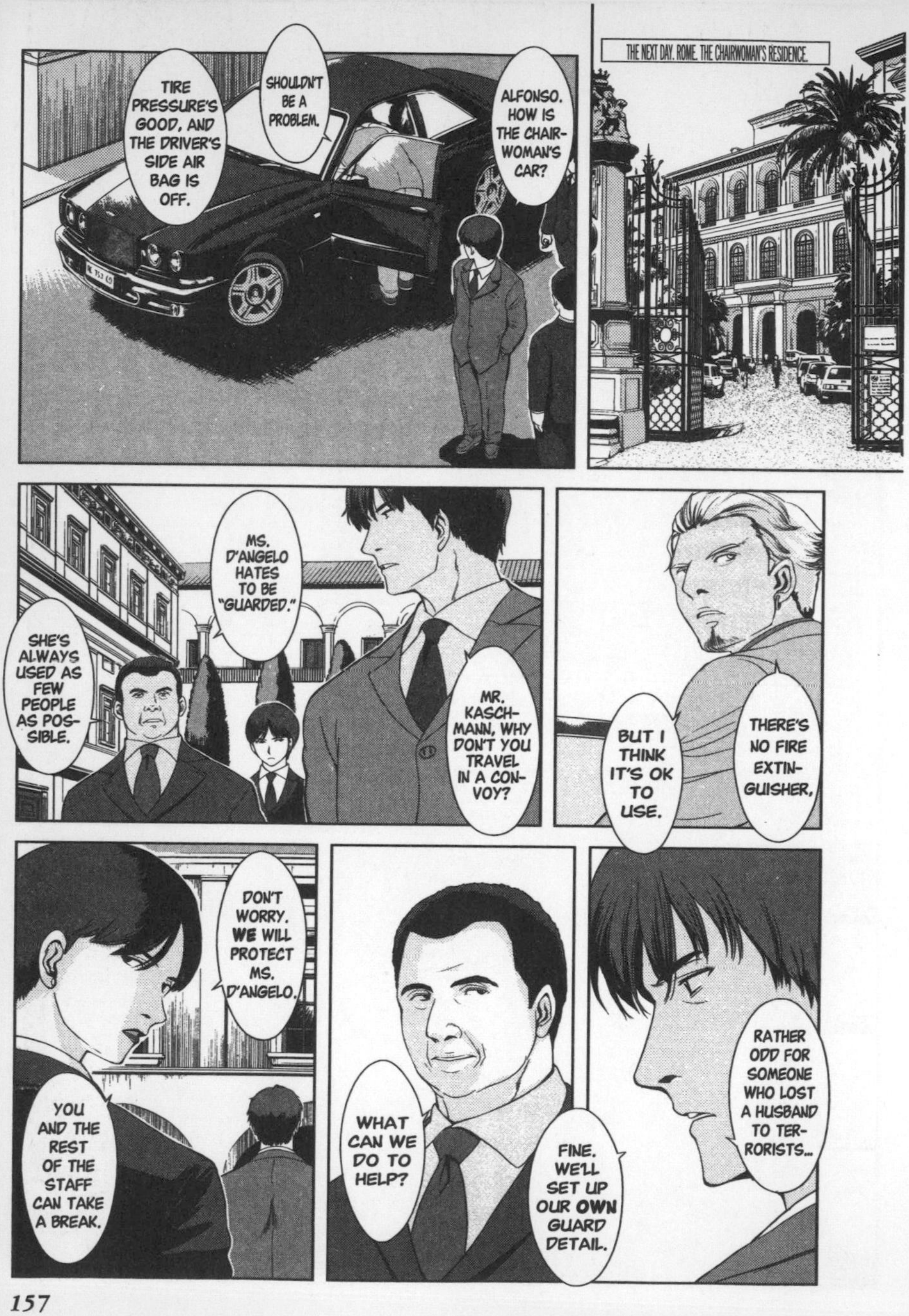
THE NEXT DAY. ROME. THE CHAIRWOMAN'S RESIDENCE.
ALFONSO. HOW IS THE CHAIR-WOMAN'S CAR?
SHOULDN'T BE A PROBLEM.
TIRE PRESSURE'S GOOD, AND THE DRIVER'S SIDE AIR BAG IS OFF.
THERE'S NO FIRE EXTIN-GUISHER,
BUT I THINK IT'S OK TO USE.
MR. KASCH-MANN, WHY DON'T YOU TRAVEL IN A CON-VOY?
MS. D'ANGELO HATES TO BE "GUARDED."
SHE'S ALWAYS USED AS FEW PEOPLE AS POS-SIBLE.
RATHER ODD FOR SOMEONE WHO LOST A HUSBAND TO TER-RORISTS...
FINE. WE'LL SET UP OUR **OWN** GUARD DETAIL.
WHAT CAN WE DO TO HELP?
DON'T WORRY. **WE** WILL PROTECT MS. D'ANGELO.
YOU AND THE REST OF THE STAFF CAN TAKE A BREAK.

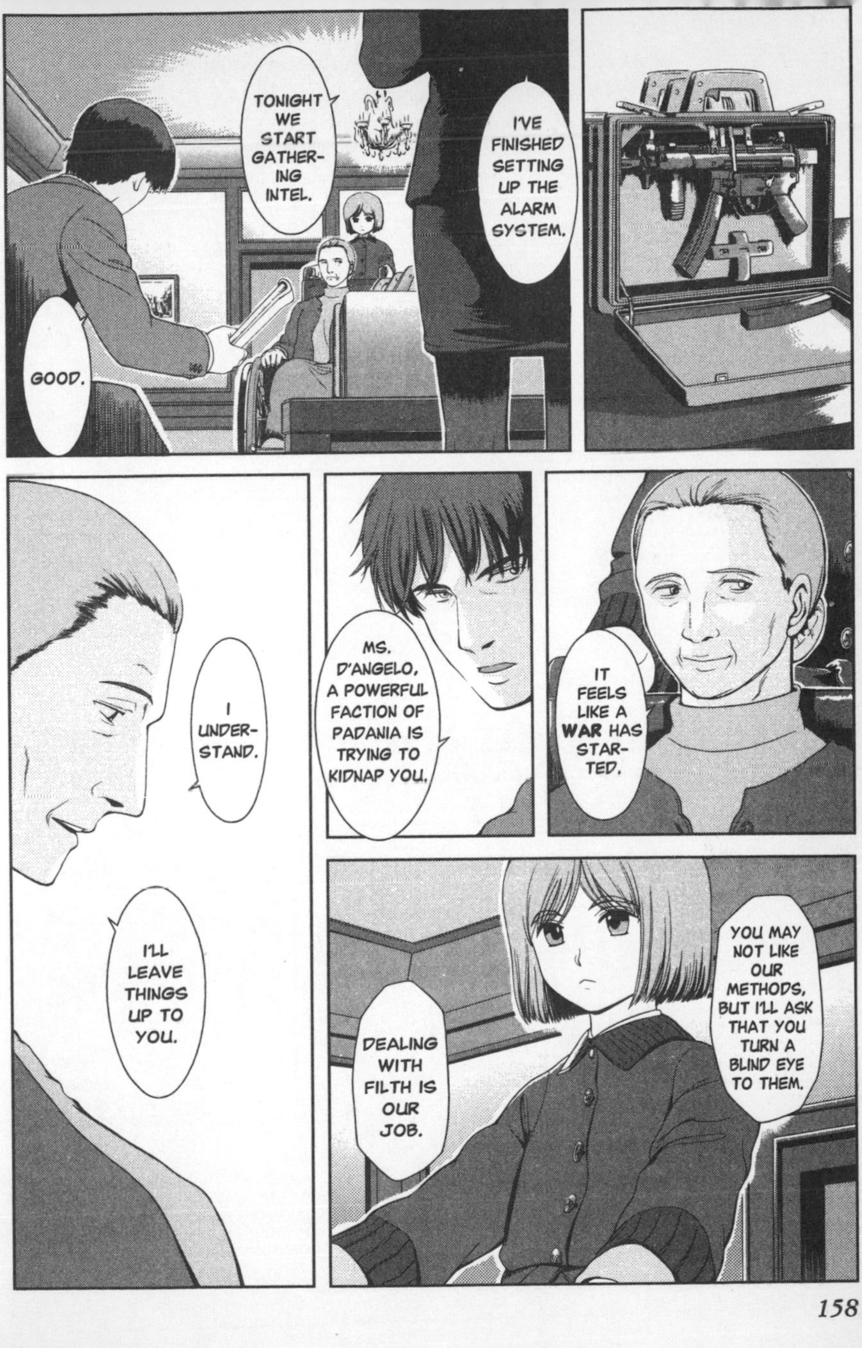
I'VE FINISHED SETTING UP THE ALARM SYSTEM.
TONIGHT WE START GATHER-ING INTEL.
GOOD.
IT FEELS LIKE A WAR HAS STAR-TED.
MS. D'ANGELO, A POWERFUL FACTION OF PADANIA IS TRYING TO KIDNAP YOU.
YOU MAY NOT LIKE OUR METHODS, BUT I'LL ASK THAT YOU TURN A BLIND EYE TO THEM.
DEALING WITH FILTH IS OUR JOB.
I UNDER-STAND.
I'LL LEAVE THINGS UP TO YOU.

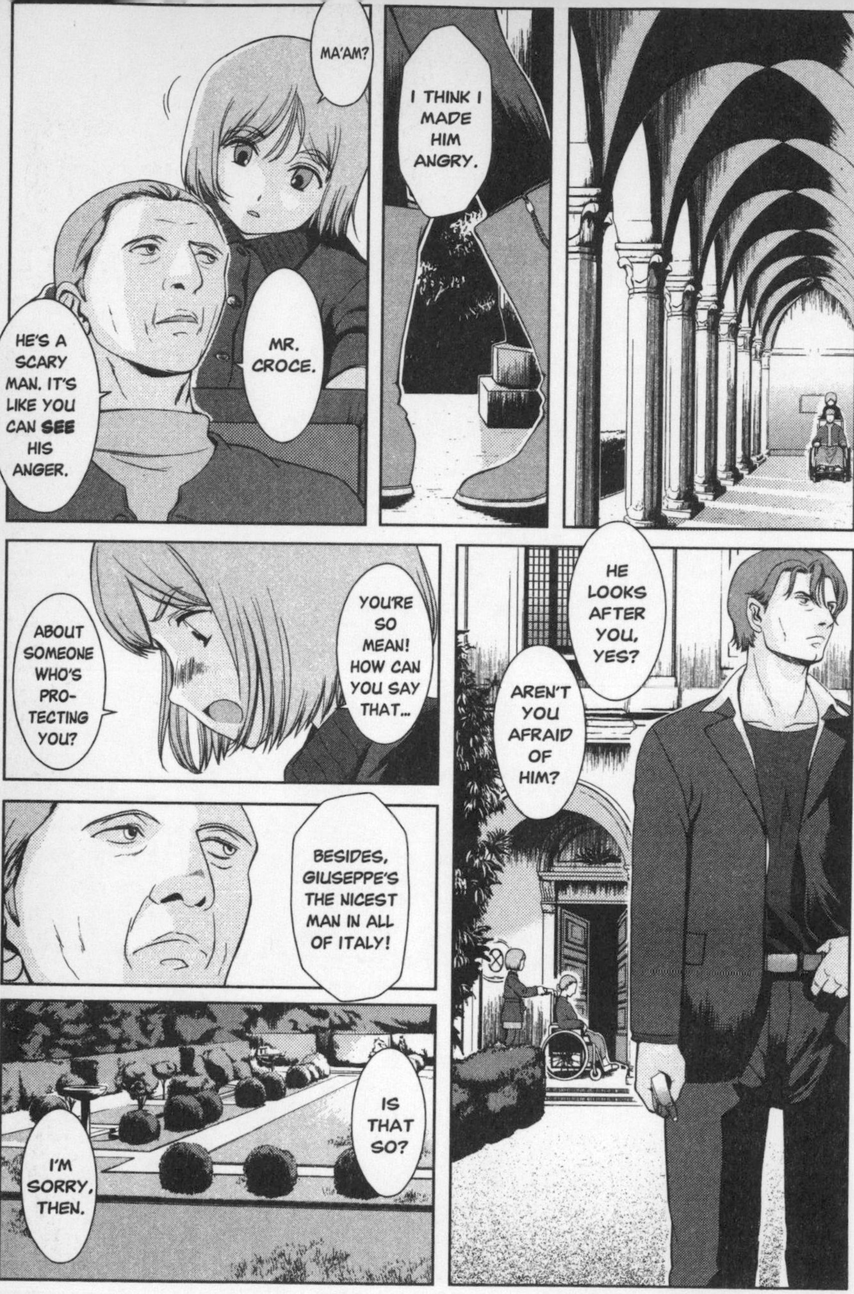
I THINK I MADE HIM ANGRY.
MA'AM?
MR. CROCE.
HE'S A SCARY MAN. IT'S LIKE YOU CAN **SEE** HIS ANGER.
HE LOOKS AFTER YOU, YES?
AREN'T YOU AFRAID OF HIM?
YOU'RE SO MEAN! HOW CAN YOU SAY THAT...
ABOUT SOMEONE WHO'S PRO-TECTING YOU?
BESIDES, GIUSEPPE'S THE NICEST MAN IN ALL OF ITALY!
IS THAT SO?
I'M SORRY, THEN.

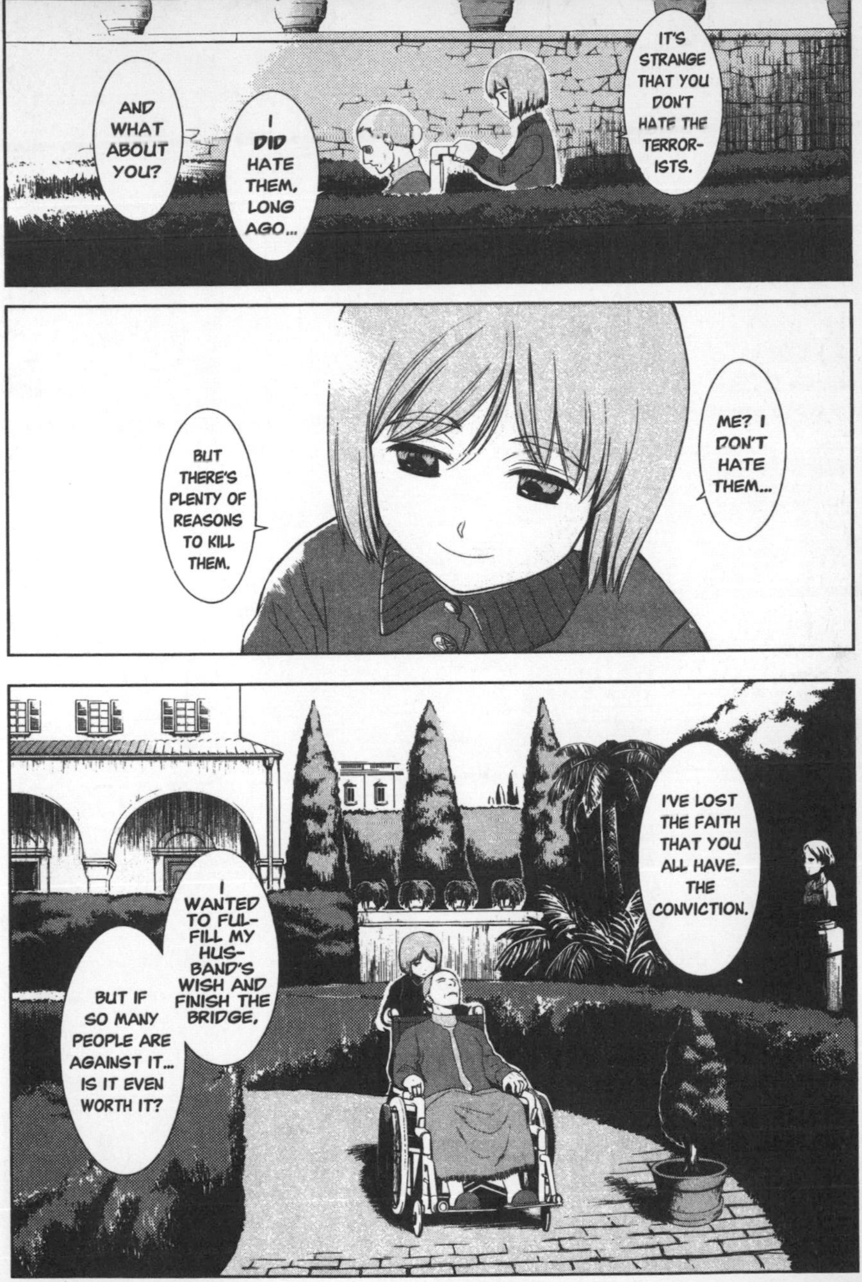
IT'S STRANGE THAT YOU DON'T HATE THE TERRORISTS.
I DID HATE THEM, LONG AGO...
AND WHAT ABOUT YOU?
ME? I DON'T HATE THEM...
BUT THERE'S PLENTY OF REASONS TO KILL THEM.
I'VE LOST THE FAITH THAT YOU ALL HAVE. THE CONVICTION.
I WANTED TO FULFILL MY HUSBAND'S WISH AND FINISH THE BRIDGE,
BUT IF SO MANY PEOPLE ARE AGAINST IT... IS IT EVEN WORTH IT?

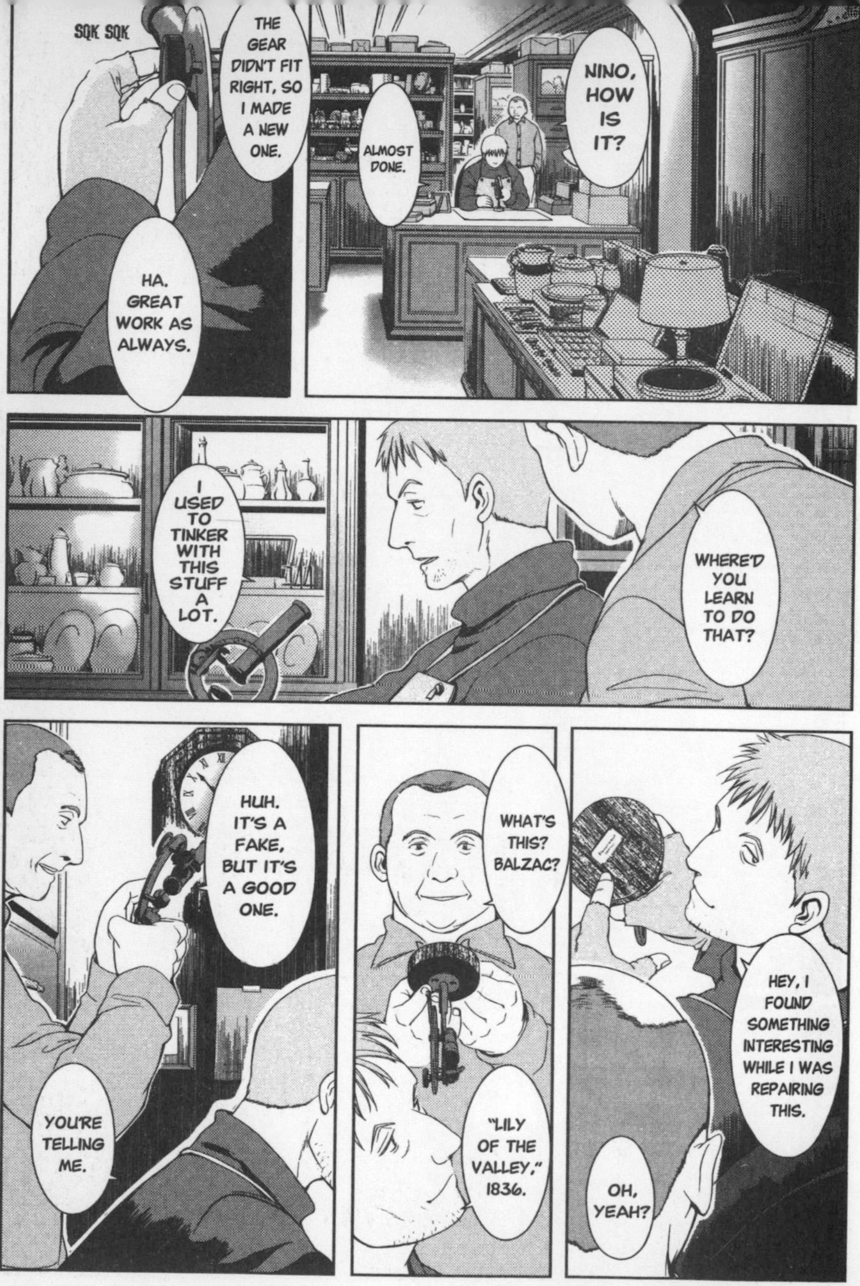
NINO, HOW IS IT?
ALMOST DONE.
THE GEAR DIDN'T FIT RIGHT, SO I MADE A NEW ONE.
SQK SQK
HA. GREAT WORK AS ALWAYS.
WHERE'D YOU LEARN TO DO THAT?
I USED TO TINKER WITH THIS STUFF A LOT.
HEY, I FOUND SOMETHING INTERESTING WHILE I WAS REPAIRING THIS.
OH, YEAH?
WHAT'S THIS? BALZAC?
"LILY OF THE VALLEY," 1836.
HUH. IT'S A FAKE, BUT IT'S A GOOD ONE.
YOU'RE TELLING ME.

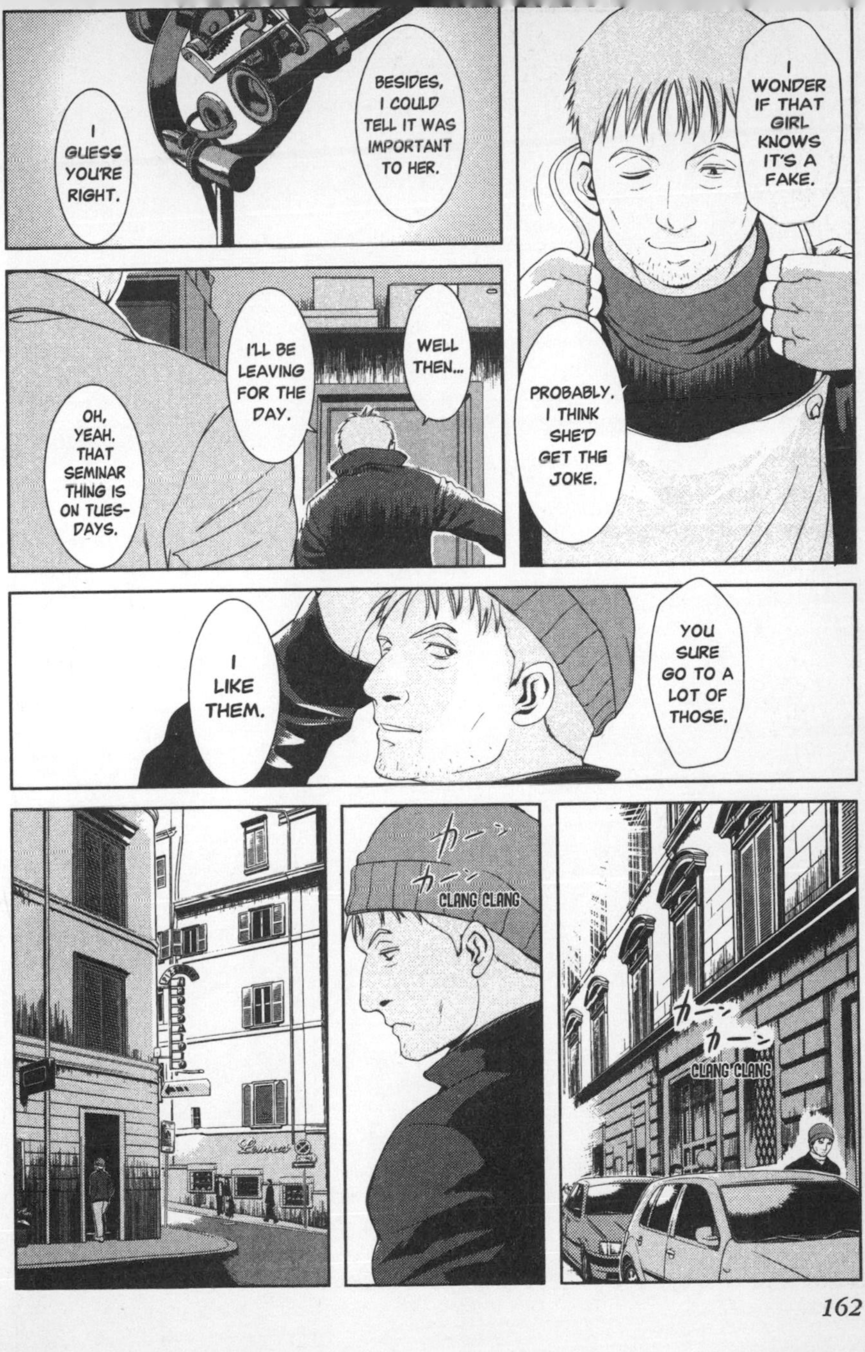
I WONDER IF THAT GIRL KNOWS IT'S A FAKE.
PROBABLY. I THINK SHE'D GET THE JOKE.
BESIDES, I COULD TELL IT WAS IMPORTANT TO HER.
I GUESS YOU'RE RIGHT.
WELL THEN...
I'LL BE LEAVING FOR THE DAY.
OH, YEAH. THAT SEMINAR THING IS ON TUES- DAYS.
YOU SURE GO TO A LOT OF THOSE.
I LIKE THEM.
カーン カーン
CLANG CLANG
カーン カーン
CLANG CLANG

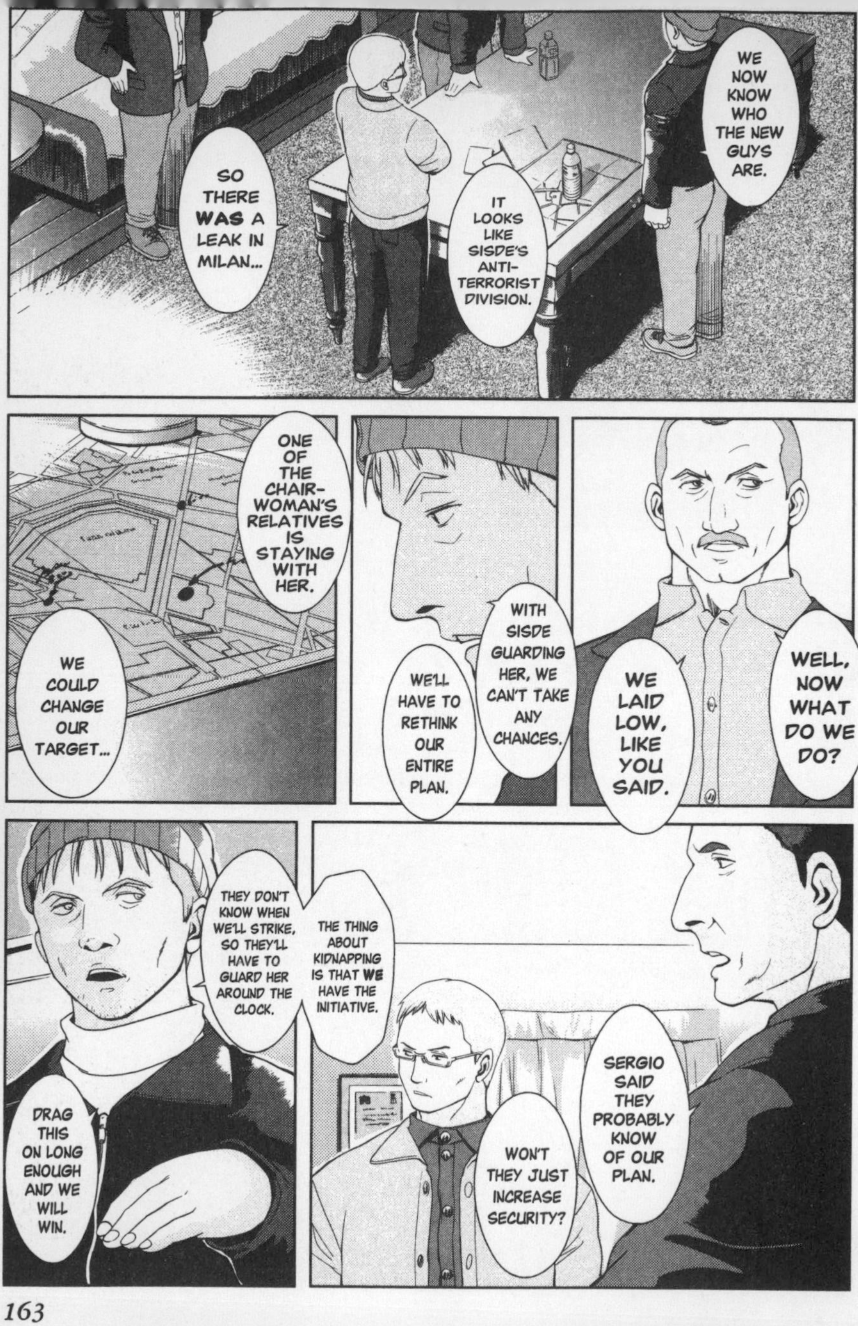
WE NOW KNOW WHO THE NEW GUYS ARE.
IT LOOKS LIKE SISDE'S ANTI-TERRORIST DIVISION.
SO THERE **WAS** A LEAK IN MILAN...
WELL, NOW WHAT DO WE DO?
WE LAID LOW, LIKE YOU SAID.
WITH SISDE GUARDING HER, WE CAN'T TAKE ANY CHANCES.
WE'LL HAVE TO RETHINK OUR ENTIRE PLAN.
ONE OF THE CHAIR-WOMAN'S RELATIVES IS STAYING WITH HER.
WE COULD CHANGE OUR TARGET...
SERGIO SAID THEY PROBABLY KNOW OF OUR PLAN.
WON'T THEY JUST INCREASE SECURITY?
THE THING ABOUT KIDNAPPING IS THAT **WE** HAVE THE INITIATIVE.
THEY DON'T KNOW WHEN WE'LL STRIKE, SO THEY'LL HAVE TO GUARD HER AROUND THE CLOCK.
DRAG THIS ON LONG ENOUGH AND WE WILL WIN.

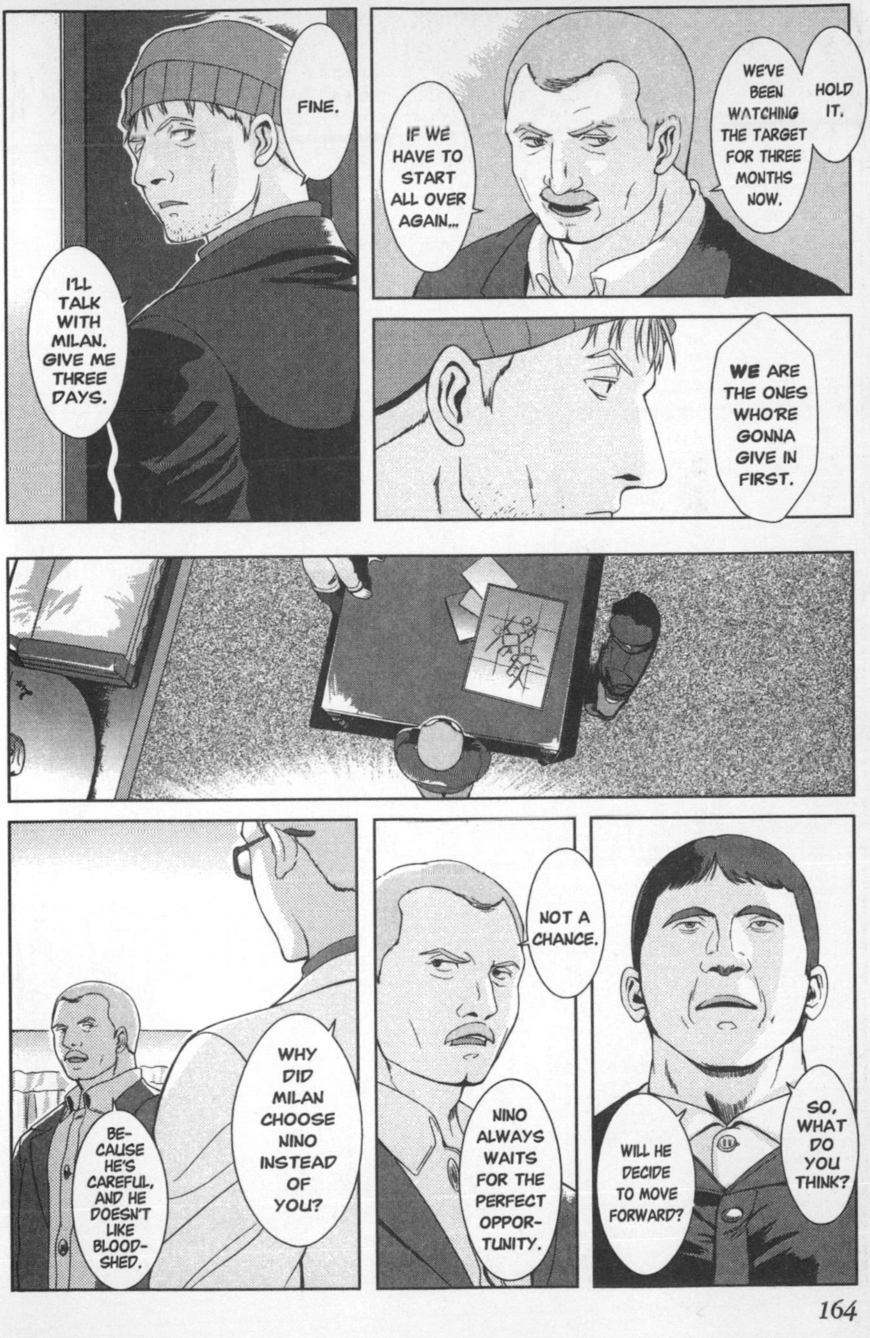
HOLD IT.
WE'VE BEEN WATCHING THE TARGET FOR THREE MONTHS NOW.
IF WE HAVE TO START ALL OVER AGAIN...
WE ARE THE ONES WHO'RE GONNA GIVE IN FIRST.
FINE.
I'LL TALK WITH MILAN. GIVE ME THREE DAYS.
SO, WHAT DO YOU THINK?
WILL HE DECIDE TO MOVE FORWARD?
NOT A CHANCE.
NINO ALWAYS WAITS FOR THE PERFECT OPPORTUNITY.
WHY DID MILAN CHOOSE NINO INSTEAD OF YOU?
BECAUSE HE'S CAREFUL, AND HE DOESN'T LIKE BLOODSHED.

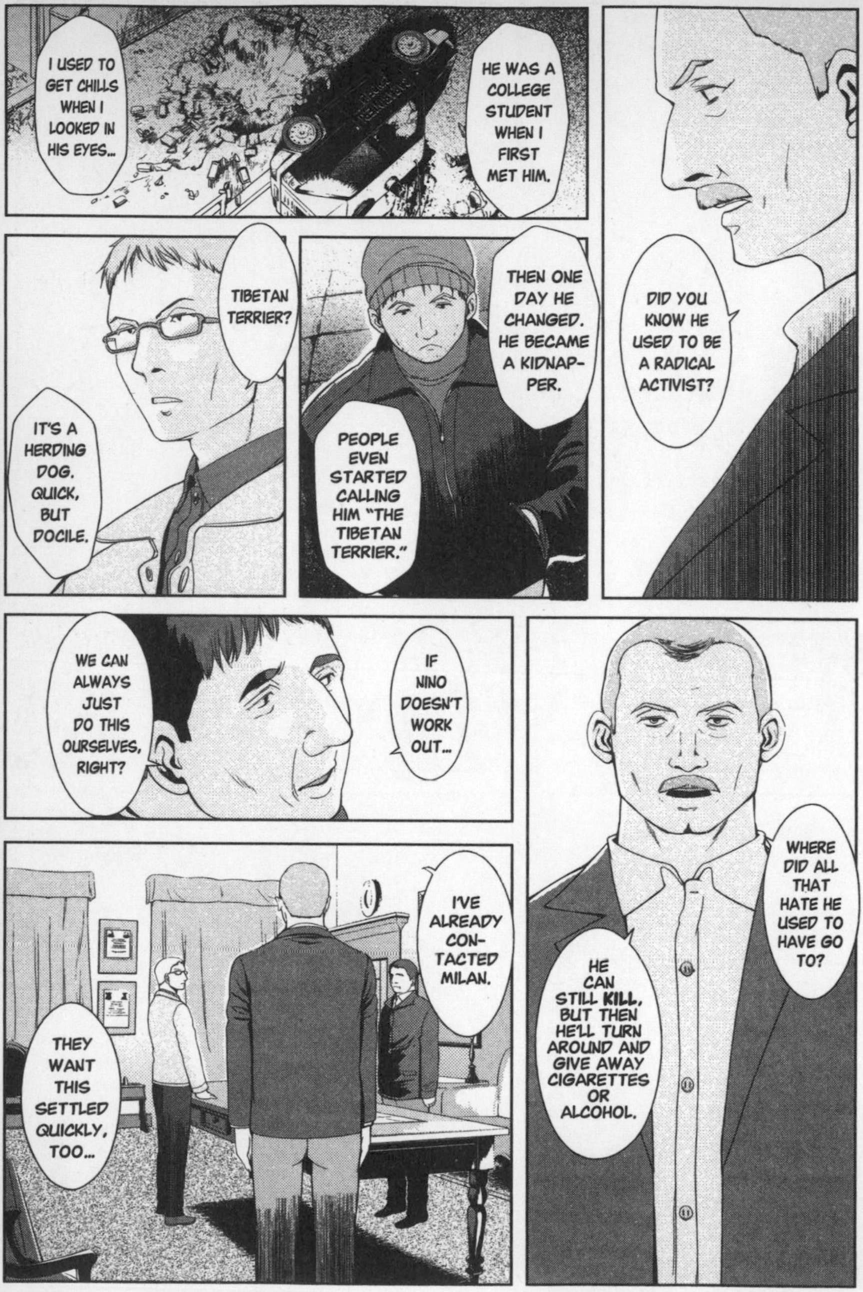
DID YOU KNOW HE USED TO BE A RADICAL ACTIVIST?
HE WAS A COLLEGE STUDENT WHEN I FIRST MET HIM.
I USED TO GET CHILLS WHEN I LOOKED IN HIS EYES...
THEN ONE DAY HE CHANGED. HE BECAME A KIDNAP-PER.
PEOPLE EVEN STARTED CALLING HIM "THE TIBETAN TERRIER."
TIBETAN TERRIER?
IT'S A HERDING DOG. QUICK, BUT DOCILE.
WHERE DID ALL THAT HATE HE USED TO HAVE GO TO?
HE CAN STILL **KILL**, BUT THEN HE'LL TURN AROUND AND GIVE AWAY CIGARETTES OR ALCOHOL.
IF NINO DOESN'T WORK OUT...
WE CAN ALWAYS JUST DO THIS OURSELVES, RIGHT?
I'VE ALREADY CON-TACTED MILAN.
THEY WANT THIS SETTLED QUICKLY, TOO...

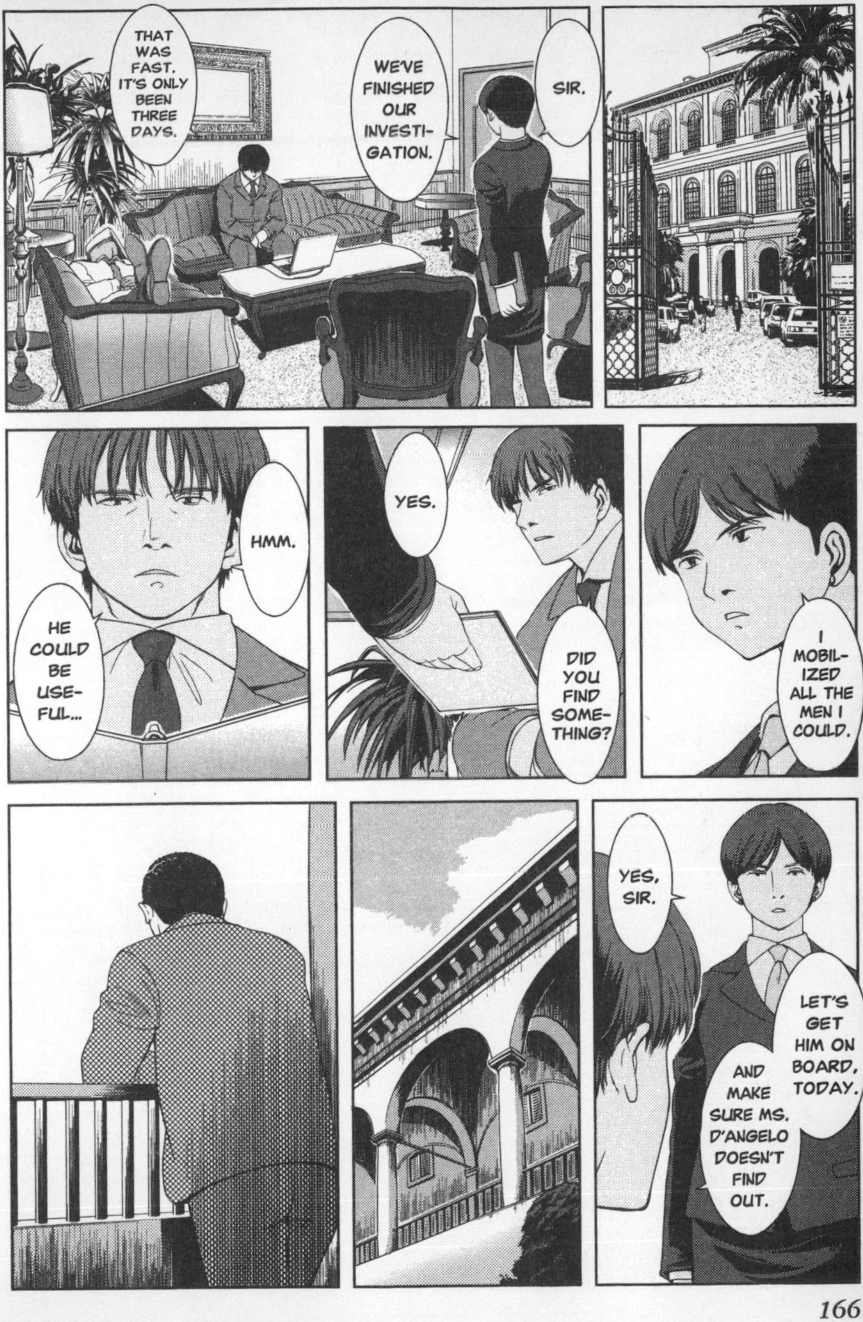
SIR.
WE'VE FINISHED OUR INVESTIGATION.
THAT WAS FAST. IT'S ONLY BEEN THREE DAYS.
I MOBILIZED ALL THE MEN I COULD.
DID YOU FIND SOMETHING?
YES.
HMM.
HE COULD BE USEFUL...
LET'S GET HIM ON BOARD, TODAY.
AND MAKE SURE MS. D'ANGELO DOESN'T FIND OUT.
YES, SIR.

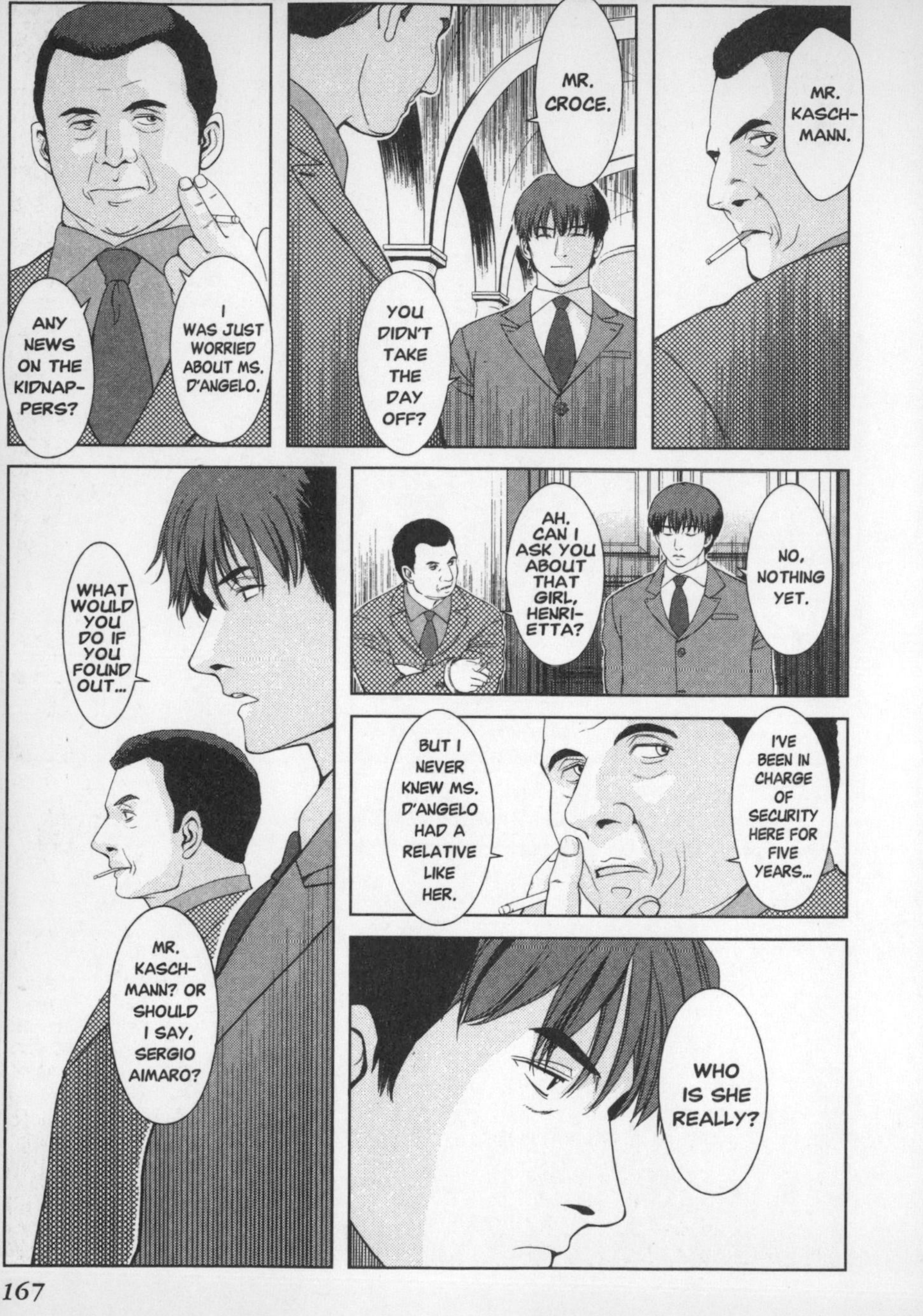
MR. KASCHMANN.
MR. CROCE.
YOU DIDN'T TAKE THE DAY OFF?
I WAS JUST WORRIED ABOUT MS. D'ANGELO.
ANY NEWS ON THE KIDNAPPERS?
NO, NOTHING YET.
AH. CAN I ASK YOU ABOUT THAT GIRL, HENRIETTA?
I'VE BEEN IN CHARGE OF SECURITY HERE FOR FIVE YEARS...
BUT I NEVER KNEW MS. D'ANGELO HAD A RELATIVE LIKE HER.
WHO IS SHE REALLY?
WHAT WOULD YOU DO IF YOU FOUND OUT...
MR. KASCHMANN? OR SHOULD I SAY, SERGIO AIMARO?

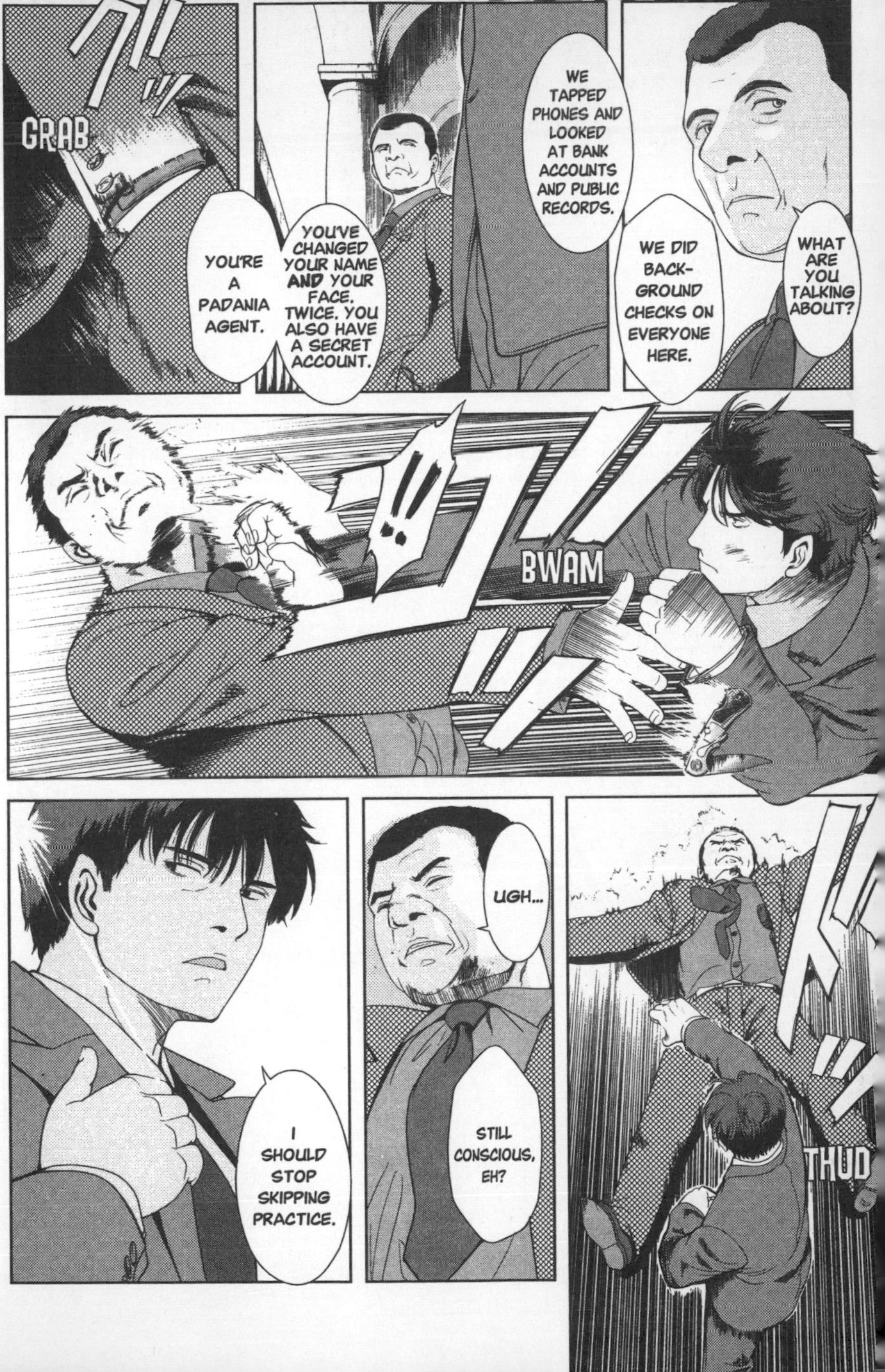
WHAT ARE YOU TALKING ABOUT?
WE DID BACK-GROUND CHECKS ON EVERYONE HERE.
WE TAPPED PHONES AND LOOKED AT BANK ACCOUNTS AND PUBLIC RECORDS.
YOU'VE CHANGED YOUR NAME AND YOUR FACE. TWICE. YOU ALSO HAVE A SECRET ACCOUNT.
YOU'RE A PADANIA AGENT.
GRAB
BWAM
!!
THUD
UGH...
STILL CONSCIOUS, EH?
I SHOULD STOP SKIPPING PRACTICE.

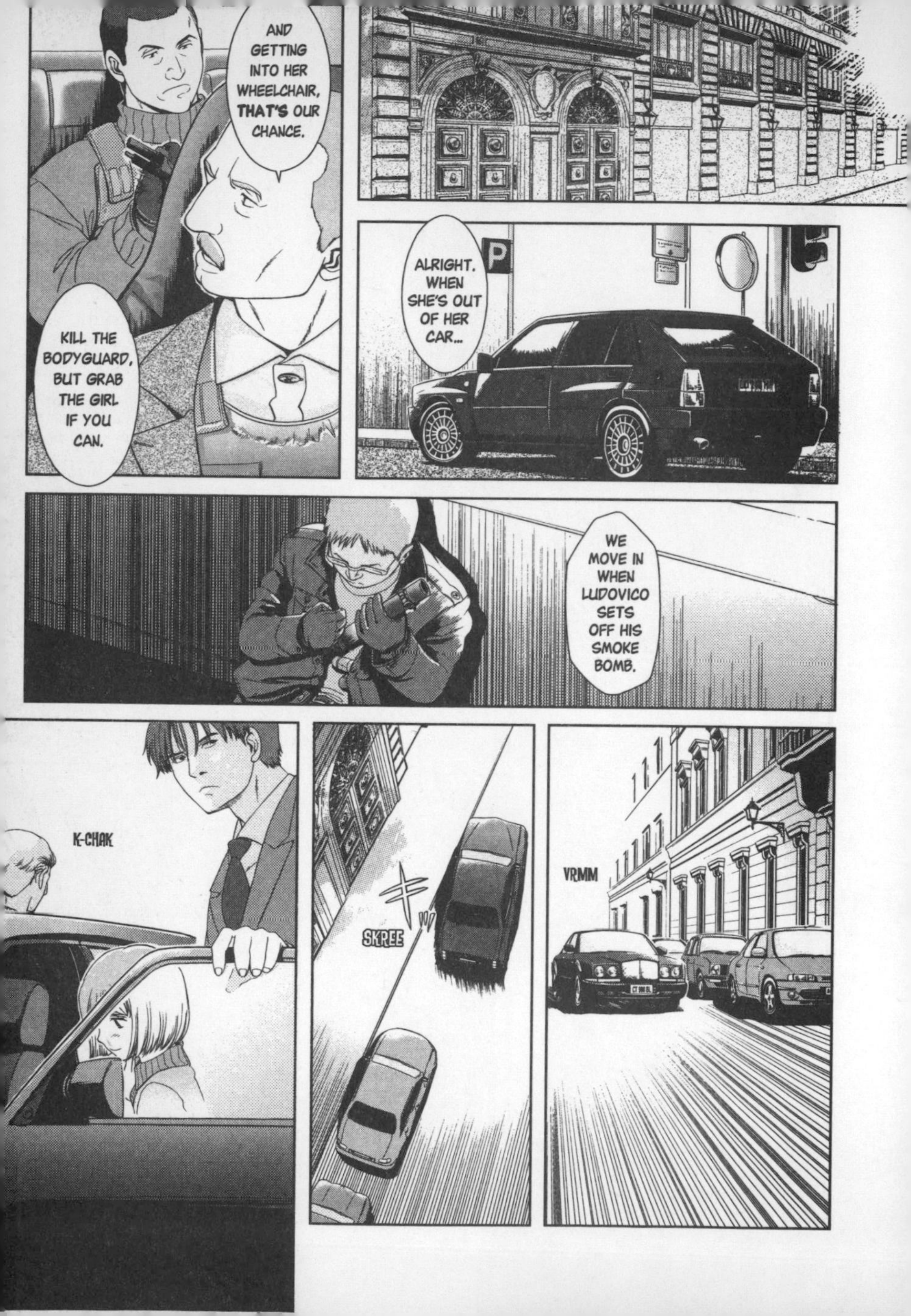
ALRIGHT. WHEN SHE'S OUT OF HER CAR...
AND GETTING INTO HER WHEELCHAIR, THAT'S OUR CHANCE.
KILL THE BODYGUARD, BUT GRAB THE GIRL IF YOU CAN.
WE MOVE IN WHEN LUDOVICO SETS OFF HIS SMOKE BOMB.
VRMM
SKREE
K-CHAK

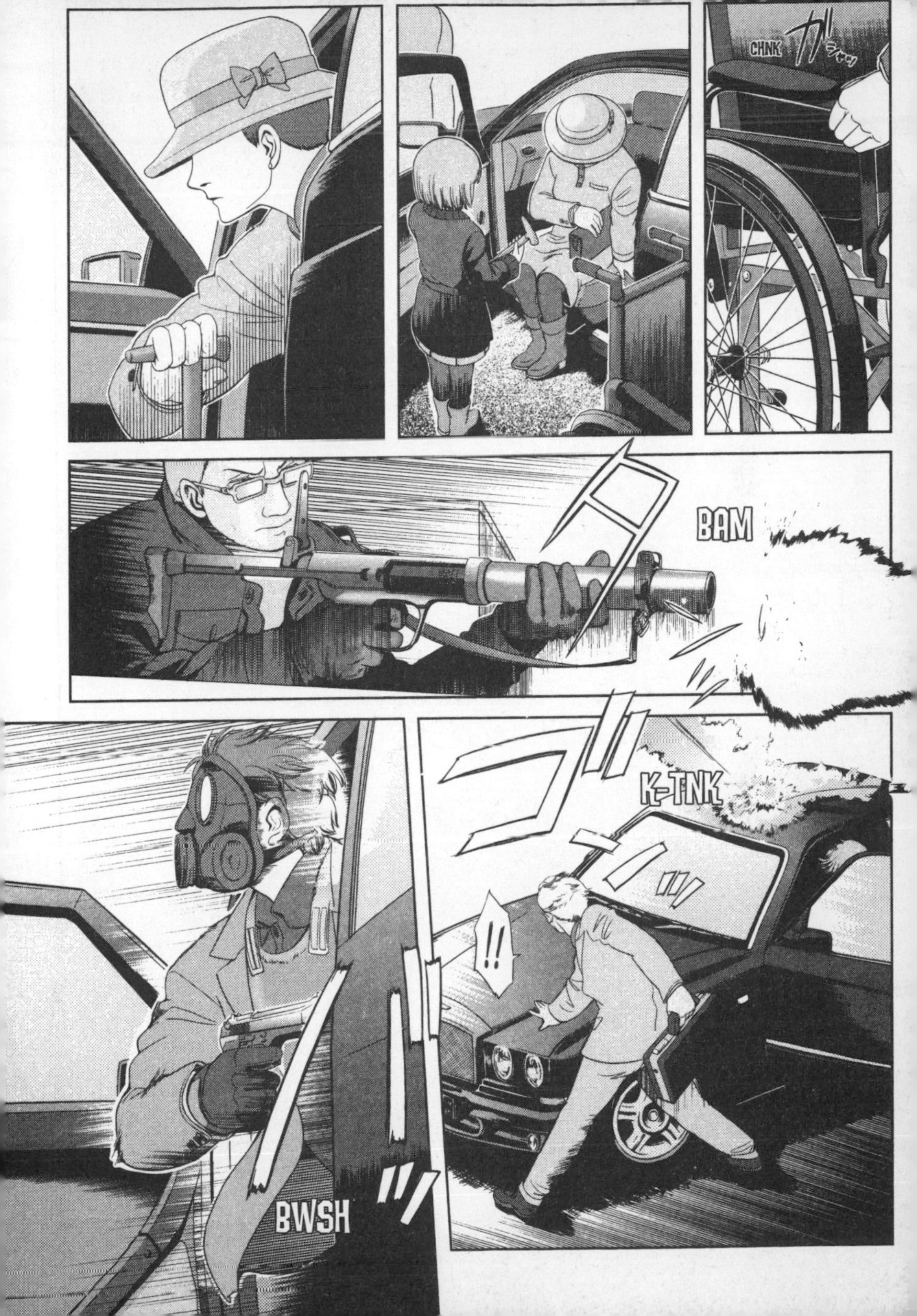
CHNK
ガシャッ
BAM
K-TNK
!!
BWSH

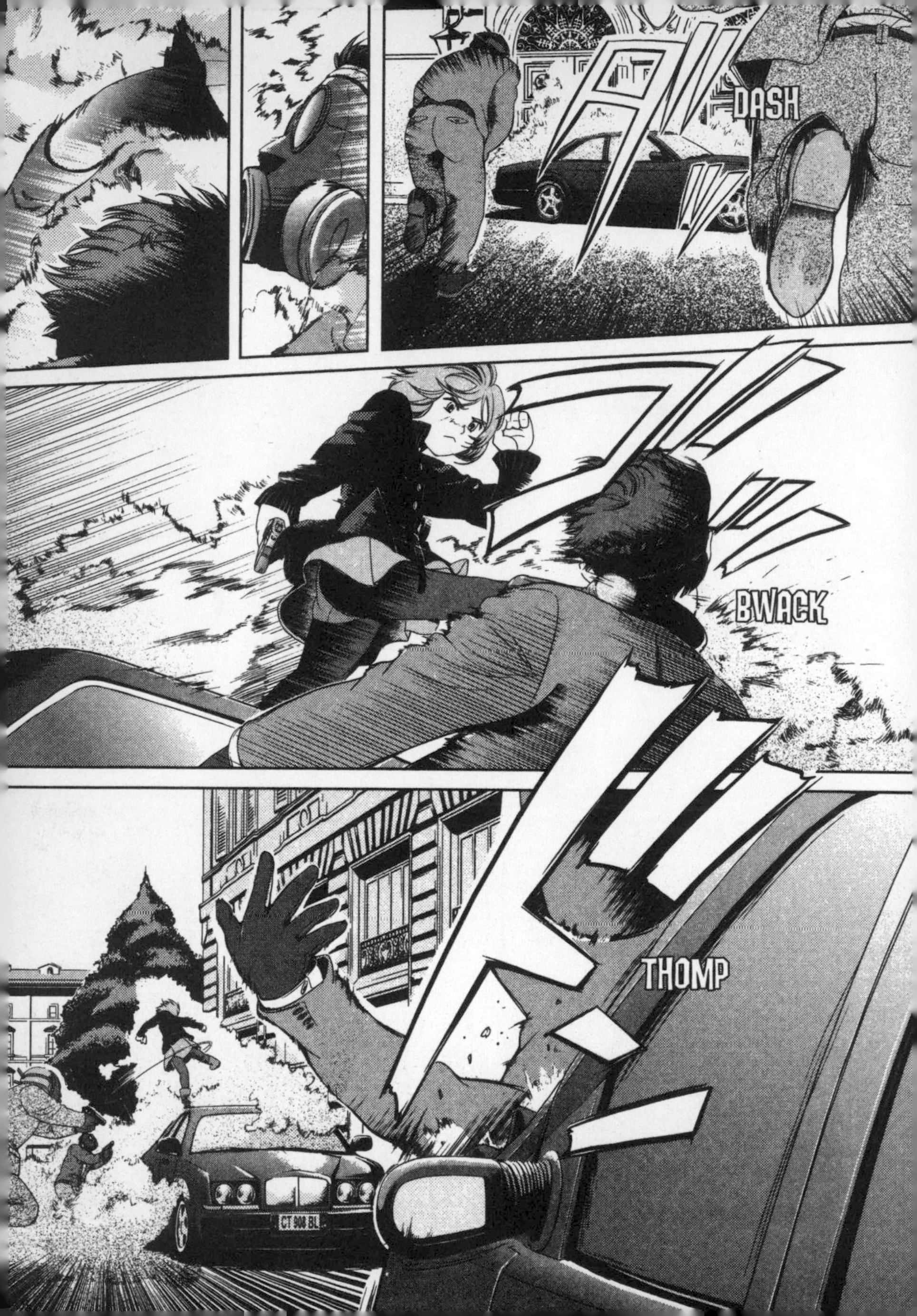
DASH
BWACK
THOMP
CT 908 BL

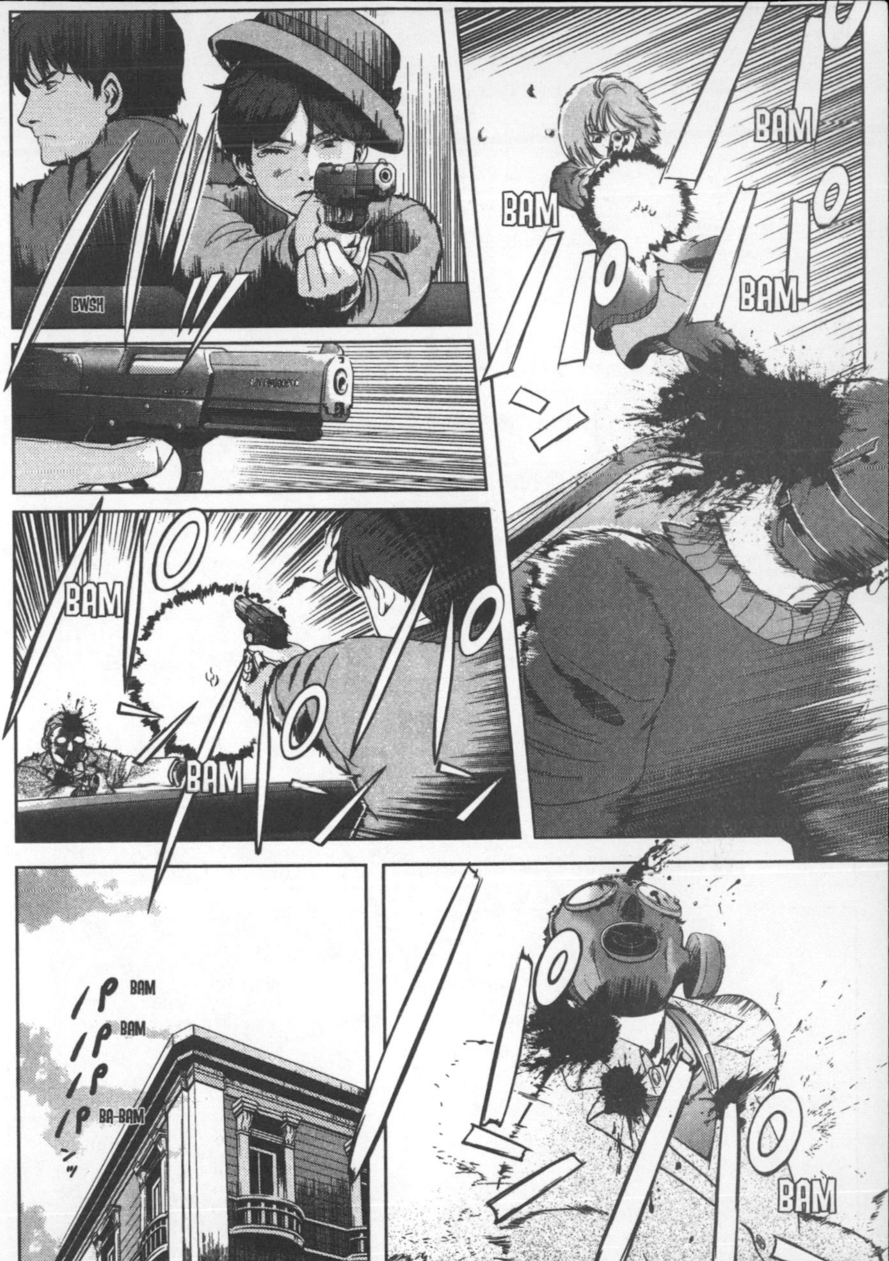
BAM
BAM
BAM
BWSH
BAM
BAM
BAM
BAM
BAM
BA-BAM

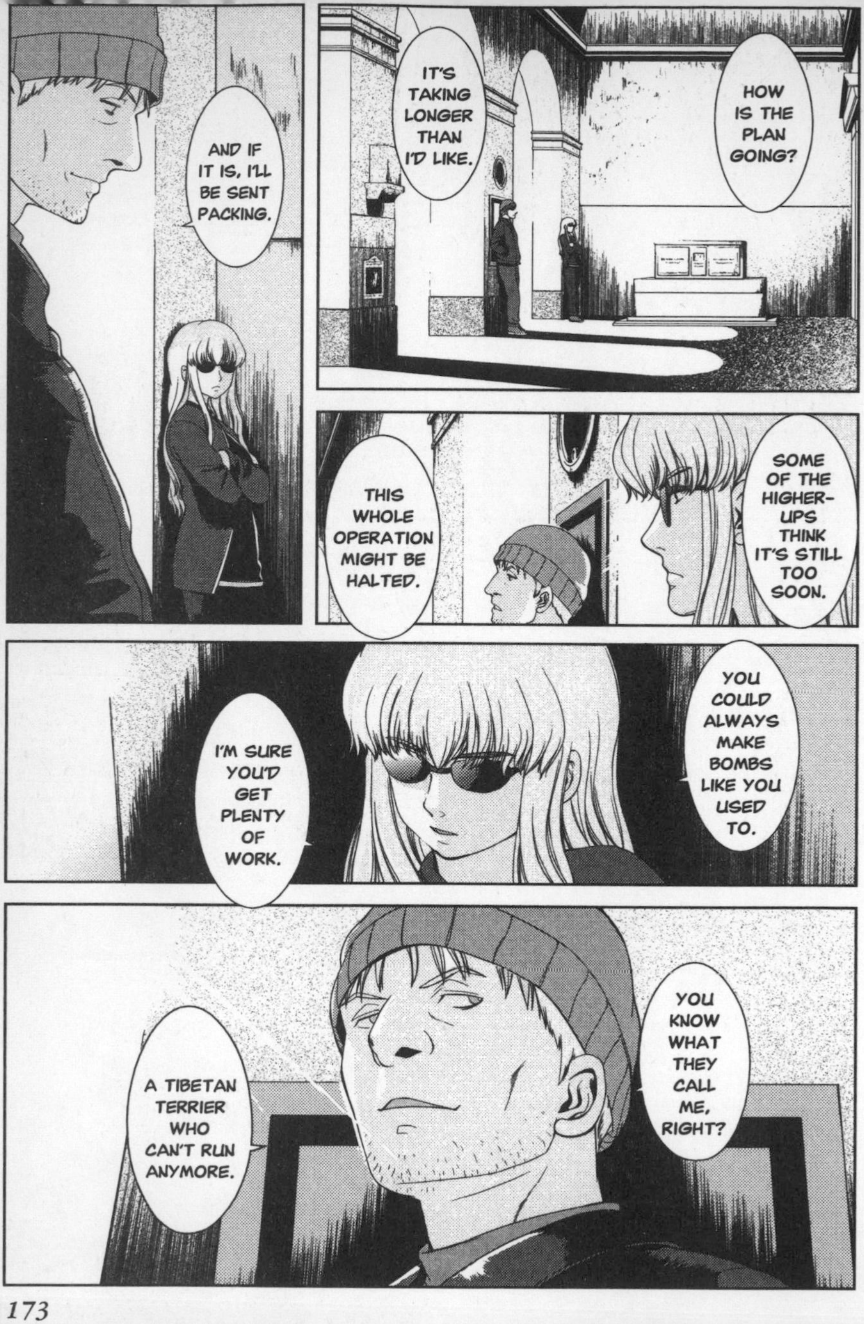
HOW IS THE PLAN GOING?
IT'S TAKING LONGER THAN I'D LIKE.
SOME OF THE HIGHER-UPS THINK IT'S STILL TOO SOON.
THIS WHOLE OPERATION MIGHT BE HALTED.
AND IF IT IS, I'LL BE SENT PACKING.
YOU COULD ALWAYS MAKE BOMBS LIKE YOU USED TO.
I'M SURE YOU'D GET PLENTY OF WORK.
YOU KNOW WHAT THEY CALL ME, RIGHT?
A TIBETAN TERRIER WHO CAN'T RUN ANYMORE.

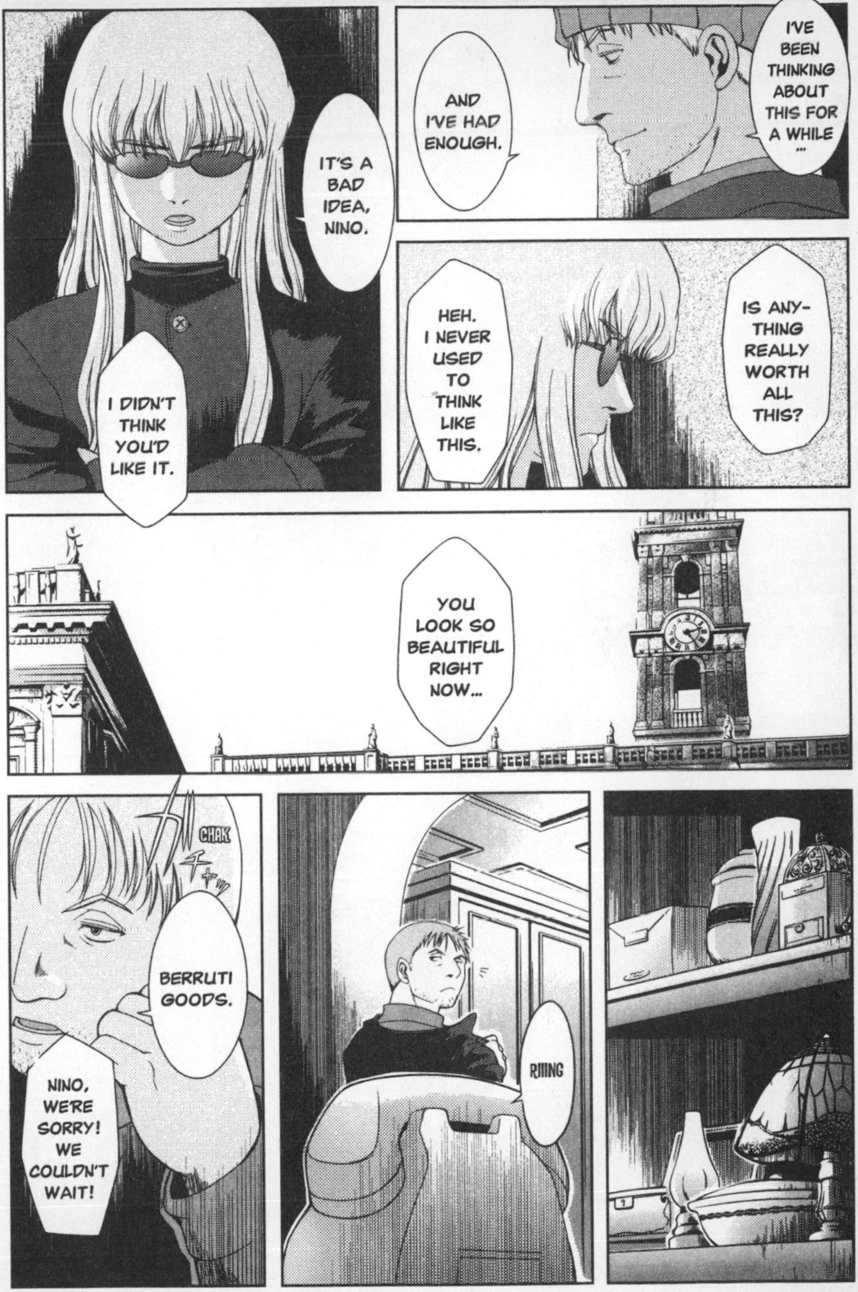

I'VE BEEN THINKING ABOUT THIS FOR A WHILE...
AND I'VE HAD ENOUGH.
IS ANY-THING REALLY WORTH ALL THIS?
HEH. I NEVER USED TO THINK LIKE THIS.
IT'S A BAD IDEA, NINO.
I DIDN'T THINK YOU'D LIKE IT.
YOU LOOK SO BEAUTIFUL RIGHT NOW...
RIIING
CHAK
BERRUTI GOODS.
NINO, WE'RE SORRY! WE COULDN'T WAIT!

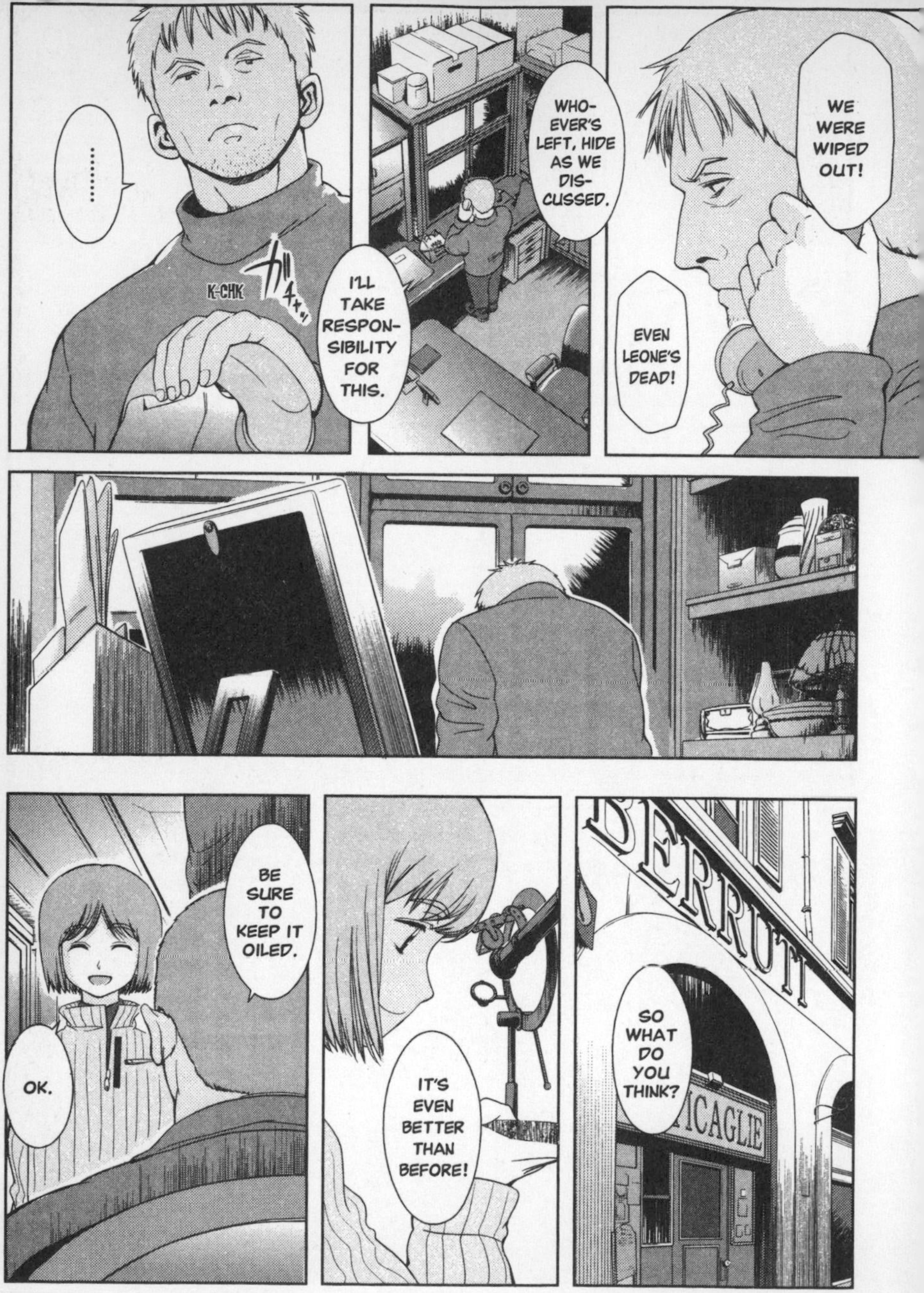
WE WERE WIPED OUT!
EVEN LEONE'S DEAD!
WHO-EVER'S LEFT, HIDE AS WE DIS-CUSSED.
I'LL TAKE RESPON-SIBILITY FOR THIS.
......
K-CHK
SO WHAT DO YOU THINK?
IT'S EVEN BETTER THAN BEFORE!
BE SURE TO KEEP IT OILED.
OK.

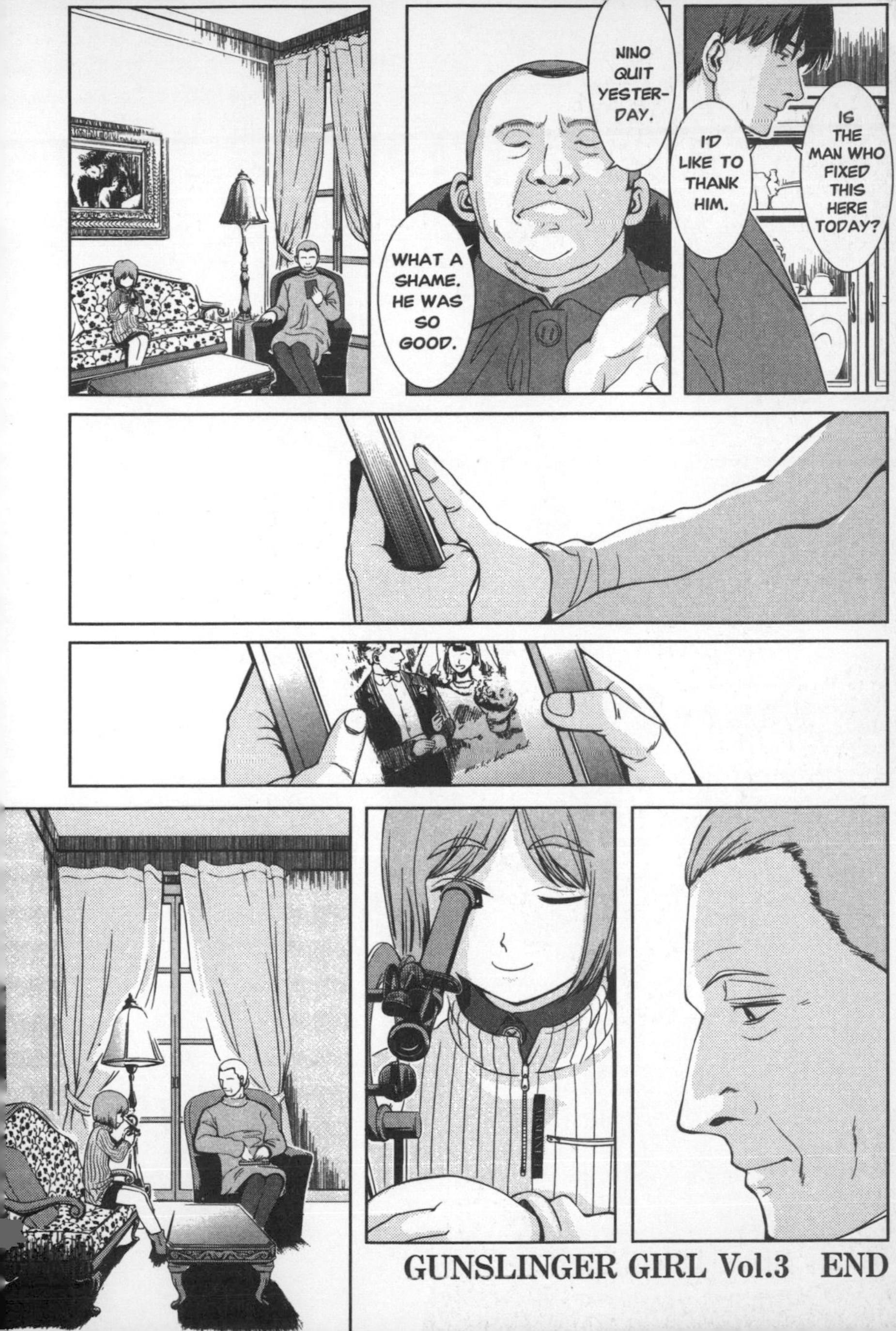
IS THE MAN WHO FIXED THIS HERE TODAY?
I'D LIKE TO THANK HIM.
NINO QUIT YESTER-DAY.
WHAT A SHAME. HE WAS SO GOOD.

GUNSLINGER GIRL Vol.3 END

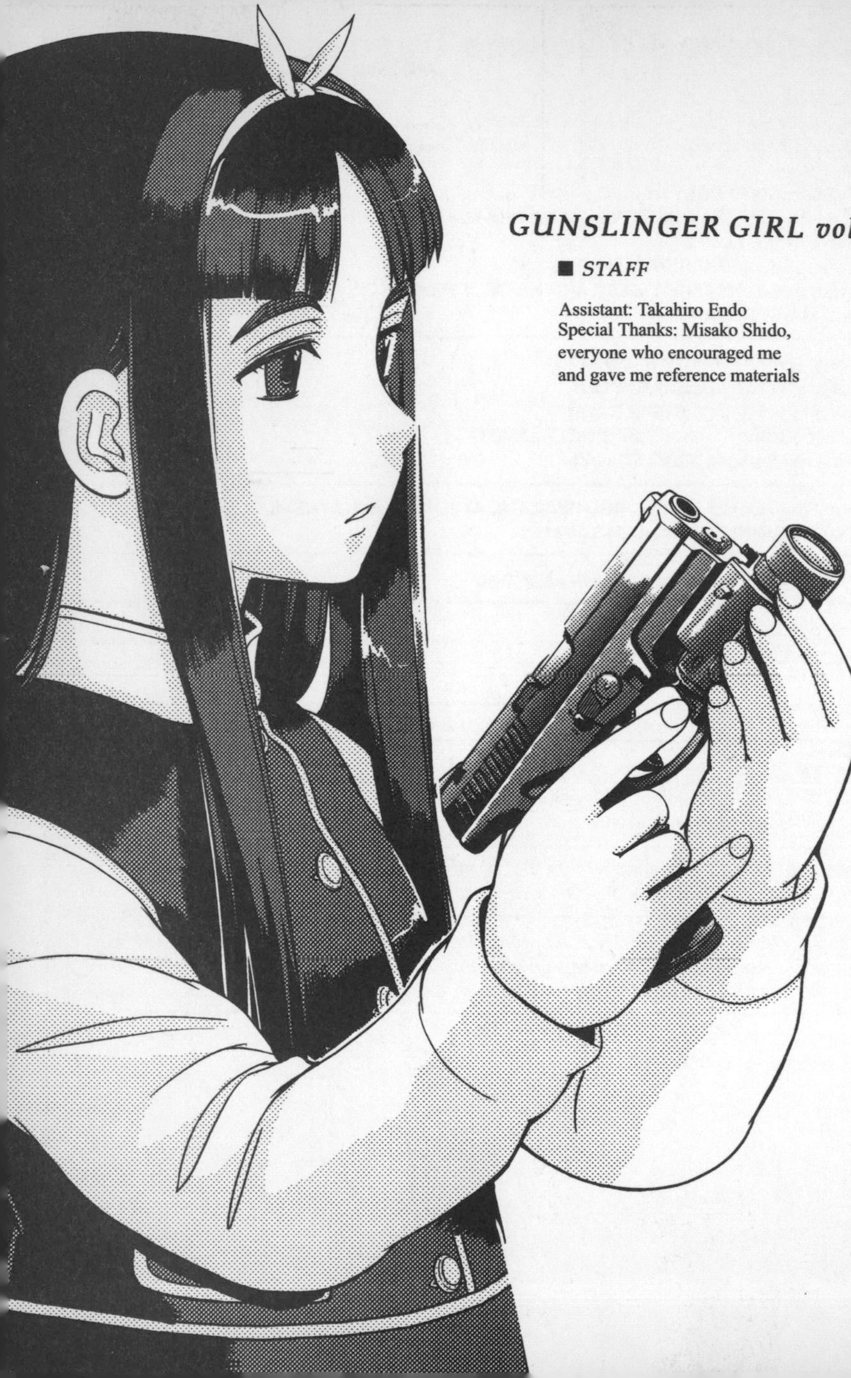

GUNSLINGER GIRL vol.3

■ *STAFF*

Assistant: Takahiro Endo
Special Thanks: Misako Shido, everyone who encouraged me and gave me reference materials

Gunslinger Girl Volume Three

© YU AIDA 2004
First published in 2004 by Media Works Inc., Tokyo, Japan.
English translation rights arranged with Media Works Inc.

Translator **AMY FORSYTH**
Translation Staff **KAY BERTRAND AND BRENDAN FRAYNE**
Editor **JAVIER LOPEZ**
Assistant Editor **SHERIDAN JACOBS**
Graphic Artists **HEATHER GARY AND NATALIA REYNOLDS**
Intern **MARK MEZA**

Editorial Director **GARY STEINMAN**
Creative Director **JASON BABLER**
Sales and Marketing **CHRIS OARR**
Print Production Manager **BRIDGETT JANOTA**
Pre-press Manager **KLYS REEDYK**

International Coordinators **TORU IWAKAMI, ATSUSHI KANBAYASHI, KYOKO DRUMHELLER AND AI TAKAI**

President, CEO & Publisher **JOHN LEDFORD**

Email: editor@adv-manga.com
www.adv-manga.com
www.advfilms.com

For sales and distribution inquiries please call 1.800.282.7202

 is a division of A.D. Vision, Inc.
10114 W. Sam Houston Parkway, Suite 200, Houston, Texas 77099

English text © 2005 published by A.D. Vision, Inc. under exclusive license.
ADV MANGA is a trademark of A.D. Vision, Inc.

All Rights Reserved. This is a fictional work. Any resemblance to actual events or locales, or persons, living or dead, is entirely coincidental. Reproduction and, or transmission of this work in whole or in part without written permission of the copyright holders is unlawful.

ISBN: 1-4139-0274-X
First printing, June 2005
10 9 8 7 6 5 4 3 2 1
Printed in Canada

TRANSLATOR'S NOTES

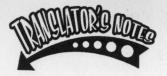

Gunslinger Girl Vol. 03

PG. 3 **Steiff Bear**
The very first of these classy (and expensive) stuffed bears was designed by Richard Steiff at his aunt Margaret's company in 1902. The following year, some 12,000 of them were sold at the World's Exhibition in St. Louis, and president Theodore Roosevelt was so taken with them that they would later be given the moniker "Teddy bear."

PG. 15 **Louise Antoinette Laure**
Also referred to as Louise-Antoinette-Laure De Berny. The "French author" mentioned here is Honoré de Balzac (see below), and Laure was his first mistress, whom he described as "more than a friend, more than a sister, almost a mother."

PG. 18 **Balzac**
Honoré de Balzac (1799-1850) was a modestly successful author credited with being one of the originators of realism in literature. The wildly prolific Balzac is best known for his *La Comédie Humaine* ("The Human Comedy"), a mammoth undertaking of nearly 100 novels and short stories and some 2,000 characters set amidst a backdrop of bourgeois France.

PG. 53 **Padania**
The name Padania (or Padana as it is spelled in Italian) refers to the valley in northern Italy formed by the river Po. Within the context of *Gunslinger Girl*, Padania is used synonymously with the Five Republics, a radical movement pushing for northern independence.

PG. 67 **SCORPION**
Constructed of aerospace-quality aluminum, this brand of silencer was designed for those times when "low profile, light weight, and world class sound suppression mean the difference between life and death."

PG. 102 **(1) SIG**
An abbreviation for *Schweizerische Industrie-Gesellschaft*. This Swiss company is one of the oldest and most widely-known manufacturers of small arms. "SIG" can be used to refer to any one of the many models the company makes.

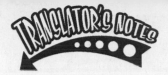

Continued...

PG. 102

(2) Glock

Another small arms manufacturer, this one being founded in 1963 in Austria. It began producing its own firearms in the 1980s, when the Austrian army contracted the company to make a service pistol.

PG. 112

NOCS

NOCS (*Nucleo Operativo Centrale di Sicurezza*) is the national police unit roughly equivalent to the SWAT of the United States, being deployed in arrest, rescue and counterterrorist operations.

PG. 112

Carabinieri

Short for *il Carabinieri Nationale*, this is an old and highly-respected Italian military police force. Coincidentally, the first time the *Carabinieri* appeared in a piece of fiction was in *Pinocchio*.

PG. 115

(1) la Scala

This is the *Teatro alla Scala*, one of the world's oldest and most famous opera houses. Located in Milan, it was built from 1776-1778, and refurbished after the war in 1945-1946. By the time of this printing, it will have completed yet another refurbishment.

(2) Red Brigade

The *Brigate Rosse* is a terrorist movement founded on Communist principles. Largely inactive since 1989, the group at one time led a campaign of kidnappings and assassinations.

(3) CQB

Short for "Close Quarters Battle." This can include hand-to-hand fighting, as well as the use of knives, sticks, bayonets and so on.

PG. 161

Lily of the Valley

Written by Balzac in 1836, this is one of the stories comprising *The Human Comedy* (see above). As mentioned previously, the heroine's name is Henriette (or more properly, Madame Blanche-Henriette de Mortsauf).

PG. 162

SISDE

This stands for *Servizio per le Informazionie la Sicurezza Democratica*. It is an Italian security agency which reports directly to the Minister of the Interior.

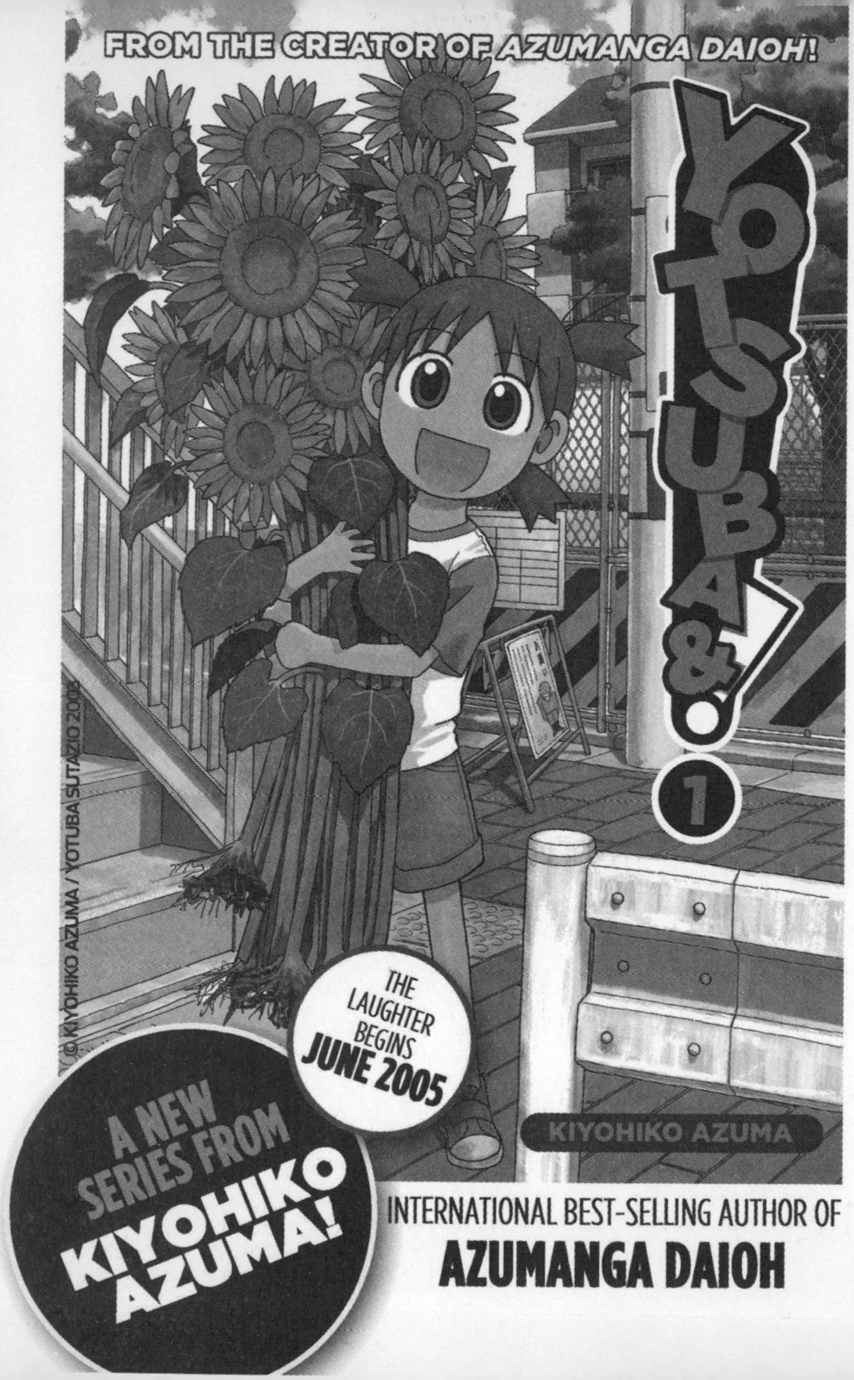
FROM THE CREATOR OF AZUMANGA DAIOH!
YOTSUBA&!
1
THE LAUGHTER BEGINS JUNE 2005
KIYOHIKO AZUMA
© KIYOHIKO AZUMA / YOTUBA SUTAZIO 2003
A NEW SERIES FROM KIYOHIKO AZUMA!
INTERNATIONAL BEST-SELLING AUTHOR OF
AZUMANGA DAIOH

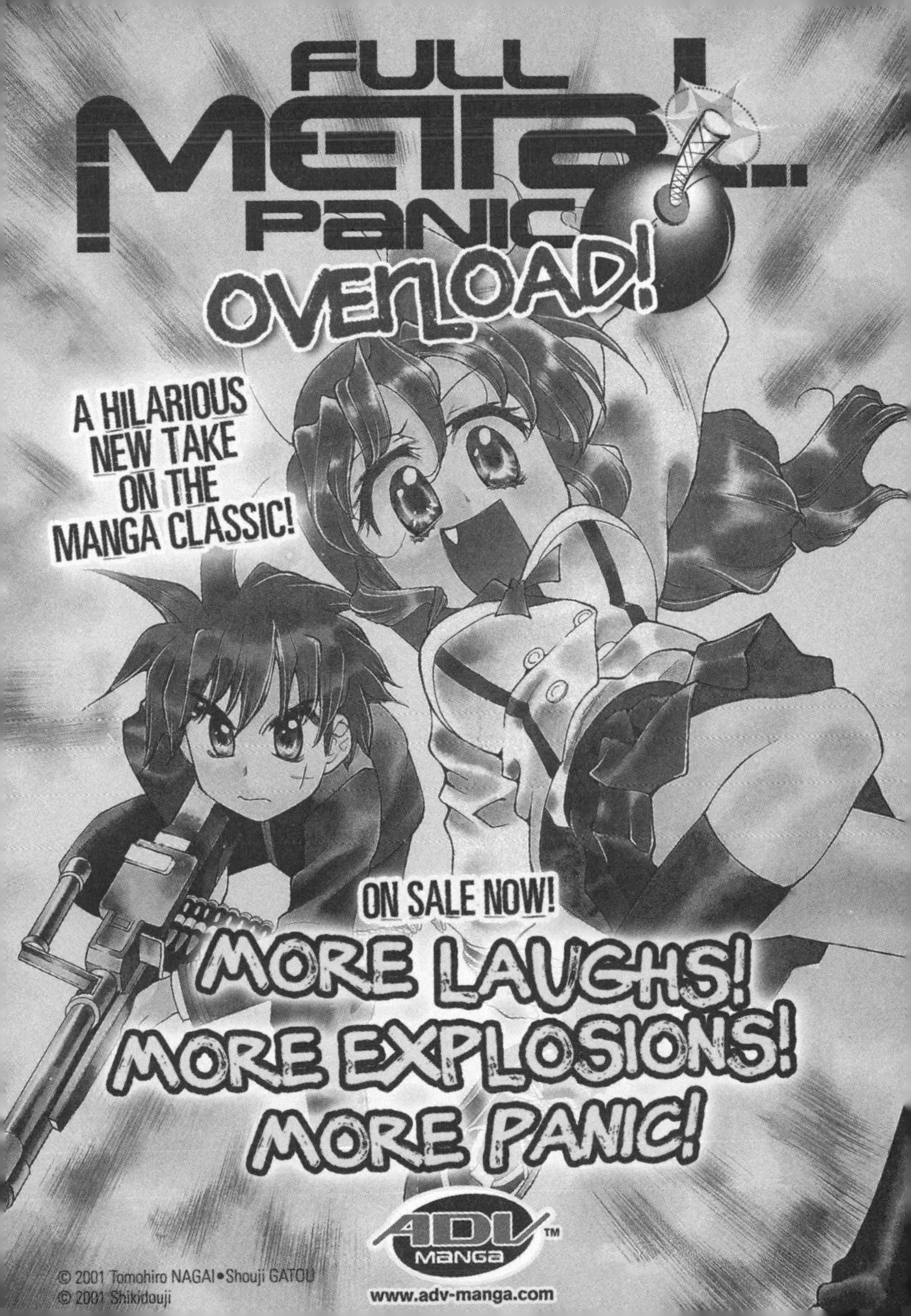

FULL METAL PANIC
OVERLOAD!
A HILARIOUS NEW TAKE ON THE MANGA CLASSIC!
ON SALE NOW!
MORE LAUGHS!
MORE EXPLOSIONS!
MORE PANIC!
ADV Manga
© 2001 Tomohiro NAGAI • Shouji GATOU
© 2001 Shikidouji
www.adv-manga.com

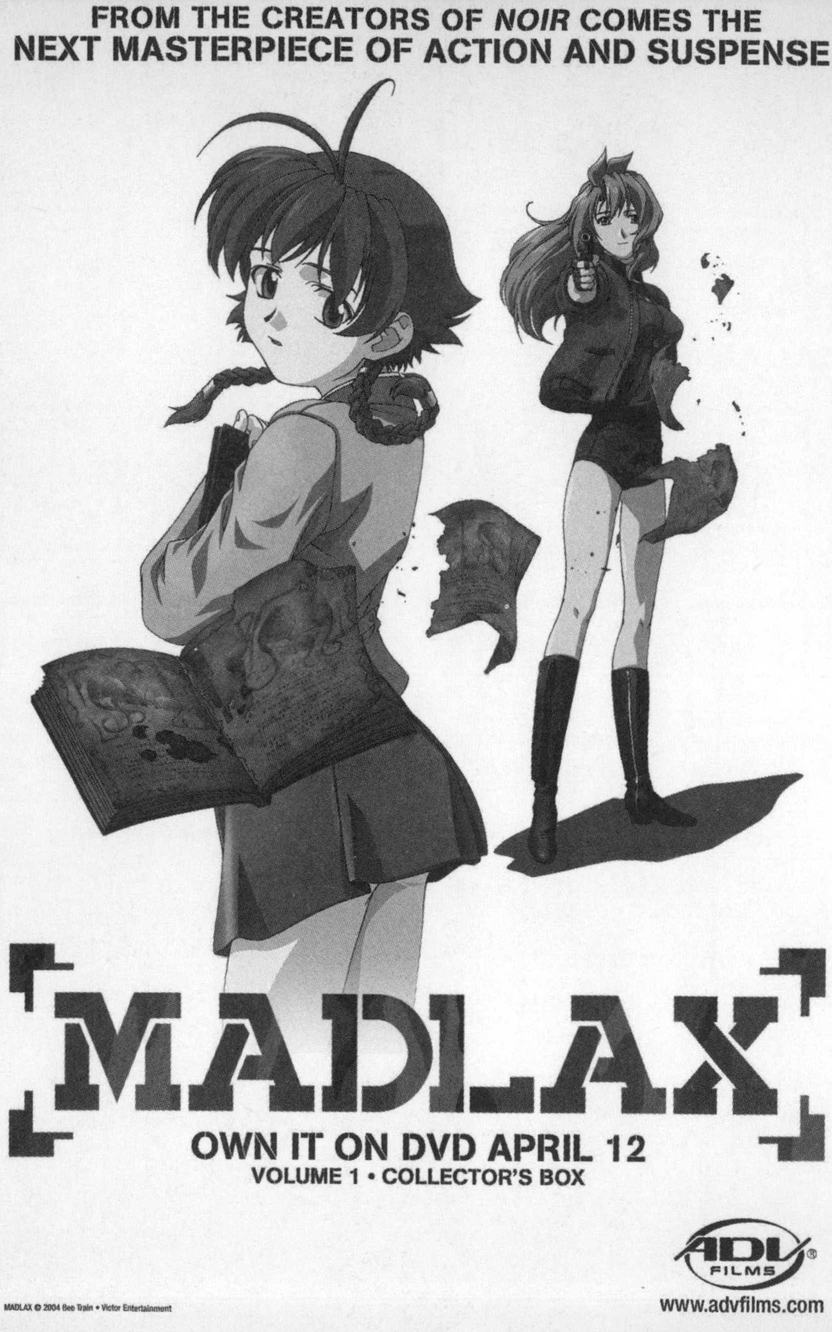
FROM THE CREATORS OF NOIR COMES THE
NEXT MASTERPIECE OF ACTION AND SUSPENSE
MADLAX
OWN IT ON DVD APRIL 12
VOLUME 1 • COLLECTOR'S BOX
ADV FILMS
MADLAX © 2004 Bee Train • Victor Entertainment
www.advfilms.com

SOMETHING MISSING
FROM YOUR TV?

 ROBOT DESTRUCTION

 SAMURAI VIOLENCE

 KAWAII OVERDOSE

SKIMPY CLOTHES

 NOSE BLEEDING

 SUPER DEFORMED CHARACTERS

 UPSKIRTS

EXTREME JIGGLING

HYPERACTIVE TEENS

MONSTER RAMPAGE

METROPOLITAN MELTDOWN

BLOOD & GUTS

Tired of networks that only dabble in anime? Tired of the same old cartoons?

Demand more from your cable or satellite operator. If they don't currently offer Anime Network as part of your channel lineup, then something is missing.

Your TV deserves better.

You deserve Anime Network.

Log on and demand anime in your home 24/7:
WWW.THEANIMENETWORK.COM

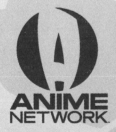
ANIME
NETWORK

© 2004 Anime Network

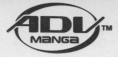

MANGA SURVEY

PLEASE MAIL THE COMPLETED FORM TO: EDITOR – ADV MANGA
C/o A.D. Vision, Inc. 10114 W. Sam Houston Pkwy., Suite 200 Houston, TX 77099

Name:_____

Address:_____

City, State, Zip:_____

_____

E-Mail: _____

Male ☐   Female ☐   Age:_____

☐ *CHECK HERE IF YOU WOULD LIKE TO RECEIVE OTHER INFORMATION OR FUTURE OFFERS FROM ADV.*

All information provided will be used for internal purposes only. We promise not to sell or otherwise divulge your information.

1. Annual Household Income (*Check only one*)
- ☐ Under $25,000
- ☐ $25,000 to $50,000
- ☐ $50,000 to $75,000
- ☐ Over $75,000

2. How do you hear about new Manga releases? (*Check all that apply*)
- ☐ Browsing in Store
- ☐ Internet Reviews
- ☐ Anime News Websites
- ☐ Direct Email Campaigns
- ☐ Online forums (message boards and chat rooms)
- ☐ Carrier pigeon
- ☐ Other:_____
- ☐ Magazine Ad
- ☐ Online Advertising
- ☐ Conventions
- ☐ TV Advertising

3. Which magazines do you read? (*Check all that apply*)
- ☐ Wizard
- ☐ SPIN
- ☐ Animerica
- ☐ Rolling Stone
- ☐ Maxim
- ☐ DC Comics
- ☐ URB
- ☐ Polygon
- ☐ Official PlayStation Magazine
- ☐ Entertainment Weekly
- ☐ YRB
- ☐ EGM
- ☐ Newtype USA
- ☐ SciFi
- ☐ Starlog
- ☐ Wired
- ☐ Vice
- ☐ BPM
- ☐ I hate reading
- ☐ Other:_____

4. Have you ACPL ITEM DISCARDED
  ☐ Yes
  ☐ No

5. Have yo _____ **e ADV website?**
  ☐ Ye
  ☐ No

6. If you have visited the ADV Manga website, how would you rate your online experience?
  ☐ Excellent   ☐ Average
  ☐ Good   ☐ Poor

7. What genre of manga do you prefer?
  (Check all that apply)
  ☐ adventure   ☐ horror
  ☐ romance   ☐ sci-fi/fantasy
  ☐ detective   ☐ sports
  ☐ action   ☐ comedy

8. How many manga titles have you purchased in the last 6 months?
  ☐ none
  ☐ 1-4
  ☐ 5-10
  ☐ 11+

9. Where do you make your manga purchases? *(Check all that apply)*
  ☐ comic store   ☐ department store
  ☐ bookstore   ☐ grocery store
  ☐ newsstand   ☐ video store
  ☐ online   ☐ video game store
  ☐ other:_____

10. Which bookstores do you usually make your manga purchases at?
  (Check all that apply)
  ☐ Barnes & Noble   ☐ Borders
  ☐ Walden Books   ☐ Books-A-Million
  ☐ Suncoast   ☐ Toys Я " Us
  ☐ Best Buy   ☐ Other bookstore:
  ☐ Amazon.com   _____

11. What's your favorite anime/manga website? *(Check all that apply)*
  ☐ adv-manga.com   ☐ animeondvd.com
  ☐ advfilms.com   ☐ anipike.com
  ☐ rightstuf.com   ☐ animeonline.net
  ☐ animenewsservice.com   ☐ planetanime.com
  ☐ animenewsnetwork.com   ☐ animenation.com
  ☐ Other:_____

All information provided will be used for internal purposes only. We promise not to sell or otherwise divulge your information.